# OPEN SECRET

# OPEN SECRET

The Autobiography of
the Former Director-General of MI5

## STELLA RIMINGTON

HUTCHINSON
London

First published in the United Kingdom in 2001 by Hutchinson

1 3 5 7 9 10 8 6 4 2

Hutchinson
The Random House Group Limited
20 Vauxhall Bridge Road, London SW1V 2SA

Random House Australia (Pty) Limited
20 Alfred Street, Milsons Point, Sydney
New South Wales 2061, Australia

Random House New Zealand Limited
18 Poland Road, Glenfield, Auckland 10, New Zealand

Random House (Pty) Limited
Endulini, 5A Jubilee Road, Parktown 2193, South Africa

The Random House Group Limited Reg. No. 954009

www.randomhouse.co.uk

A CIP record for this book is available from the British Library

Papers used by Random House are natural,
recyclable products made from wood grown in sustainable forests.
The manufacturing processes conform to the environmental
regulations of the country of origin.

ISBN 0 09 179360 2 (Hardback)
ISBN 0 09 1794358 (Trade Paperback)

Typeset in Sabon by MATS, Southend-on-Sea, Essex
Printed and bound in Great Britain by
Mackays of Chatham PLC, Chatham, Kent

*For Sophie and Harriet*

# ILLUSTRATIONS

*Second Section*

Viktor Lazine is expelled, 1981 (© *Topham/Press Association*)
Georgi Markov (© *Topham/Press Association*)
The miners' strike, 1984: at Corton Wood (© *Tony Prime/Camera Press*)
Arthur Scargill at Orgreave (© *Camera Press*)
In the garden of Spion Kop, 1978
With John Rimington, 1983
Leaving Spion Kop, 1984
Harriet at Alwyne Villas, 1984
In my check coat, the *New Statesman* photo (© *Rex Features Ltd*)
Robert Armstrong on his way to Australia (© *David Parker*)
The CAZAB kangaroo, cleared for security, 1988
Provisional IRA shooting in Holland, 1988 (© *Topham/Press Association*)
Vadim V. Bakatin (© *Novosti, London*)
In Dzerzhinsky Square, 1991
Sightseeing in Moscow, 1991
'Looking dishevelled on a Saturday morning' (© *Mail on Sunday*)
JAK cartoons from the *Evening Standard*, 9 March and 19 July 1993 (© JAK)
With Michael Howard at the launch of the MI5 booklet, 1993
With Jonathan Dimbleby before the Dimbleby Lecture, 1994
With Louis Freeh, director of the FBI, 1996
John Major opens the new MI5 building, 1994
Receiving an Honorary Degree at Exeter, 1996
Playing in *The Fifteen-Minute Hamlet*, 1999

Cartoon reproduced on page *x* by Blower, 18 May 2000 (© *Evening Standard*)

*Unless otherwise attributed, all the illustrations are from the author's collection*

# ACKNOWLEDGEMENTS

I would like to thank those who have supported and encouraged me in writing this book. They include one or two of my former colleagues in MI5, whom I will not name to avoid embarrassing them, my husband John, who helped especially with the India episodes; and my two daughters Sophie and Harriet who have unfailingly supported me in this as in everything else I have done.

Thanks go also to the team at Random House: Gail Rebuck and Simon Master and their colleagues and Sue Freestone and Tony Whittome of Hutchinson, in particular for the way they have handled the sensitive issues connected with publication.

Finally, I want to thank my successor as Director-General of MI5, Sir Stephen Lander. He and I have been friends and colleagues for years and as I would expect he has kept cool throughout the hysteria which has sometimes surrounded the preparation of this book. He has said that he would rather I had not written it, but in that I did, he has done his best, in difficult circumstances, to ensure that our relationship remains friendly.

# PREFACE

This is a straightforward and honest account of my life so far, as I remember it. That life includes some twenty-seven years spent working in the Security Service (MI5). But I have not set out to write a history of British counter-espionage or counter-terrorism during that period, just a recollection of what now, in retrospect, seem to me to be the personal highlights. It has been written without access to any papers or official information and I have never kept a diary.

As the first publicly named Director-General of MI5 and the first woman to hold that post, my career has generated much interest, particularly among other women. It was in response to that interest that I decided to try to write an autobiography, though I realised that it would be difficult to strike the balance between readability and the necessary discretion when I came to write about my time in MI5. I did not know what the reaction would be when, as I was obliged to do, I submitted my first fairly raw draft to the official clearance process. Although I had written it very carefully, acutely aware of the needs of secrecy, I did not expect it to be received with enthusiasm. It goes without saying that those in charge of the intelligence community at any given moment will feel that the less former members say, the better. If everyone goes off and keeps quiet it is much easier to keep things under control. No doubt Prime Ministers feel the same about their predecessors and former Cabinet colleagues. But I did hope that when they saw the sort of thing I wanted to write, they would not think it damaging. I certainly did not expect the ferocity of the reaction I received. Perhaps I was too out of touch by then and not sufficiently aware of the other fish various parts of the intelligence community were trying to fry – the whistle-blowers, the leakers and those accused of breaking the Official Secrets Act.

I started the book in August 1998, and the writing of the first draft took until Christmas 1999. Then, on 14 February 2000, in truly covert style, I handed my manuscript in a black briefcase to a former colleague, after a pleasant lunch at the Orrery Restaurant in Marylebone High Street. The manu-script was accompanied by a letter asking what omissions would need to be made before it could be published. Looking rather startled, she disappeared with it in her car. Then, apart from a brief letter of acknowledgement, I heard nothing at all for two months.

I now know that during that period Whitehall went into full damage-limitation mode. The draft was sent to the Cabinet Office and circulated to everyone who could have any angle on it. No-one will ever know how many copies were made. Not surprisingly in the circumstances, everyone did have an angle – mostly, so far as I have gathered, hostile, negative and worried. After enquiries on my part as to what was happening, I was summoned down to Whitehall to see the Cabinet Secretary, Sir Richard Wilson. His brief was to deter me and he fulfilled it very well. By the end of an hour or so of being bullied, threatened and cajoled in the more-in-sorrow-than-in-anger way the Establishment behaves to its recalcitrant sons and, as I now know, daughters, I was very shaken. My protests that at that stage I had done nothing except submit a draft manuscript for clearance in the proper way seemed to fall on deaf ears. I felt that I had become an outsider, a threat to the established order. I tried to keep my end up, while I waited to see what his fall-back position was, and eventually I was told that if I co-operated on the content (something I had always intended to do) and if we could agree, he would recommend that the book could be published, though he could give me no guarantee what ministers would decide. When at the end of it all he walked me to the door of the building, patted me kindly on the shoulder and said, 'Never mind, Stella, go off and buy something,' I did not feel any better.

After that the leaking began. In a rather laddish covert operation conducted presumably by someone in one of the departments which had been consulted, a copy of the draft I had submitted was sent anonymously in a black cab to the *Sun* newspaper and I woke up in the middle of the night to hear the BBC World Service on my radio, which I had left on when I went to sleep, telling the world that I was wanting to publish my memoirs. Then a version of the record of my meeting with the Cabinet Secretary, which had presumably also been circulated widely, was leaked to a newspaper. Selective briefings were given, including that one department or agency wanted me to be arrested. Everyone had something to say about the issue whether they had read the draft text or not. The story was kept going when the *Sun* kindly returned the manuscript with much fandango to No. 10 Downing Street. As a result of the premature publicity, I received a torrent of advice from the media, including abuse for even thinking about writing a book and offers to serialise it, sometimes from the same source.

Meanwhile, in a series of friendly meetings over the next year and a half (I was, I can now admit, so shaken I could not bear to look at the text again for some time), while all the leaking and huffing and puffing was going on, I discussed the content with the present Director-General, Sir Stephen Lander. With the best intentions in the world, it is not possible to know, once you are on the outside, exactly what will be regarded as damaging. Some things I wrote appeared to the intelligence community to go too close to the bone. I agreed to accept their judgement and omit them. Any intelligence operations I have referred to are well disguised in various ways.

When we had agreed a final text, which was not difficult, it was submitted for clearance to ministers and eventually, on 6 July 2001, I (and simultaneously the press) duly received the information that I was authorised to publish, though as a matter of principle the government regretted and disapproved of my decision to do so. At the end of it all, it is only a slight exaggeration to say that even I, a seasoned Whitehall insider, was starting to feel the sense of persecution and fear of the main character in a Kafka novel, in the grip of a bureaucracy whose ways and meaning could not be discerned.

As far as I know, I am the first former head of one of the intelligence agencies to ask permission to publish a book since 1955, when Sir Percy Sillitoe published his autobiography, *Cloak Without Dagger*, and that may account in part for the reaction I received. Intelligence and security services are vital to democracies, and to be effective they must be able to conduct their operational activities in secret. When I first joined MI5 in 1969, that was taken to mean that practically nothing at all could be said in public about the Service, about what it did, where its offices were, the people who worked there. Over the years that has gradually changed. Thinking has moved on, and it will move on further, with developments in the law and in the arrangements for oversight of the secret services. There is already much information publicly available for those who care to seek it out, in print and on the web. But it is clearly still true that revelations about specific operations, details of sources of information, human or technical, or about the precise way in which intelligence is gathered are damaging and risk undermining the effectiveness of the intelligence machinery and eroding the confidence of the human sources of information, who often provide the best intelligence and risk their lives to do so. There are no such revelations here.

The wholly disproportionate fuss stirred up as soon as this book's existence became known shows in my view that there is still a wish among some parts of the intelligence world to keep too much secret. Excessive secrecy harms the position of our vital security services rather than protecting it. Being more open is a risk that has to be taken in the 21st century, if the support and understanding of the public are to be obtained. Similarly it is neither necessary nor appropriate nowadays to try to hold to total silence people who have worked in the public service, whether as civil servant, diplomat, member of the armed services or intelligence officer. It won't work and it is better to accept that and focus rather on what it is important to protect. It is clearly essential that what is said or written should be considered and submitted to a clearance procedure and not just uttered off the cuff. But that means establishing a properly run clearance procedure which people are encouraged to use, instead of one that is, as it was in my case, intimidating, conducted in semi-public and confusing to everyone.

# PROLOGUE

When I first opened my eyes, in May 1935, I might have thought, if I'd been capable of it, that I had not got too bad a deal. The world was a fairly safe and settled place and my family seemed a satisfactory though hardly glamorous one to be born into. Admittedly, my father had been unemployed and forced to try to earn a living selling the *Encyclopaedia Britannica* three years before, when my brother was born, but by the time of my birth, he had a secure job as a mechanical engineer in a firm with some good contracts. My parents had just bought a house with a garden in the new suburb of South Norwood. It would have seemed to most people, observing me as I first saw the light of day, that I was pretty well set up. But the fact that it was snowing on that May day should have warned that all might not be quite as secure and predictable as it seemed. And it wasn't.

By the time I was four, everything had changed. The world was at war; my father's job had disappeared; we had left our nice new south London suburb, by then far from the secure place it was intended to be, for a series of rented homes in the north of England. My safe life had become dangerous and insecure and I had become a frightened little girl.

From then on, nothing in my life ever turned out as expected. Having chosen a rather dull and safe career, I ended up as leader of one of the country's intelligence agencies and a target for terrorists. Having conventionally married my schoolfriend, I ended up separated, a single parent. Having begun work in the days when women's careers were not taken at all seriously and most lasted only between education and motherhood, I ended up advising ministers and Prime Ministers.

During my career, I have seen myself portrayed publicly in various different guises; in the 1980s I was Mrs Thatcher's stooge, the leader of an arm of the secret state which was helping her to beat the miners' strike and destroy the NUM. I was portrayed as the investigator of CND and even as the one who had ordered the murder of an old lady peace campaigner. In 1992, when I first emerged into the public gaze as Director-General of MI5, I became a sort of female James Bond, 'Housewife Superspy', 'Mother of Two Gets Tough with Terrorists'. And finally, with the writing of this book, I have become to some a villain, 'Reckless Rimington', careless of our national security, opening the door to floods of reminiscences and damaging revelations. I don't recognise myself in any of those roles.

The unexpected course of my life has involved me closely with some of the significant issues of the late 20th century: the rise of terrorism, the end of the Cold War and some of the big social questions – women's place in society (how can work and family be combined?) civil liberties (how far should the state intrude on the citizens' privacy to ensure their safety?) and open government (how much should the public know about the secret state and how should it be controlled?).

I have observed and participated in these issues from an unusual position, inside the secret state. But that does not mean my perspective is distorted or warped. Ian Fleming and John le Carré in their different ways have done the intelligence world few favours. The vast majority of those who work inside it are balanced, sane and sensible people, with a well developed sense of humour and a down-to-earth approach to the difficult issues they have to deal with. They have all the same problems in their lives as everyone else but they are, as I said publicly in 1994 in the Dimbleby Lecture on BBC TV, 'positive, forward-looking and flexible and work hard to defend this country and its citizens against threats to its security'.

# I

On a May day in 1940, when I was just five, I had my first experience of the 'need to know' principle in action. My brother Brian and I attended the primary school in Ingatestone in Essex, some five miles from the house in Margaretting which my parents had rented to get us all out of London at the beginning of the war. That day, we came out of school as usual and waited at the bus stop outside the bank for our bus to take us home. But on that particular day, though we waited and waited, no bus came. As it later turned out, all the buses, as well as all other transport, had been commandeered to help in the evacuation from Dunkirk. I suppose because it was Top Secret no warning had been given, and there we were aged five and eight, completely cut off from home, waiting and waiting for a bus to come while at the other end my mother waited and waited for us to turn up, with no idea of what had happened to us. There were no telephones and no cars and no way for the two ends to communicate. Eventually, the bank manager noticed us standing there and arranged for us to be taken home in someone's pony and trap, the only transport available. From then until we moved on, the pony and trap became our normal mode of transport to school.

Like those of most people born in Europe in the first half of the 1930s, all my earliest memories are dominated by the war and its anxieties and uncertainties. My father was on the high seas when war broke out, returning from working on an engineering contract in Venezuela. Though I was only four, my mother's anxiety easily transferred itself to me. I can remember her coming out into our back garden, where Brian and I were playing in the sun. She was wearing one of those flowery wrap-around cotton aprons, which 1930s suburban housewives seem always to be wearing in photographs of that period. She had come out to tell us what she had heard on the wireless about the outbreak of war, and the latest news of where Father was. She was worried and she needed to share her anxiety. Even though I didn't understand it all, I felt anxious for the first time in my life. It was an anxiety that was to last a long time.

Father got home safely, and he told us about the boat drills the crew had carried out for all the passengers on board ship, in case they got torpedoed, and how they had painted a huge stars and stripes on the deck of the ship to indicate to enemy aircraft that they were neutral. Father greeted the arrival of the Second World War with immense sadness and depression. He had been seriously wounded in the Great War at Passchendaele, attempting to mine the German trenches. He had volunteered young, disguising his real age. He thought he was fighting in the war to end all wars, for a world fit for heroes to live in. He had been unemployed during the Depression and now a second war seemed to him the crowning blow.

We lived at the time in the new house in South Norwood, which my parents had bought in 1929, shortly after they got married, in high hopes of a prosperous future. But it was obvious to Father that we could not stay there now war had broken out; the London suburbs were much too dangerous a place for his wife and young family. For a time he and Mother toyed with the idea of sending my brother and me to America to spend the war with his sister, who had emigrated to Philadelphia. In fact everything was in place for us to go, when one of the ships carrying children to Canada was torpedoed. Mother, who had never liked the idea of sending us away in the first place, decided that whatever happened we would all stay together.

So instead we rented what seemed to me an enormous house – but was in fact a moderate-sized detached dwelling, 'St Martins' at Margaretting in Essex. This was the first of a whole series of rented houses which we lived in throughout my childhood. That move was financially disastrous, and effectively made it certain that my parents would never be even moderately comfortably off by middle-class standards. They let our London house to an unmarried lady for a trifling rent – the only sort of rent you could get for a house in South Norwood in 1939. She thus established a protected tenancy and, as we never returned to live in London, my parents were never afterwards able to get her out so that they could sell the house. In the 1950s, despairing of getting any of their capital back, they sold it to her for a song.

Moving to St Martin's in September 1939 was hugely exciting for us children. First of all came the journey in a taxi with a black fabric hood and a very small, almost opaque, cracked yellow window, through which I tried to look back as South Norwood disappeared. We went through the 'Rotherhithe Pipe' as the driver called it, the tunnel under the Thames, and into what was then the countryside of Essex. I remember the house well. It had a big galleried hall and a kitchen that was old-fashioned even by 1930s standards, with a door at each end. This meant that small children could rush through the kitchen and round the passages in circles, yelling with excitement and causing vast annoyance to anyone working in the kitchen. Less excitingly, for my mother at least, the house had rats in the roof, which scampered loudly overhead and seemed in imminent danger of falling through the large number of cracks in the ceiling into the bedrooms.

My mother was a great coper. She lived through a very disturbed historical period – born in 1901, she experienced two world wars and a depression. She had trained as a midwife and worked in the 1920s in the East End of London at the Jewish Hospital. She remembered the visits paid to the hospital by Mrs Rebecca Sieff, who was a patron, and particularly that she was always sacking her chauffeurs. Every time she came to the hospital she had a new one. She used to tell the nurses that you had to keep a very sharp eye on chauffeurs or they would use up too much petrol. Mother's experience at the hospital, particularly in going to East End homes to deliver babies, convinced her that you should make the most of what you had, and she was not given to complaining nor was she sympathetic to anyone who did.

This stoical attitude was certainly well tested in those early months at Margaretting. The winter of 1939–40 turned out to be excessively cold. All the pipes froze. There was no water and little heat. All able-bodied men had gone off to the Armed Forces and there was extreme difficulty in getting a builder or anyone in to help. To increase the gloom, both my brother and I got bronchitis and to his he added German measles, so he had to be isolated. Our bedrooms were kept warm with Valor paraffin stoves and I had to breathe in the fumes of Friar's Balsam brought up steaming in a big brown bowl every few hours. The smell of paraffin and Friars Balsam still bring back to me those early days of the war.

Father was working in London at this period and though she coped, Mother became increasingly exhausted and un-characteristically bad-tempered, particularly when we were beginning to recover from our ailments. Spring and the warmer weather must have come as a great relief to her. We had quite a carefree early summer, spent feeding the pigs which lived in the field at the back of the house with bucket-loads of rotting apples which we found in a shed in the garden. But with May and my fifth birthday came Dunkirk. All day long and as we lay in bed at night, lorries and buses rumbled past the house, including presumably the bus which should have picked us up from school, going down to the coast, as we later found out, to help in the evacuation.

Towards the end of 1940 Father got a job as Chief Draughts-man at the Barrow Hematite Steelworks in Barrow-in-Furness. We gave up the house in Margaretting and my mother, brother and I moved north to stay with my mother's mother and sister in Wallasey, while Father looked for a suitable house for us in Barrow.

My maternal grandmother was a rather beautiful, ladylike and gentle person. She had been born into a fairly prosperous Liverpool family and had married the son of another solid, middle-class Liverpool family, the Parrotts. He is described on their wedding certificate as an 'African trader'. For some unknown reason, my grandfather had gone off to Canada when my mother was quite small, leaving Grandmother in Liverpool with their three children, promising to send for them when he was established. He corresponded for a while and then she heard no more from him. The years passed and she brought up the children as best she could, on her own, with help from her family. Then one day, in 1917, she was contacted by the War Office, to be told that her husband was on a hospital ship in Liverpool docks on his way back to Canada, seriously wounded. He had become a Canadian citizen, had been conscripted into the Canadian army and had fought in France in a Canadian infantry battalion. If she wanted to see him before the ship sailed, she must go straight down to the docks. She did, and my mother then aged sixteen went with her. Neither of them ever talked about what was said at that meeting but it must have been a traumatic occasion. It was their last meeting for he died not long after his return to Canada.

Wallasey in 1940–41 was not a good place to live. Night after night the German bombers came over to try to flatten the Liverpool docks. My grandmother had a flat in a large Edwardian house in Church Street, just up from the Wallasey sea front and opposite the docks. My brother Brian and I slept on bunks behind a thick curtain at the end of a long corridor. It was thought to be safer than sleeping in a room, where the windows might break and the glass cut us. We didn't like the dark, so we drew the curtain back after we had gone to bed. Looking up the corridor one night as the bombs descended, I saw a picture falling off the wall and a nightlight on a table flickering and going out with the blast of a bomb which had fallen very near by. Until recently my mother still kept that particular picture with a crack in the frame where it had hit the floor.

After a few weeks of this, the bombing became so intense that, when the sirens sounded, we left our house and went next door to a ballroom dancing school, where there was a windowless basement. We and several neighbours sat there night after night till dawn came and the all-clear sounded. The first time we decided that it was too dangerous to stay in our own house, we delayed until the middle of an intense air raid. As we went outside I looked up and saw the sky lit up by the flames of the burning docks, with a pattern of spotlights, anti-aircraft fire, barrage balloons and an aircraft falling on fire out of the sky.

For months during this period, Brian and I did not go to school. There probably seemed little point as we were awake most of the night and in any case we did not know how long we would stay in Wallasey before moving on again. I think Mother did not really want us to go to school in case there was an air raid and we got separated, because by then the sirens were sounding during the daylight hours too. Being separated from us was her biggest anxiety at the time. We used to sleep during the day and sometimes play in the park, but eventually the school inspectors got on to us. Rather surprisingly they were still working and they told my mother we had to go to school. I can't remember many lessons, though, when we did, just more time spent sitting in the white-tiled school cellar during daytime raids.

Later in 1941, we moved to Barrow-in-Furness, to join my father. By then, night after night, the Luftwaffe was bombing the Vickers dockyards at Barrow. At first we lived in rooms in a tall house on Abbey Road, where the safest place during a raid was under the stairs. We went there every night, the landlady's family, my mother, brother and I, while my father was out on the streets as an air-raid warden.

After a short time in Abbey Road, we moved to yet another rented house, No. 5 Ilkley Road, a pebble-dashed semi, where, like our neighbours, we turned our back garden into a vegetable patch, stuck tape over the windows to stop the glass shattering in the blast and battened down to see out the war. But before that time came we had yet more nights of bombing to endure. In this house the safest place in a raid was judged to be under the dining-room table and we were all sitting there one night during a particularly ferocious attack, when the blast from a nearby bomb drove the soot down the chimney and covered us all from head to toe. On that night my parents decided again, in the middle of the raid, that the bombing was too close for safety and we set off in our nightclothes, covered with soot as we were, to walk the hundred yards or so to the municipal air-raid shelter. I was terrified, as yet again I saw the sky full of the lights of anti-aircraft fire and burning planes and buildings. I remember urging my parents to run, but my father insisted we walk. No Nazi was going to make him run, and in any case he took the view, difficult for a six-year-old to appreciate, that if we were to be hit we would be hit whether we walked or ran. That night I had a very narrow escape, when a piece of shrapnel missed me by inches. I felt the draught as it passed my shoulder.

After that experience, we acquired an air-raid shelter, a mighty structure of steel plates, which was actually a blast shelter from a quarry. It entirely filled our sitting room but was rapidly absorbed into the family and became accepted as part of the furniture. We could sit up in it, and we had beds in there too. We spent every night in that shelter while the bombing went on. My brother colonised it and used it as a base for his model railway. It made a really satisfactory reverberating sound when hit, and on it I learned the Morse code. Air-raid shelters were a part of life in those days – everyone had one. I used to envy some of my friends who had neat table shelters, which could be much more easily disguised than ours. They made wonderful hiding places for games at birthday parties, but in fact they must have been horribly claustrophobic in an air raid. Others had Anderson shelters in their gardens, deep dangerous places, which hung around long after the war and often seemed to be full of stagnant, smelly water. The father of one of my friends once used his to drown a family of kittens – an execution which I still remember with horror to this day.

During one night we spent in our air-raid shelter, the houses across the road were landmined. Amazingly, my brother and I must have gone to sleep during the raid and been put into our beds still asleep when it was over. But later in the night our ceilings collapsed and we woke to find our beds covered with dust and to see my mother and father sweeping up the ceiling plaster from the floor. Our windows had all been blown in and the staircase had shifted inches from the wall. I had been delighted when we moved into that house. It was the first house of our own we had had since we left London and I felt that at last we had settled somewhere. When I woke up and saw the state of things I was heartbroken, and according to family legend, I said 'Oh, look what's happened to our nice little house,' and burst into tears. We lived with the house in that state until towards the end of the war, when the bomb-damage people came to repair it.

Looking back on my early childhood, I realise now how frightened I was for most of the time. After some months spent wide awake in cellars and shelters, listening to aeroplanes and the explosions of falling bombs, I began to shake uncontrollably when the siren sounded and the shaking did not stop until we heard the all-clear. Obviously my experiences came nowhere near the horror of those of many children in Europe during the war. But even what I went through would be thought nowadays to require instant counselling. In those days you just absorbed the experience and dealt with it however you could. I was left with some tangible symptoms of anxiety. In my teens, I began to suffer claustrophobia which lasted for years, even after I was married, and had the effect of making it very difficult for me to sit in the middle of a row at a concert or the theatre or in church. I had to know where the exits were and to have planned how I would get out. If I found myself in a situation where I could not easily get out of a room, I would come out in a cold sweat and start to shake. Perhaps less clearly attributable to the war, I developed a quite pessimistic and anxious personality. I grew up feeling that it was no good having great expectations, nothing in life was going to be easy and there wasn't much certainty around; so you'd better depend on yourself to make the best of whatever came along. And heaven only knew what that would be.

I suppose I caught that attitude from Father, whose experiences had given him a fairly dour attitude to life. He was a self-educated Yorkshireman, who had obtained his engineering qualifications at night school, after working during the day at Cochrane's Ironworks in Middlesbrough. He held strong Christian beliefs and taught us that hard work and devotion to duty were the most important things and that they would be their own reward.

When we lived in Barrow, we had a dog called Billy. Actually, when he came to us, from an old soldier who had died, his name was Buller, after General Sir Redvers Buller, the Boer War general, but we renamed him. When Billy died I was heartbroken. As little girls do when their pet dies, I cried and cried and went on crying into the night. I know Father was really sorry that I was so upset, but his reaction was to say in a rather stern way, 'Well, we shall certainly never have another dog, if this is what happens.' We never did, and I felt really guilty and silly for being so upset. All my life I have felt that showing emotion is somehow a bit of a weakness. Emotions are what other people are allowed to have and show and people like me are supposed to be strong, to help when others are in difficulties. It's a very stark philosophy.

Both Father and Mother believed most strongly that you must never give up – there was no place for weakness and above all no time to be ill. Father suffered all the time I knew him from stress-related illnesses, particularly constant nervous indigestion, but he never gave way to them. His experiences during the First World War had been horrific, and he could not be persuaded to talk much about them. He sometimes mentioned his time in the military hospital, recovering from his head wound, which left him with a large depressed fracture of the skull. I think he had been very ill at first, but later he had found being cooped up in hospital very difficult and he talked with some shame about an incident, which must have occurred when he was recovering. Having been woken by the nurse at some incredibly early hour to be washed, he had thrown the washing water at her.

Probably as a result of his head wound, he tended to be anxious and pessimistic. He had some form of nervous breakdown at the beginning of the Second War in 1939, when all the horror of his experiences of the First came back to haunt him. He was kind and took a great interest in his two children, and later in his grandchildren. But he was very conscientious, he always had to work hard and there was not much time or money for relaxation. Perhaps not surprisingly, I do not remember much lightheartedness about him.

Most of the burden of bringing us up and of keeping Father going fell on my mother, who died at ninety-five during 1997. She was a truly stoical person. She believed, and these beliefs were tested almost, but not quite, to destruction during the war, that whatever the circumstances one should remain as cheerful as one possibly could; that one should never complain and that one should try to cause as few problems or difficulties for others as possible. She taught her two children the importance of perseverance. She used to tell us that nothing that is worth doing can be achieved easily, but that at the end of the day you can do no more than your best. When, later on, I used to moan about exams and say, as I always did, that I was going to fail, she used to reassure me quietly and say that nobody could blame me if I tried my hardest, and so of course I did, and I usually passed.

With the end of the war came more peaceful nights and what was remarkable freedom in comparison with the life of present day children. With very little traffic about, we played hopscotch and football in the street and bicycled to school. During the war, playing in the street could be a bit hazardous because bands of soldiers used to come and practise urban warfare in our area, hiding round corners and shooting at each other with blank cartridges. When they weren't there we enjoyed our own war games. My brother always wanted to be Rommel, because it meant he could ride around the street on my tricycle, wearing a long overcoat and a cap.

I started school in Barrow at the local infants' school at the top of our road. I must have been a regular little Southerner when I first went there. On my first day I was asked to read to the class, and they all roared with laughter because I pronounced 'castle' as 'carstle', whereas they all said 'casstle'. I soon lost my Southern ways after that, and learned how to speak Lancashire. When my brother went on to Barrow Grammar School, I was sent to a little convent school for girls, Crosslands Convent at Furness Abbey on the outskirts of Barrow. The teachers were nearly all nuns and were all characters. There was Sister Borromeo, who taught us history, a long lean ascetic lady, who, whenever she wrote on the blackboard, put a sideways cross over one of the words. This puzzled me for a long time and one day I summoned up the courage to ask her why she did it. 'To remind me that all my work is done for God,' she replied. I never worked out whether that was profound, or profoundly dotty. Sister Borromeo was a nervous lady and it was due to her that I transferred my fear of bombing raids to a fear of lightning. I remember one particular history lesson, which was disturbed by ferocious claps of thunder. I had been told that thunder-storms were not dangerous and was quite prepared to shrug them off, until I noticed that after every clap of thunder Sister Borromeo would anxiously cross herself and whisper, 'I thought I saw lightning.'

At the convent I was among the group apart, known as the 'Non-Catholics'. We were excluded from interesting-looking occasions, when incense was burned and rosaries were said. From time to time, a very important-looking figure came to visit the school. He wore a long, purple gown and all the way down it at the front, in a sort of semi-circle over his large protuberant stomach, were tiny little round purple buttons, covered with the fabric of his robe. I used to stare at him, trying to count his buttons, but he never stayed still long enough for me to get all the way from top to bottom. I never knew who he was, though he was clearly some dignitary in the Roman Catholic hierarchy and we all had to call him

'Monsignor'. The Catholic girls were allowed to kiss his ring, but we were supposed just to curtsy to him.

But even as a non-Catholic, I did learn to recite the Hail Mary, which was said in chorus several times a day. Or at least I thought I did. No-one ever taught it so I just picked it up, but for years I thought it went, 'Hail Mary, full of grace, the Lord is with you, blessed art thou swimming and blessed is the fruit of thy, whom Jesus.' It was only when I thought about this, much, much later, that I realised that could not have been right.

I was never quite sure how to take the nuns. I had never met any before. We all called them 'Sister' and some of the Catholic girls bobbed to them as though they were royalty. But I couldn't help noticing how oddly they behaved. Sister Dominic was a scatty and very untidy nun whose habit was always dirty and torn, with the tears held together with huge tacking stitches. But she had a heart of gold. She used to bring in to class, as prizes for mental arithmetic tests, pieces of cake of dubious origin, which emerged from the folds of her none-too-clean habit and which certainly should have had a health warning attached. We gobbled them up, both because we were greedy and because we didn't want to hurt her feelings. Sister Dominic claimed to be lame and was allowed to travel from the convent to the school and back in a wheelchair, a journey of about 200 yards over a rough, stony track. Presumably her sister nuns pushed her to school, but we girls vied for the privilege of pushing her back. Three or four of us would seize the handle of the wheelchair and run as fast as we could, bashing the poor lady and her wheelchair over the stones in what must have been a bone-breaking journey. She seemed to enjoy it though, and when, as regularly happened, a wheel flew off the chair, she would leap out, take off her shoe, and using it as a hammer, bash the wheel back on. It was this sprightly readiness to leap out which made us all wonder just how lame she really was.

Sister Cecilia was quite a different cup of tea. She terrified me. She was an exceptionally neat nun; her habit was always clean and beautifully pressed but her character matched her appearance and she was extremely severe. She taught art, and her lessons should have been pleasant occasions, but I was not very artistic and she was very sarcastic. My fear of art came to a head one Christmas when she decided we would all make crackers. I was unable to grasp that you had to get the crêpe paper one way round and not the other. I kept getting it wrong and when all the other children had a box of lovely crackers to show for their pains, I had just a few sticky, mangled messes because I had had to keep taking mine to bits. I stayed awake many nights worrying about those crackers, and to this day the sight of a certain kind of shiny string, which is still sold at Christmas, the kind we had been given to tie up those crackers, gives me the shudders.

In spite of Sister Cecilia, this was a happy period for me as a child, once the bombing had stopped. Life was no great effort. I was one of the brighter children at the school and had plenty of friends. We went on Saturday mornings to the children's picture show at the Roxy cinema, where some weeks Flash Gordon and his gang got into the most nerve-racking adventures, and sometimes, for the girls, we had Carmen Miranda and her fantastic fruit-covered hats. We marvelled at the cinema organ, which came up out of the floor changing from livid pink to vivid green as the mood of the music altered. My uncle played the piano for the silent films in Redcar, so he told us all about mood music and the difficulty of keeping the music in time with the pictures. We sometimes went down to the sea at Walney Island, though it was a dangerous place in those late wartime days, as much of the beach was mined and enclosed with barbed wire and there were frightening notices, saying 'Danger of Death'. At the weekends the whole family went walking in the Lake District, practically deserted and quite unlike the crowded tourist area it later became. We stayed for holidays at the Crown Hotel in Coniston, and watched the Victorian steamboat, 'The Lady of the Lake', rotting away quietly on Coniston Water and much to my satisfaction I climbed Coniston Old Man on my tenth birthday.

However in 1947, when I was twelve, my father took a post in the Drawing Office at Stanton Ironworks in Ilkeston, on the border of Derbyshire and Nottinghamshire, and very sadly on my part, we left the Lakes and the sea and the north of England and my little convent school for the Midlands.

# 2

The nuns at that convent school must have been better at teaching than I have allowed. At the age of twelve, without too much difficulty, I was accepted at Nottingham Girls' High School, one of the Girls' Public Day School Trust group of schools and then the best girls' day school in the area. At the beginning, this was the only thing that worked out well about the move to the Midlands. There was no place for my brother, then fifteen, at Nottingham High School, the much older and rather grander boys' school, neighbour of the girls' school in Arboretum Street. He had to go to Ilkeston Grammar School, which was considerably less academically distinguished. As he was very clever, much more so than I, that was a disappointment to my mother, though eventually he did very well there.

We found ourselves living in a house which belonged to Stanton Ironworks, a small Edwardian semi in Longfield Lane, on top of a hill just outside Ilkeston, which overlooked the valley in which the Ironworks lay. The view was the best thing about it; you couldn't quite see the works from the house, but when the wind was in a certain direction, you could smell the sulphurous odour of the coke ovens, or 'Duckhams' as they were called, after the manufacturer, Messrs Woodall-Duckhams. 'Duckhams is strong today,' people would remark, in the same way as you might say 'Turned out wet again,' in other parts of the country. The house itself was gloomy and old-fashioned. I remember coming home from school on my first day and finding my mother close to tears after a day spent scrubbing the red-tiled floor of the kitchen. She had made no headway at all, because it was damp. As well as the damp tiled floor, that room had a black iron stove in the fireplace, with little baking ovens, and in the scullery there was a low stone sink with an open drain beneath it. It was the authentic version of what the kitchen designers try to reproduce nowadays, and it was extremely uncomfortable. The milkman brought the milk in a can, and poured it out into a jug, which we had to have ready for him. There was no refrigerator. To my mother, who had lost her new suburban house in London, with all the family capital tied up in it, to the controlled tenant, it was all deeply unsatisfactory. But there was no chance whatsoever in the circumstances of their buying anything else, so she had to put up with it.

We stayed in that house until I was about eighteen and it did not improve. In fact for Mother it got worse, as her only sister, my Auntie Lilian, to whom she was very close, came there to die when she developed cancer. That was a very grim period. I had been very fond of Auntie Lilian, with whom we had shared our wartime experiences in Wallasey. After my grandmother's death she had continued to live in the big flat in Church Street which they had shared and where we had stayed during the bombing. She came to stay with us often and always at Christmas, when it was her job to set the table for Christmas dinner and I often went to stay with her on my own. I loved going there; she had kept my grandmother's furniture, which dated from the time when their lives had been rather grander – brass bedsteads, a big mahogany table and chairs and a heavy mahogany sideboard with fantastic carvings on it. My brother and I used to look at the carvings through a magnifying glass to frighten ourselves when we were young. She also had a piano stool, with a green top that spun round and round; we used to play Wallasey buses with that. My brother had an encyclopaedic knowledge of the stops on all the local bus routes, and he would be the driver with the piano-stool wheel, while I was the conductor, ringing the little brass bell. My mother used that same bell to ring for attention when she got very old. There was one other particularly marvellous thing in that flat, which was an old knife-cleaner.

You put the knives in slots at the top and some grey powder in another slot and then you wound a wheel round and round as fast as you could and there was a satisfying grinding noise and the knives came out shiny. I saw a similar one in an antique shop not long ago. When things from your childhood start appearing in antique shops, you know time is beginning to run out for you. It is the same sort of shock you get when you learn that children are studying the period of your childhood as history.

Auntie Lilian worked on the telephone switchboard in the warehouse of a firm called J. Langdon and Sons in Duke Street, Liverpool, crossing the Mersey on the ferry-boat from Seacombe every day. It was a job well beneath her capacity, for she was intelligent and well educated, but she was a casualty of her times, and of their curious family history. She had not been brought up to work, but found herself having to do so. Although I was so fond of her, I feel ashamed to remember that I found myself almost unable to go in to the bedroom to see her when she lay dying in our house. We had only three bedrooms and Brian had to sleep downstairs so Lilian could have his room. She was next door to me and I could hear her drumming on the wall when the pain got very bad.

My mother's gloom about the move to the Midlands was not helped by my arriving home on my first day and announcing that I hated my new school and I would never settle down there. It must have been the last thing she wanted to hear at the end of a frustrating day spent scrubbing an intractable floor. I found Nottingham Girls' High School a bit of a shock after the cosiness of the convent. Apart from anything else, I had exchanged my bike ride along quiet roads for a journey which involved a walk down the hill, a trolley bus ride, and then a seven-mile bus journey into Nottingham. It is a sign of the big social changes that have taken place since then that I was despatched on that journey quite alone at the age of twelve with as far as I know no particular anxiety on the part of my parents. I can only once remember anything alarming happening. It was on one return journey when I must have been about thirteen, that a man came and sat next to me on the top deck of the bus. He put his hand on my thigh and all through the journey he stroked it, gradually pulling up the side of my skirt. I was far too scared to say anything to him or to get up and change seats, but he can't have been too determined as he had not succeeded in reaching my bare leg before it was time for me to get off the bus. When I got up, though, I realised that my skirt was all crushed where he had been folding it into his hand. I was too embarrassed ever to mention this to anyone.

It was a big change for me to go from a small school in large grounds to a large school with no grounds. The school was a series of houses in a then run-down street in a city and it was a most impractical arrangement. It had grown gradually by acquiring more and more houses, not all of which had been joined together, so the girls had to go out in the open air, come rain come shine, as they went from one lesson to another. On the other side of the street was a row of houses which have now been knocked down to let the school extend over the road. A few years ago, when I gave away the prizes at the school speech day, I told the girls that when I was at the school, I had whiled away my time during boring history lessons by gazing out of the classroom window into the windows of the houses across the road, and watching people having their tea. 'I was a spy at school, says MI5 boss,' announced the *Nottingham Evening Post*.

In fact there was not a great deal of time to be bored at that school. There were some fiercely efficient teachers there, like Miss Pretty who taught History. She drummed information into us by a combination of sheer strength of personality and fear. She would regularly announce at the end of the lesson, 'Test tomorrow,' and we knew we had to go home and learn up everything that had gone before. She never forgot. The next day she would come striding across from the staff-room in her sensible lace-up shoes and mid-calf tweed skirt and as she swept into the classroom she would be already saying, 'First question: What was the date of the *Drei Kaiserbund?*' She was not the only terrifying teacher in that school. Miss Todd was equally efficient at dinning Latin and French into us. We learned from those teachers largely I think through fear of their scorn should we fail. The younger teachers could not match their power, though we much preferred their lessons.

I soon settled down and learned to operate in the bigger pond of that school. In the late 1940s, Nottingham Girls' High School was providing an extremely sound and traditional education for girls from all social classes. Although it was a fee-paying school, the fees were small, something like £12 per term, a sum my parents could afford without too much difficulty. But it also provided a considerable number of free places for those whose families could not afford the fees and the result was a group of girls from very mixed backgrounds. One of my closest friends was Jean Hardy, a girl whose father had disappeared fighting in the Far East, and was later found to have died in a Japanese prisoner-of-war camp. Her mother had been left, not knowing for years whether her husband was alive or dead, to bring up their two daughters with very little money in a prefabricated house in Nottingham. Both girls went to the High School and Jean's time there totally changed her life, opening up opportunities and giving her contacts which she could never otherwise have had. My education seems to me superior in every way to the education my daughters received at similar schools in London in the 1980s. We came away with an ability to spell, a sound understanding of grammar, helped by a grounding in Latin, French and German, a certain facility in mental arithmetic, although mathematics was never my strong suit, an outline knowledge of the history of Britain and Europe and of English literature, including, as far as I am concerned, a store of quotations which once learned have never been forgotten. They seem to have acquired very little of this.

What the school did not provide was any focus on what the girls were going to do with their lives. There was no career information offered and no thought of choosing a university course with a career in mind. The teachers thought that their responsibilities began and ended with getting us with credit through the public examinations, and encouraging the brighter of their charges to go on to university and then getting them in. They made it very clear to us, too, that the only subjects worth taking at university were the academic ones – English, History, the Sciences or Mathematics for example. Jean Hardy, who was a bright girl, deeply upset the teachers by announcing that she wished to take Sociology, and although she successfully obtained a place at Bedford College, she was regarded as having in some way let the school down.

What all this focus on university and nothing beyond really indicated was that we all, even the girls, thought, subconsciously if not overtly, that any career we did have was not going to last. It would be only a temporary interlude until we got married, when we would stay at home to look after our husbands and children. So the important thing was the education, not what you did with it. Nobody, least of all the teachers, would have admitted that, but I am sure that is how it was. Others, even less enlightened, thought that it was not worth sending girls to university at all. I can remember one of my father's friends saying to my parents in my hearing, 'Surely you are not going to send that girl to university. She will only get married and that will be a complete waste.' Of course, adults were always asking us what we wanted to be, as they always do of children, but when that question was asked of a girl, it was never meant seriously. I had no idea how to answer the question, partly because I knew it was not serious and partly because the only thing I knew at that stage was that I wanted to do or be something out of the ordinary and exciting. So I used to reply that I was going to be an airline pilot, which was something women could not do in those days, so the conversation was effectively brought to an end. Not surprisingly, as a result of all this, girls did feel that most of the focus was on the boys and they were taken less seriously. If there were a limited amount of money to be spent, it would be spent on the boy, because he would eventually have to be the breadwinner for his family. To do my parents credit, I personally never felt that I was denied anything that mattered to me because I was only a girl, but I know some girls did.

Today the focus has changed. It is expected that girls will have long-term careers. Career advice or 'counselling' as all advice seems to be called nowadays, is offered from the age of fourteen. But now I am afraid that the sort of schools I went to may have swung too far the other way, almost to the point of making girls feel inadequate if they decide that they would prefer to spend more time looking after their homes and family. I know how hard it is to cope with a full-time job and small children, particularly in circumstances where there is not enough money to pay for qualified child-care at home. It is difficult, and even the toughest and most determined can wilt under the strain. Not everyone can cope, though many have no choice. But if schools like the one I attended are not quite careful and subtle about the message they give to their pupils, they may make a generation of young women feel that they are inadequate failures, if they are not both high-flying career women and successful wives and mothers.

I grew to enjoy my time at Nottingham Girls' High School, where at first I was always in the top few in the class. But by the time I was about sixteen, I began to make less effort and to cease to conform. The terrifying but excellent teachers passed out of my life, and we were in the hands of young women who had just left university, and did not have the power to force learning. I easily got bored and when things started to become more difficult I was not prepared to make the effort. My attitude to school changed and school's attitude to me changed too. From being quite highly thought of by the teachers, I began to be regarded as something of a rebel, though as rebels often do, I kept a large group of friends. When I reached the sixth form, and elections for Head Girl were held – the election was by voting by the sixth form and the teachers – though I believe I was the choice of the girls, I was blackballed by the teachers. Teachers in girls' schools in those days did not have a great deal of time for those who did not conform. All this ended by my failing one of my three A Level subjects, Latin, and having to stay at school for another year to re-sit. It was decided that the only person who would teach me enough Latin to get me through was Miss Todd, one of the old school, so I fell back into the hands of the real teachers again and of course passed easily the second time round. What they did, those female teachers of the old school, was subtly to imply respect for the ability of those they were teaching, so that in some way a partnership was formed, neither side of which could let the other down. It was very effective. As I had stayed on for a third year, it was decided that I would sit the Oxford and Cambridge entrance exams, and I applied to Newnham. I was called for interview but when I got there I felt very much a fish out of water, wearing the wrong clothes, from the wrong background and quite unable to deal with the sharp and rather patronising female dons. They sat so cosily on their sofas, quizzing me about an interesting theory I had put forward about some poet in my essay, that I had in fact lifted lock stock and barrel from a book one of them had written.

It was during my journeys on the bus to school that I met John Rimington whom I was later to marry. His father was a Coal Board official and they lived in a Coal Board house called 'The Grange', in Trowell, that gloomy village between Ilkeston and Nottingham which surprised the world in 1951 by being pronounced 'Festival Village' for the Festival of Britain. Whoever chose it must have been suffering from an excess of political correctness. Confused foreign tourists used to arrive there looking for what they thought was going to be some thatched cottage idyll only to find themselves contemplating the main road to Nottingham, passing through a ribbon development of redbrick semis which did not even have a pub.

'The Grange' seemed to me extremely grand. It was a brick-built detached house in its own quite sizeable garden. Its drawbacks were that it was just beside the railway line, and it suffered even more than we did from 'Duckhams' as the wind was more frequently in their direction than ours. John and I met on the bus when we were sixteen and both just entering the sixth form of our respective schools – he was at Nottingham High School. I thought him rather quaint and old-fashioned. He used to write verse in a perfect, neat handwriting in a black stiff-backed notebook and would occasionally send me letters, equally beautifully written. Our acquaintance was reinforced at the dancing classes, at which the sixth formers of the two schools were allowed to meet and fraternise.

On our side, Miss Pretty presided to make quite sure there was no hanky-panky. I think she terrified the boys even more than she did us. She made very sure that we were all dressed in a seemly manner – we were allowed not to wear school uniform. Her standards were severe and unwavering. I remember once wearing what I regarded as a rather fetching scarf tied round the neck of my jumper. This did not meet Miss Pretty's exacting standards.

'Have you got a sore throat, Stella?' she asked.

'No Miss Pretty.'

'Then take off that silly scarf.'

So ended my fashion statement.

John's and my acquaintance did not get much beyond the dancing classes and occasional visits to each other's houses for tea during our school days. He got a scholarship to Cambridge and went off to do his National Service and, after successfully completing my A Levels, I got a place at Edinburgh University and set off there in October 1954 to read English. I never expected to see him again.

# 3

I spent my last summer at school, the summer of 1953, working in Paris as an *au pair*. In those days young people did not routinely go off travelling in the year between school and university, and this sort of experience was the alternative. It was quite a shock, and helped me to sympathise with some of the young girls we later employed as *au pair*s in London. I was working for a French doctor and his wife, who had five children. The oldest was a boy of about nine and the youngest a baby. I was totally ill equipped for this experience, a provincial girl with no knowledge of anything much outside my narrow upbringing. I had only been abroad once before, on a school trip to Brittany, when we stayed in a convent in Lamballe and were shepherded everywhere by the nuns. My main recollection of that holiday was the anxiety struck into the nuns by the arrival of a telegram addressed to me at the convent. It was delivered just as we had sat down to dinner and I was called out to be given this missive by a very caring-looking nun, who was obviously convinced that my nearest and dearest had been struck down with some dreadful tragedy. I opened the envelope and inside was a telegram form with, written on it in pencil, in spidery French handwriting: '*Tassed* (sic) *all subjects*.' These were my O Level results which my parents, instructed by me before I left, had opened and telegraphed on. I was happy, but the telegram really set the cat among the pigeons, as nobody else's family had sent anything. There was a wild scramble for the one and only phone, which totally disrupted dinner and greatly upset the nuns who took meals rather formally.

The French family was very kind to me, considering how

useless I must have been. I knew nothing about children at all, I could not cook, my French was schoolgirl O Level, and I had never been away from home totally alone in my life. The family lived on one of the main roads out of Paris, avenue General LeClerc, at Antony, in a house which to me with my English provincial ideas of comfort, seemed bleak and almost bare of furniture, but which I would probably now regard as elegant. It was a 19th-century house, with wooden floors and tall shuttered windows and double doors between the rooms. The doctor was a charming, sophisticated but to me, at least, rather remote figure. He had been a supporter of de Gaulle and the family had, so I understood, lost many of their possessions, looted as the German Army left Paris in 1945. Compared to what *au pair*s are required to do nowadays, my job was not onerous. Madame did not work, so I was left alone with the children only when she went out. I found them terrifying, particularly the oldest boy, who had murderous tendencies and spent his time trying to hit his sisters on the head by launching the heavy wooden seat of a garden swing straight at them.

There were lots of surprises for me during the weeks I spent with Doctor and Madame Thouvenal. There was the fig tree in the garden, on which large ripe figs were hanging. I had only seen a fig in pictures, and had certainly not seen one growing on a tree. As a war-time child, I had only recently got used to seeing bananas freely available in the shops, and in the 1950s there was nothing like the variety of fruit on sale that there is today. Another shock was the bathing arrangements. There was no bath that I could use and the only shower was in the cellar, which I knew contained rats. I had seen them in the garden, where I had watched with horror as Madame Marie, who came in to do the washing, lobbed her shoe at one. One day, I was sent out to buy meat for dinner. I was told to go to a certain butcher's shop and buy two kilos of steak. It was only when I saw the horse's head above the door that I realised what I was buying. That was yet another shock – until then I did not know that anyone ate horse.

I was in Paris during July and August, and, homesick, I used to lean out of the window and enviously watch the French families setting off for their holidays. That summer, public transport in Paris went on strike, and the army ran lorries to replace the buses. I was keen to use them, but Madame, knowing a great deal more about the French army than I did, was quite sure they were not safe and was equally sure that my mother would not want me to travel on them. So I was not allowed to go anywhere except by bicycle, which rather restricted my sightseeing and was probably a good deal more dangerous. I remember being whistled at furiously by a gendarme as I bicycled along a motorway near Versailles, not realising that I should have been on the cycle track. '*Voulez-vous être écrasée?*' he bellowed at me. It was a very hot summer, and there is a certain combination of smells, a mixture of petrol fumes, floor polish, French bread and coffee beans which I have occasionally met since, which always reminds me of that summer in Paris in the 1950s.

Having failed with Cambridge, I chose Edinburgh University, I think, because of a rather romantic attraction to Scottish history and Celticness and also because it was a very long way from home. By then home and family was beginning to seem very restricted and I could not wait to get away. My father had been promoted within the drawing office at Stanton Ironworks and by 1954, when I set off to Edinburgh, he was Chief Draughtsman. He had joined the Rotary Club in Ilkeston and my mother had had a year as President of the Inner Wheel. Their lives had broadened out, there was a bit more money around and they socialised more. We had moved to a larger and better-appointed company house, Glen Maye, in Sandiacre, on the road between Nottingham and Derby. It was still fairly old-fashioned. Stanton Ironworks did not spend a great deal on updating their officials' houses in those days. There was no heating, except fires, which was not unusual, but it was a particularly cold house in winter and as I poked my head out of bed I could see my breath steaming in the cold air. Even so, it was nothing like as cold as some of the lodgings I later found myself living in in Edinburgh. In the bathroom of one particular flat, when I put my toothbrush in my mouth one morning, I found I was scrubbing away with a small block of ice on a stick.

In one way, Edinburgh University quite lived up to my romantic expectations. It seemed to me, when I arrived there in 1954, to be still very close to its 16th-century origins. The 18th-century lecture rooms in the Adam Old College on South Bridge were still very much in use and many of the lectures I attended in my first year were held there. Some courses of lectures were hugely popular, such as the Moral Philosophy lectures of Professor John Macmurray, which would attract two or three hundred students. The old tiered wooden benches would be full and people would be sitting on the steps and on the floor. It was the custom for the students to express their appreciation by stamping when a particularly popular lecturer arrived and left. The sound of all those feet drumming on the wooden floor in those ancient lecture rooms, just as they must have done for hundreds of years, made me feel I was part of some on-going historical process and this I enjoyed.

One part of the 18th century that was still alive was the election of the Rector, accompanied by the battle of the fish-heads. I remember well the Rectorial election of 1957, when James Robertson Justice, the actor, was elected. The fish-head battle, in which supporters of one candidate hurled fish-heads and other portions of fishes' anatomy at each other across the Old Quad, was particularly enthusiastic that year. The Old Quad was awash with foul-smelling water and slimy pop-eyed heads were whistling through the air and slopping around for hours. I don't think any side ever claimed victory in those battles. The whole satisfaction came from the mess of the fight. The actual election was a much more sober affair, conducted elsewhere by the usual democratic means of crosses on ballot papers.

The fish-heads and the lectures were not the only 18th-century aspects to my life in Edinburgh. The living arrangements had a touch of that century from time to time too. I have mentioned the frozen toothbrush I wielded in the flat in Learmonth Gardens in my second year. That was in fact quite a civilised place because it did have a bathroom. In my third year I moved into a flat in a block of tenements just off the Royal Mile overlooking Arthur's Seat, called Prince Albert Buildings, now demolished, presumably regarded as not fit for human habitation. Ours had no bathroom or hot water, though it did at least have a lavatory. We used to go for our baths to the public bath-house where you got a cubicle with a deep, old-fashioned bath in it and lashings of hot water for just a few pence. The only problem with the bath-house was that the walls of the cubicles were made of pine boards and some of them had holes poked through, so that bathers on the men's side could peer through at the naked ladies in the baths on the other side of the board. We became quite adept at bunging up the holes with soap. As far as I remember there was no time limit on how long you could stay and I managed to get through large parts of Richardson's *Pamela* and *Clarissa* sitting in my lovely deep hot bath, with the holes in the wall suitably plugged. Later, I did quite a lot of my exam preparation in the bath-house. It was a very cosy place to work and provided there was no queue, no one seemed to bother.

I must have had an extremely retentive memory in those days. At Scottish universities, Honours students had to take a number of subjects outside their Honours course in their first and second years. I was advised to take Latin, amongst others, in my first year. It was Latin which had been my Waterloo at A level and I failed it again in my first year at Edinburgh. I did not seem able to get to grips with the grammar and I decided that the only way I was going to pass was to achieve such immensely high marks in the set books and the Roman History components that they couldn't fail me on the rest. So I sat down and to all intents and purposes learned off by heart the translations of the set texts, chunks of Livy and Virgil, which you could buy in James Thin's university bookshop. If someone showed me a few lines, I could recite the translation word by word, without actually being able to translate the Latin for myself: an esoteric skill which I have lost now.

Alongside my enjoyment of the tradition went a strong feeling that the whole Arts faculty was frozen in the past. Those Moral Philosophy lectures had been being delivered for years in exactly the same form and style. If you couldn't be bothered getting out of bed in time to go to the lectures, you could buy, in the Student Union, the notes taken at the same lectures years ago by some enterprising student who had reportedly got a First on the basis of them. Our English Literature course ended at T.S. Eliot, and 'the novel' came to an end with Hardy. But what we actually read for pleasure was *Lucky Jim* and what got us talking was *Look Back in Anger*, and the other writings of the 'angry young men'. I resolved the problem in my third and fourth years by going right back into the past and focusing on Anglo-Saxon and Middle English.

I found life at university enjoyable and on the whole un-stressed. I was not an intellectual and was more concerned with enjoying myself than acquiring knowledge, though I did want to end up with a decent degree. Coming from the English higher education system, I had already done the first year's English for A level, so this caused me no bother at all. The Scottish system of outside subjects and yearly exams did force me to do some work, even in my first and second years, but on the whole life during those first two years was pretty much devoted to pleasing myself and having fun. We had fairly innocent amusements in those days. As it was Scotland, there was a lot of partying and quite heavy drinking. There was a constant search for ways to get drunk cheaply and quickly, in which strange combinations of beer or, very popular, Merry-down cider and spirits figured frequently. But there were no drugs around, or at least I never came across any, and in the early 1950s it was not even automatically expected that you and your boyfriend would sleep together.

In the first term of my third year, I was struck down with glandular fever, the result, I always thought, of a walking holiday in Belgium and Luxembourg in the late summer of 1956 with Jean Hardy. We had slept in some damp and insalubrious places and eaten and drunk some odd things obtained from farms by the wayside. The European Community had not got its grip on Luxembourg in those days and it was still quite rustic. Of course the glandular fever may have originated in the tenement flat in Prince Albert Buildings, which I was sharing with my Highland friend Isolyn. There was only one bed, so I slept on a very dubious-looking sofa, in which anything might have been lurking. Anyway, I fell sick and had to go home for a term.

I was at home and feeling very ill during October 1956 when the world seemed to be lurching from one international crisis to another. In bed I listened avidly to radio accounts of the invasion of the Canal Zone and then of the Soviet invasion of Hungary. Although my friends at Edinburgh were not particularly politically active, they were all involved in demonstrations and protests, and they kept me in touch with what was going on. I was quite well enough to be very frustrated at missing it all. At home, my father was sure the world was slipping back into war again and he used to come up to my bedroom when he came home from work and sit on my bed going on at length about the iniquities of Colonel Nasser and Mr Khrushchev. The fact that my brother was away doing National Service in the Tank Corps in Germany did not make the household any more cheerful. As far as we were concerned he would be at the forefront of resistance when the Russian forces swept into the West across the German plains. But we did reflect that at least for the moment he was better placed than the sons of some of my parents' friends who were doing their National Service in Cyprus, and were sending home hair-raising accounts of camping in orchards while EOKA terrorists attacked them in the night from the trees.

I had had my chance to protest earlier that year when Bulganin and Khrushchev, the Soviet Russian leaders, paid a visit to Edinburgh as part of their tour of the UK in 1956. It was supposed to be a 'friendship' trip, but there wasn't much friendliness in our welcome. I can't remember what aspect of their visit in particular we were protesting about but I was in the jeering crowd, carrying a banner bearing the immortal slogan 'Bulge and Krush Go Home'. It had no effect at all, of course, and they went on to finish their tour, clearly quite unmoved by my protests.

In my last year at Edinburgh I met John Rimington again. His parents had moved up to Edinburgh when his father had become Finance Director of the Scottish Coal Board. They were living in Fairmilehead and he had gone up to Cambridge. I was at a dance at the Students' Union with my then boyfriend, a large Scottish geology student called Fergus, and we were dancing to Jimmy Shand and his Band, when John suddenly showed up. He was at a territorial army camp just outside Edinburgh and with several of the young officers had gatecrashed the Union dance to see what female talent was on offer, when he saw me. Fergus, and he, who were at opposite ends of the spectrum, physically, intellectually and in every other way, took an instant dislike to each other. That chance encounter led to my renewing my friendship with John. I went to have supper at his parents' house and we kept in touch when he went back to Cambridge.

It was not until the Christmas of 1957, when I was at home for the holidays and working for my finals, that I started to give any serious thought to what I was going to do next. Most of my female friends at Edinburgh were automatically drifting into teaching, largely because they could not think of anything else to do, but I was determined that I would not do that. Teaching seemed to me to be the end of all interesting life; I was still hankering after something a bit out of the ordinary. I had been to the Careers Advisory Service but they had come up with no suggestions that made any impression on me. I don't think I made much impression on them either. Even in those days I was quite good at reading upside down, and I could read the notes the interviewer was making on her pad. She wrote down 'Ill-made face' and I felt so insulted that I would not have taken any advice from her, even if it had been worth taking. In fact she made only one suggestion that appealed to me at all, which was the British Council's Voluntary Service Overseas Scheme (VSO). There were interviews taking place in an Edinburgh hotel for posts in Scandinavia – Finland I think it was – and I went along. The interviewer impressed on me that one would be all on one's own in some remote part of the country, expected to teach English to people who understood none, and very much dependent on one's own resources. I thought it sounded rather fun, but when, using my upside down reading skills again, I saw that the interviewer had written 'All nerves' on his pad as he interviewed me, it was obvious I was not going to be selected, and I wasn't. If there was a covert recruiter for the intelligence services in the Careers Advisory Office at Edinburgh in those days, and I expect there was, I clearly did not strike them as suitable material and the intelligence services certainly did not enter my mind as possible employers. Indeed, probably the only time I had ever heard of them was when Burgess and Maclean defected to the Soviet Union in 1951, when I can remember my father fulminating about the inefficiencies of MI5 which had let them get away.

So it was with a certain desperation at Christmas 1957 that I thought about how to earn my living. Teaching seemed to be looming if I could not think of anything else. I certainly had to do something. My parents could not afford to keep me indefinitely and there was no kindly welfare state waiting to welcome me with open arms onto the unemployment register. A degree in English Language and Literature seemed to qualify one for nothing and it did not occur to me to apply to a company or to look at the financial world or the City. In my book, that was what the men did, and I have no recollection of anyone suggesting it to me. The only solution seemed to me to do another course in something but by then I would have already spent four years at university and my father took some persuading that I needed to be supported for another year. After all, I was only a girl, who would probably get married before long, surely four years was long enough. My brother, after two years in the Army doing National Service and three years reading Engineering at Cambridge, had got a very satisfactory job with British Rail. So why did I need yet another year of education?

Eventually my mother persuaded him that they would never forgive themselves if they denied me a proper chance in life and anyway perhaps I would get a grant for part of it. In the end he agreed, without too much persuasion, and so I went on scouring the handbooks and eventually came up with the idea of taking a postgraduate diploma in the Study of Records and the Administration of Archives, which qualified one for a post in a County Record Office, the Public Record Office or a private archive. The slightly weird combination of courses in the diploma appealed to me. They included mediaeval Latin and French, palaeography, social history and the law of property. Only two universities offered the diploma in those days, London and Liverpool. Thinking it would be the cheapest option, I agreed with my parents to apply to Liverpool and I was accepted, conditional upon my degree, and what's more the Derbyshire County Council came up with a contribution. My degree was a quite satisfactory 2nd, so in autumn 1958 I set off for Liverpool.

I had lived in some inhospitable places while I was at Edinburgh, but my room in 17 Canning Street, Liverpool, was as bad as any. The house, a once-elegant Georgian building, was at that time divided into flats. I had a room in a flat at the top of the building, let to me by a lady who lived there on her own, who seemed to resent my presence. She occasionally locked me out by putting the bolt on the door if she disapproved of the man I had gone out with, or thought I was out too late. The house was dominated by cats. Hundreds of them, it seemed, lived in the basement and garden and ten at a time would appear outside my bedroom window, sitting sunning themselves on the flat roof of an extension. There was another dominating animal presence too. From my window I could see into the yard of a meat factory across the road in which a guard dog was left chained up every night and all weekend.

The dog, an Alsatian, was fastened by a fairly short rope to a line, which ran along the wall of the yard. It would run up and down the line, barking hysterically all weekend and waking me up early every Saturday and Sunday, when I wanted to stay in bed. But even if it had not been there, I would have been woken by the bells of Liverpool Anglican cathedral, which was just down the hill. The cathedral was surrounded by rows of empty, semi-derelict bomb-damaged houses which had not been touched since the war. One of them had a fading Union Jack painted on and the slogan 'Welcome Home Mick', a memento of some hero's return.

I did not much enjoy my time at Liverpool. The course was interesting and enjoyable enough but we were a small group of only five or six and, as a postgraduate, I was out of the main stream of the university. All my friends were still in Edinburgh and whenever I could afford to I went back there for weekends. However, I was moving inexorably towards earning my own living and towards the end of my year at Liverpool, I applied for a job as an Assistant Archivist in the Worcestershire County Record Office in Worcester. I went off for an interview to the Shirehall in Worcester and was interviewed by the Chief Clerk and the County Archivist. I must have impressed them more than I impressed the British Council, as I got the job and, much to my father's relief, I am sure, started work in July 1959 at a salary of £610 per annum, my formal education finally over.

# 4

The twenty-four-year-old girl who turned up for the interview at the Shirehall in Worcester in 1959 cannot have been particularly impressive. I was a thin-faced, rather anxious looking young woman, diffident and quietly spoken, with a slight Scottish accent, which mingled rather oddly with my short Midlands vowels. I had big eyes, a fringe which hung down into them and long hair in a ponytail, and I slouched. One of the panel must have commented on my posture during the first part of the interview, because before I went in for the second part, the County Archivist, who had obviously decided that he wanted me to get the job, advised me firmly to 'sit up'. I was not socially at ease, except with my own friends, I had no small talk and I found meeting new people difficult and embarrassing. But, once I got started in that first job and realised that I could cope with it perfectly well, I loved everything about it. And at twenty-four I felt really free and independent for the first time in my life. I lived in a charming double-fronted Georgian house in Chestnut Walk, just a stone's throw away from the Shirehall, which was my main place of employment. The house was owned by Miss Clarke, who was taking a degree at Oxford as a mature student and was away a good deal of the time. I shared the house with a young woman who taught at the Alice Otley Girls' School in Worcester, who was also a lodger, and we each had our own little flat. No-one was using the garden, so one year I grew potatoes and broad beans. Worcester was a delightful town to live and work in.

The County Record Office had two premises, one in the Shirehall, where the County Archivist, E.H. Sargeant, had his office up a cast-iron spiral stair above the entrance, and the other in a disused church, St Helen's, at the other end of the High Street. I could walk to one and the other was just a bicycle ride away. That meant that although we started work at 8.30, I did not need to get up till 8. I could go home for lunch if I wanted to and I was home in the evenings by 5.30. The Record Office Staff consisted of Mr Sargeant and his Deputy, Miss Henderson, a very sensible down-to-earth lady, who wore flat brown sandals and cycled everywhere, and two Assistant Archivists, myself and Brenda. Brenda and her husband had been among the first undergraduates at Keele University. They lived a rather hippie lifestyle with their baby, whom the husband looked after during the day while Brenda was at work – a sufficiently unusual arrangement in those days to cause raised eyebrows. Mr Sargeant, who had been a sergeant in the Army in the war, regarded their lifestyle as beyond the pale, and was always exhorting Brenda to 'smarten up', advice which she happily ignored. There was also a group of young clerks, all addressed as Mr This and Miss That – the use of Christian names was frowned on by Mr Sargeant to whom good order and discipline were very important. He ran that office like an army camp. He had rigged up a series of electric buzzers to communicate from his office to other parts of the Shirehall where members of his staff might be working. The archives were stored in a series of muniment rooms in the basement of the building and we had a subsidiary office in the Judge's Lodgings, where members of the public who came in to consult the archives could read them.

The first thing any new member of his staff had to do was learn the Morse code, so that when he buzzed the Morse letter T on the buzzer you knew it was tea time. I was regarded very favourably, because I had already learned it tapping on our air raid shelter during the war. We were expected to assemble in his room at the top of the spiral stairs for morning and afternoon tea breaks and briefing. We each had our call sign, and if he wanted any of us in his office or there was a telephone call for us when we were working in one of the muniment rooms, he would buzz our call sign on the buzzer, and we would be expected to come running. He used to time how long it took us to get there, and if it was too long we were firmly told to do better next time. It is a wonder none of us ever broke our neck on the spiral stairs.

One of his favourite tricks, which he liked to play on new arrivals in the office, was to ask them, with no warning, to address the assembled group on a subject of their choosing for five minutes. It caused great anguish for the victim, but once you had done it successfully, addressing the Women's Institute or the local school sixth forms, which was a regular part of the job of the archivists, did not seem quite such a daunting experience. Mr Sargeant made no distinction between the archivists and the clerks in the way he treated us. My first job on arriving in the Record Office with my Honours degree and my postgraduate diploma was to make the tea. He thought no one could be of any use in that office unless they knew how to make tea to his satisfaction. He bullied us all, but it was meant well and was taken by us in that spirit. The atmosphere in the office was friendly and cooperative and we all enjoyed it. In his eccentric way he was in fact an excellent trainer of staff.

The Archives were split between the two buildings. In the Shirehall were all the modern records of the County Council, all except those in current use were the responsibility of the Archives Department, and in St Helen's church were the ancient records of the County and Diocese of Worcester, including those of the cathedral and many of the parish records. In St Helen's too were the 'private collections', the archives of some of the local families, such as the Beauchamps of Madresfield Court which had been placed with the Record Office on so-called 'permanent loan', for safekeeping and so they could be used by researchers. In St Helen's too was the Worcestershire Photographic Record, which Mr Sargeant had started and for which he had recruited a band of enthusiastic local photographers to photograph all the old buildings in Worcestershire. We were on the verge of the 1960s. Much that was ancient and interesting had fallen into disrepair. New buildings were being put up, motorways were being built and Mr Sargeant could already sense that much of Worcestershire's history was in danger of destruction. It was his intention that at least it should be recorded photographically before it disappeared.

The Worcester Record Office contained a fine collection and was much used by everyone from County Council officials to historians, authors and schoolchildren. Our job was very varied. One of the first things I was given to do was to create a new filing system for the Highways and Bridges Department's staff to use for their current papers. This was not the sort of thing I had imagined doing when I had been studying mediaeval Latin and 14th-century handwriting at Liverpool. But when I had completed that job to Mr Sargeant's satisfaction, I was allowed to escape to St Helen's. There our oldest document was a charter from the reign of King Stephen and we had a fine collection of early Bishops' Registers and a set of the records of the Archdeacons' Court, which went back for centuries. Some of our most frequent customers were the Mormons and their representatives. They were researching the ancestors of fellow Mormons, by searching for names, usually in the parish records. My understanding was that if the ancestors could be identified their names would be written down and they would be posthumously baptised so that their spirits would pass from wherever they were into the Mormon heaven. I was rather uneasy about this particular activity. It occurred to me that the ancestors might not wish suddenly to be moved about, particularly without being given an opportunity to express an opinion.

I loved working in St Helen's church, and not only because one was away from the boss's eagle eye and his buzzer. The church itself, down at the bottom of the High Street and close by the cathedral, was an office full of atmosphere, and working there, surrounded by the history of the county and the diocese, gave me much satisfaction. It was not all academic peace and quiet though. We had many visitors with a wide variety of questions and research projects, all of whom needed our help and from time to time the peace was punctuated by the sound of china breaking, as the Worcester Porcelain factory next door smashed up its rejects in the yard.

I was at my happiest when I was asked to go out in the little grey office van to visit a vicar in his parish, or a stately home owner or families who had interesting historical papers. It was my job to catalogue what they had and ultimately to try to persuade them to deposit their documents in the Record Office on permanent loan. My pet hate at that time was the lampshade makers. It was fashionable at that period to have lampshades made out of real old parchment deeds and the manufacturers' agents were going around offering people money for such things. I thought it quite scandalous that our history was being destroyed in this way. In my effort to beat the lampshade makers, I developed my powers of persuasion, ruthlessly using my charm to persuade people that their social duty lay in giving me their old records for safekeeping in the Record Office rather than making money by selling them to the lampshade makers. It was these same powers of persuasion, which came in very useful years later, when in MI5 I had to try to persuade people to do much more unlikely and sometimes dangerous things on behalf of their country. You could say that I cut my teeth on those vicars.

At weekends John, who had by then finished Cambridge and started work in London as an Assistant Principal in the Board of Trade, used to come up by train from London whenever he could afford it. We would walk the county, visiting the churches and villages and in the evenings I would practise my cooking on him, a skill which was still at a fairly early stage of development. When he was not there, the two young articled clerks in the Clerk's Department, just down from university, kept me company. When there was nobody around, I used to cycle around the county, making rubbings of the memorial brasses in some of the churches. Later, I acquired a Heinkel bubble car, and I went everywhere in that. I was a fairly new driver and I and anyone who travelled with me must have been at considerable risk. With my university friend Isolyn, I even took it to France on the car ferry aeroplane which used to fly from Lydd to Le Touquet, and we drove to the Black Forest. I can remember looking up through the bubble top at the huge lorries bearing down on us menacingly on the French motorways. Looking back on that whole period, in the light of everything that has happened since, I remember it as a carefree idyll.

My job was interesting, I met some eccentric and amusing people and at the end of the day it did not much matter if it was not particularly well-paid or leading anywhere. I was sure I would get married one day; I would probably stop work before long and live on my husband's income, so I might just as well do whatever I fancied. Worcestershire was a beautiful county, full of charming villages with wonderful half-timbered houses. Because I learned all about the county through my work, and worked at the heart of its administration, I felt very much at home there.

Of course it had its unhappy moments, and there were some things about it which would raise the hackles of my modern-day equivalents. For one thing, women did not have equal pay. If there had been a male Assistant Archivist in that office, he would have been earning more than I was for doing the same work. That was something women took for granted in those days, though I think if there had been a man there, which mercifully there was not, and I had been confronted with the inequality at close quarters, even in those days I would have found such unfairness hard to swallow.

There were other things that were taken for granted too, like the office party. The Record Office was part of the Clerk's Department of the County Council and the Christmas party was for the whole department. Mr Sargeant tried to warn me against going, without actually directly telling me not to and I realised why, when at a certain stage of the evening things started to hot up and a series of pairing games began. In one I remember particularly, the women were expected to throw one of their shoes into a heap in the middle of the room and the men each chose one. The paired-off couple would then go into one of the offices for whatever purpose occurred to them when they got there. My partner, who was a singularly unattractive clerk in the Finance Department, did not get very far with me, once I realised what the game was all about. Nowadays, I think a few charges of sexual harassment might have resulted from that evening, but in those days women were expected to look after themselves.

Towards the end of 1961, the idyll was over and I was beginning to feel that it was time to move on. I felt thoroughly unsettled. My relationship with John had gone into what appeared to be its terminal decline, and I seemed to have done everything there was to do in Worcester. I have found throughout my career that, after about three or four years in any job, I have begun to get bored and started to look round for the next one. I applied for a number of jobs in record offices in other parts of the country, including one as Archivist at St Andrews University, which seemed to me at that time about the right distance away from both London and Worcester. Mercifully I did not get the job because, shortly after that, John and I made it up and decided to get married. From then on I was interested only in jobs in the capital. I applied unsuccessfully to the British Museum, and shortly afterwards I was appointed to a post in the European Manuscripts Department of the India Office Library (which at the time was part of the Commonwealth Relations Office) and I moved to London.

## 5

That move to London firmly put an end to any idyllic quality my life might have had up to then. In those early-60s days London was still a rather grim place to live. The last of the great smogs was in progress as I arrived and I saw everything through a thick yellow haze which left my eyes sore and watering and a line of grime round my nose where I had breathed in the filthy air. There were still huge bomb craters in the City of London, full of buddleia bushes and campion in the summer, but they were rapidly being filled in with great shoe-box buildings, which seemed ugly and out of proportion even in those days. Millbank Tower was being built and a huge crane with 'Mowlem' picked out in lights towered over Millbank and Pimlico where John lived. Swinging London had not happened, and our idea of an evening out was to take ourselves, very occasionally, to what we thought of as a posh restaurant. It was usually Au Père de Nico in Chelsea, where we could dine for less than £4 if we were careful. One evening, celebrating John's first promotion, we went to Leoni's in Soho and found ourselves sitting at the next table to Dr Beeching, who was at the time responsible for closing down half the country's railway system. We watched with awe as he and his companion ate their way through what seemed to us an immensely lavish meal. He demolished his food very quickly with the same avidity with which he was dismembering the railways.

All the problems experienced by anyone coming to live and work in London began for me at that time. The first, of course, was where I was to live. John was sharing a flat in St George's Square in Pimlico and there was no room for me. In any case, my parents would not have approved of my sharing accommodation with him before we were married. At the beginning of the 1960s that was still regarded by people from my sort of background as rather risqué. So I had to find something else, and my first recourse was to the YWCA in Tottenham Court Road, where I stayed for a few weeks. Meanwhile, I trawled the flat agencies of Kensington and Westminster, and was shown some places which to me, straight from my double-fronted Georgian house in its large garden in Worcester, seemed totally unfit for human habitation. I went round with an agent recommended by the Commonwealth Relations Office and became quite depressed by the seemingly endless supply of squalid rooms, described as 'one room flats', made out of badly partitioned floors of decrepit houses in Victoria and Pimlico. Some had people in bed in them, who were clearly not meant to be there. Some of these were obviously prostitutes. To me, the provincial girl come to town, it was all quite a shock. Over the years I have watched most of those same houses being gentrified to be lived in in something like the style for which they were originally built. The squalid rooms still exist of course, but now they are mostly further out of the centre of the town.

I wanted none of that style of living; it would have been too much like going back to Prince Albert Buildings, an experience I did not wish to repeat. I would obviously have to share, if I was to find anywhere I wanted to live. So one day I found myself being interviewed by Ann and Susan who had a flat in Roland Gardens off the Old Brompton Road in South Kensington. It was like a palace compared with some of the places I had seen. The fact that anyone who wanted to go to the bathroom had to walk through what would be my bedroom was, admittedly, a bit of a disadvantage, but not enough to put me off. I moved in.

We were a very odd household. I was the naive provincial girl and they were the sophisticates who knew what it was all about. The disadvantage of the sleeping arrangements soon became apparent to me when I found that Susan worked in the evenings at the Establishment Club, Peter Cook's immensely popular theatre revue club in Greek Street. Susan used to come home at about 3 a.m., walk rather noisily through my bedroom and take a bath, invariably waking me up. She also used occasionally to purloin her employers' cutlery, and my kitchen cutlery drawer to this day contains some of the Establishment Club's knives and forks, which have gone round the world with me. One night she smuggled John and me in past the long queue waiting in the street and we joined the fascinated audience watching the youthful cast (I have no idea who they were but they are probably all famous now) anarchically and enthusiastically sending up various aspects of '60s society and politics.

After a year or so, Ann got married and Susan started a relationship with a waiter at the club who moved in with us and occupied the bedroom off the bathroom. Then it was I who was walking through his bedroom to go to the bathroom, often while he was in bed with Susan. It was all very '60s but by then I was used to London ways and took it in my stride. Ultimately they moved out too, and when John and I married in March 1963 we lived in the flat as our first home.

The India Office Library had become part of the Commonwealth Relations Office when the India Office was disbanded after Independence in 1947 but in spirit and appearance it still was the India Office. It occupied its original rooms in the old India Office building, the St James's Park end of what is now the Foreign Office. The furniture in the Reading Room was 19th-century and the old East India Company clock, ticking loudly, presided over everything. The books were stored in Victorian cast-iron bookshelves on rails, which when pulled rolled out with loud creakings and groanings. The office I shared with a colleague had a coal fire, banked up for us every hour or so by a brown-coated 'paperkeeper', Mr Brewster. The paperkeepers were the porters, who were responsible for getting the books and manuscripts from the shelves when they were wanted by readers or the staff and bringing them to us. But these were no ordinary porters. Mr Brewster wrote down our requirements in a beautiful copperplate handwriting, which seemed entirely in keeping with our surroundings. The fire made our office a very cosy place; it kept our kettle constantly on the boil and we were able to make toast whenever we felt peckish. There were leather button-backed chairs for our visitors, and we sat at high desks on tall stools, like Bob Cratchit.

The Library's rooms, high up overlooking King Charles Street, at the Clive Steps end, have now been modernised by the Foreign Office; the old furniture has gone and they have lost their charm. The Library itself moved, just after I left, to a grim 1960s glass block in Blackfriars Road and lost most of its character in the process. Now it is housed in the new British Library. In those days it was a hive of activity, frequented by students, researchers and writers of many nationalities. Many of the most notable writers on India and the East India Company shared our room with us as they worked on the manuscript collections. There were others, like old Dr Ghosh, a Bengali poet who had fallen on hard times and lived in an uncomfortable room in Belsize Park, who came to the Library every day. To him the Library, and in particular our office with its cosy fire, was a sort of haven, particularly on winter's days.

The manuscript collections were extensive, and included the private papers of many of the Governors General, Viceroys and Secretaries of State for India, as well as more personal papers, letters and diaries of British men and women who had served, lived and frequently died in India over the long period of British involvement there. On another floor were the official papers of the India Office itself, the India Office Records, which were separately kept, and were also available to be consulted by readers. They included a series called 'Political Papers', which contained the official records of the 'Great Game', the intelligence operations in India, and presumably recorded what was really going on on the North-West Frontier, as 19th-century Britain battled it out with Russia for influence in that part of the world. I was not allowed to see this series, which was kept separately and was only available in part and then only to selected persons.

The Library included a fine collection of Indian miniatures, and paintings and drawings of all types and periods connected with India, which was the responsibility of Mildred Archer, who with her husband W.G. Archer, who was in charge of the equivalent collection at the Victoria and Albert Museum, were the acknowledged experts in the field. There were collections of books and manuscripts in the indigenous languages of the subcontinent, as well as Persian and Tibetan and a huge collection of printed books on every aspect of India. Many of the staff of the India Office Library and Records were scholars in their own right, experts in the languages they worked with. Miss Thompson, the Tibetan expert, occupied the office next door to ours, a room lined with glass-fronted cupboards containing manuscripts written in Tibetan on strips of palm leaf. A strange oriental odour used occasionally to waft out from under her door, and I imagined her puffing at a hookah with her eyes fixed on distant Himalayan heights. But in fact the smell came from the oil with which she would occasionally anoint the palm leaves to stop them cracking.

I felt extremely lucky to have landed that job. I knew nothing about India when I started, but it was there that my life-long interest in and love for India began. And I enjoyed working right at the centre of things, next door to Downing Street and free to wander around the Commonwealth Relations Office and the Foreign Office. That building, which has now been so splendidly restored, was very run down in those days. The glass-covered courtyard, the Durbar Court, was full of wooden huts and packing cases, and some of the offices had been crudely divided up with cheap and nasty partitioning which cut most unsympathetically into the elegant cornices round the ceilings. Many years later I thought of its former condition when as head of MI5 I found myself attending the Foreign Secretary's grand dinners for the Diplomatic Service in an elegantly restored Durbar Court.

I walked to work every morning from St James's Park

Underground Station, across the park and up the Clive Steps. In those days that end of Downing Street was open and members of the public could walk along, right past No. 10. On some mornings I would find myself following through the park an odd-looking old man with a white beard, who wore a skull-cap and carried a mat and a black book. I followed him once into Downing Street and realised that every morning he knelt down and prayed outside No. 10. It was quite comforting to know that someone was taking the governing of the country so seriously.

I was working in King Charles Street through the period of political intrigue and scandal in 1962 and '63, towards the end of the Macmillan government. We used to sit in our office next door to Downing Street, wondering what on earth went on in there. What were these orgies that the newspapers told us they were all indulging in and who could the 'headless man' in the photographs be? What was the relationship between Christine Keeler and Stephen Ward and the sinister Russian Naval Attaché, Ivanov? Like half the nation, I found it all fascinating. So much so that, on the morning of the publication of the Denning Report into the Profumo Affair, I deviated from my normal journey to work to call in at a bookshop in Charing Cross Road, where I waited in a queue to buy one hot off the press. I have read the Denning Report on several occasions since and often remembered that morning in 1963.

I married John Rimington on 16 March 1963 at Blidworth Parish Church in Nottinghamshire. My father had just retired, and he and my mother had built themselves a bungalow for their retirement at Ravenshead, opposite the gates of Newstead Abbey. Though this is now a small housing estate, in 1963 there were very few houses there and the field opposite their house was full of larks, which sang loudly on the morning of my wedding. I was immensely nervous. I was not good at formal occasions in those days or at being on show, and I reacted, as I always had on the day of exams, by being sick. It took a strong brandy and lots of encouragement from my mother to get me to the altar at all. I later found out that the car in which John was being driven to the church by his best man had almost expired going up Blidworth Hill, so he nearly did not get there either. Perhaps it was an omen that all would not be straightforward. John and I had been friends since we were sixteen and had kept in touch with each other with only a short break between the ages of eighteen and twenty-six, though our relationship had been rather an off-and-on business. We had been engaged for over a year, though that had also had its ons and offs. Some of our friends must have wondered whether we would ever make it to the altar, and indeed whether it would not be better if we didn't. For someone like me, who had always thought they wanted excitement in their life, marrying a childhood friend was an extraordinarily safe thing. I think we both had considerable doubts about whether it was the right thing, though I had never doubted that I wanted to marry, and at the age of twenty-seven I thought it was about time to do it. I certainly needed the security and the social reinforcement that comes through being part of a couple. I had no confidence at all that if I stayed on my own I would be able to travel or to see and do exciting things or to move in interesting social circles and I thought that John, who seemed to have the prospect of a glittering career in the Civil Service, would be able to achieve all that for both of us. I assumed, as women did in those days, that my job would be to back him up and go with him wherever he went. I took it for granted that my career was less important than his, and indeed that it was merely a temporary affair until we decided that I would stop work. I did not resent that assumption at all, indeed it seemed to me quite appropriate.

The first few months of married life were very difficult. For a year or so, I had been suffering from a recurrence of the claustrophobia which I had suffered quite acutely in my teenage years and which now made it very difficult for me to travel to work on the Underground. I had to sit or stand close to the door or I would start to sweat and gasp and feel faint. If the train stopped for any length of time in the tunnel, I found it very difficult indeed to keep control. To make matters worse, I began to suffer for the first time from severe migraines, with partial blindness and zigzag lines disturbing my vision. I am convinced now that this was caused by the newly-invented birth-control pills which I was taking, which, they tell us now, contained huge levels of oestrogen and were probably slowly poisoning me. I started to get curious brown splodges on my face and a moustache-like brown line above my top lip. All in all I felt extremely unwell and it was not a happy beginning to my married life. I think John began to feel that he had married a rather feeble invalid.

We were living in the flat in Roland Gardens, which I had first moved into when I came to London. We were constantly concerned by the thought that we would never, as far as we could see, be able to afford to buy a house of our own. We had no capital and no prospect of acquiring any. In fact, at the time we got married, and before counting the wedding presents, I was the proud possessor of £25, a plastic washing-up bowl, a small carpet, a basket chair and a few ornaments. John did not have much more. How we were going to turn that into the deposit for a house on our two rather meagre public service salaries, was something we constantly discussed. One thing we were clear about was that we did not want to live in the South London suburbs, like many of our friends. We were determined to stay in central London if we could and every weekend we would go for walks around areas where we thought we might like to live, sussing out what was going on in the housing market.

We kept returning to Islington, which in the early 1960s had what the estate agents described as great potential. The Victoria Line had not yet been built, though it was planned. A few houses had been done up, but there were many more which had not, and there were opportunities to buy houses with protected tenants occupying a floor or a basement, which we thought might be affordable. We were very attracted to a tall, decrepit Georgian house, with a long, thin garden running down to Liverpool Road, which was going remarkably cheaply, and another in more down-market Dalston, which we thought we might just about be able to afford, if we borrowed what seemed to us an enormous sum. By then John had been promoted to Principal on the salary of £1960 per annum and we were feeling rather better off. He went out and bought a case of Châteauneuf-du-Pape to celebrate. He put it on top of the cupboard in the hall and we started having wine with our dinner on Saturday evenings.

But it was difficult to feel particularly confident in the early '60s; the world seemed a very insecure place. In 1962, as the Cuban missile crisis unfolded, we wondered with the rest of the world whether we were about to be plunged into nuclear war, and the following year I looked out of our bedroom window and saw that the flag on the El Salvador Embassy across the road was flying at half mast. I wondered casually whether some Latin American statesman had died. It was only later in the day that I learned of the murder of President Kennedy.

All our ideas of settling down in London were wiped out at the beginning of 1965, when John turned up unexpectedly at the India Office Library to tell me that he had been offered a foreign posting. By a curious coincidence it was to the British High Commission in New Delhi as First Secretary (Economic) to deal with financial aid to India. As far as I was concerned, the answer to the offer was Yes. I was in no doubt at all that I would go to India; this was just the sort of adventure that I had been waiting for.

# 6

After the euphoria of learning that we were to go to India had passed, I began to worry. My first anxiety was whether, with my migraines and claustrophobia, the Foreign Office doctor would discover that I had some incurable illness and was unfit to travel. He did not, and probably as a result of that, and of stopping taking the pill, because we thought that this was the ideal time to start a family, I started to feel better shortly afterwards. My next worry was whether I had the right clothes. I was given a copy of the Post Report on India, dated January 1964, a strange buff-coloured booklet which had been written by members of the British High Commission in India with the aim of giving staff who were going there for the first time some suggestions on how best to prepare. It was meant to be helpful, but I found its long lists of things to bring quite daunting. We were told we would need a lot of summer dresses, a minimum of a dozen.

> It gets really hot in the summer so choose dresses in which you can be as cool and comfortable as possible i.e. without sleeves, with low necklines and if possible without belts. On the other hand unless you really feel comfortable in a strapless bra, try to find dresses under which you can wear an ordinary one. You will require [it went on], a few smart dresses to wear to summer evening parties and at least one dress suitable to wear to a lunch.

In another section we were told

> One of the pleasant aspects of life in India for a woman is

51

that, as you have few domestic chores to worry about, you have time to dress carefully before you go out. You have time in fact to take a critical interest in your personal appearance. So try not to do your shopping in too much of a hurry.

You will need plenty of cotton underwear. Waist-slips are more useful than full-length petticoats. Take a supply of elastic with you. All elastic rots very quickly but Indian elastic rots twice as fast.

Whatever the fashion is, there is one important thing you must bear in mind; winter evenings in Delhi can be really cold. Decolleté dresses can look very charming – but they lose much of their glamour when they expose shoulders covered in goose-pimples. A mohair or fur cape will be welcome and a light fur coat, if you have one, although this is not essential.

'Thank God for that,' I thought, as I had no fur coat and no prospect of getting one. I went into an orgy of sewing to make myself a wardrobe which would meet these stringent requirements and be suitable for this great adventure.

Then there were the provisions – a long list of them which the Post Report advised were worth taking. It seemed that many of the basic requirements for civilised life were unobtainable in India, including custard powder, vanilla essence and cocktail cherries – 'not necessary to bring cocktail onions'. Decent lavatory paper was extremely expensive, we were advised, and we should definitely bring all the make-up we would require for the entire posting. Thank goodness we did not have any children; the list for them seemed endless.

We pored over the catalogue of Saccone and Speed, the diplomatic suppliers, and went one exciting day to their offices in Sackville Street with a long order for quantities of strange things we did not know existed, like butter and bacon in tins and huge whole Edam cheeses. A lot of this stuff was wasted, partly because it did not keep in the heat, and partly because when we got there we found that India was nothing like the gastronomic desert we had been led to believe. One Saturday morning we went off early to Sainsbury's in Victoria Street and filled three trolleys with domestic necessities including what seems in recollection to have been hundreds of toilet rolls. And we ordered a car, something we had not imagined we would be able to afford for a long time. It was a white Ford Escort with a sun visor and it took us to many strange places, and let us down badly in some alarming circumstances. All these assorted worldly goods were to travel with us on the Anchor Line's ship RMS *Caledonia*, which sailed from Bootle on 9 September 1965.

In giving up my job at the India Office Library I took back the pension contributions which had been transferred from Worcestershire, thinking it unlikely that I would ever work again. If our plan to start our family in India worked out, I expected to spend the rest of my life as a wife and mother.

I can well remember the excitement of leaving our flat in Roland Gardens, early that September morning, with all our cabin trunks and suitcases labelled and packed, to catch the train to Liverpool. There had been doubt right up to the last minute about whether we would go. The Indians and the Pakistanis had decided to start one of their periodic wars over Kashmir, so the Commonwealth Relations Office had waited before confirming that we should go. John's sister, Rosamund, who had just come to London to start a job in the House of Commons Library and was taking over our flat, was hanging out of the kitchen window with tears streaming down her cheeks that morning to wave us good-bye. My parents came to Bootle to see us off and board the ship to have tea with us before we sailed. There was a party air about the whole occasion; my mother had bought a new hat but I think they were secretly wondering if they would ever see us again. They stayed the night in a hotel overlooking the Mersey and we went up on deck in the dark after we had sailed to look at the shore and imagine them watching the ship as it sailed past.

The sea journey to India was an unforgettable experience for someone who had never been further away from home than Italy. It divided two eras in my life and, as it turned out, our stay in India also crossed a watershed in the modern development of that country.

The RMS *Caledonia* had been built in 1923 to carry out to India officials of the Empire, tea planters, missionaries and businessmen whose lives were to be spent there. In 1965 it still did so, though we were the rather humbler substitutes for the Imperial officials. Underneath an awning at the stern of the ship a cast of traditional characters assembled at noon each day to drink their chota pegs. There were planters in knee-length khaki shorts, going back from leave to their lonely lives in the hills around Darjeeling or to Assam, businessmen and engineers and plant managers bound for Bombay, Calcutta, Delhi and upcountry too. There were missionaries, lots of them, travelling on the bottom decks of the boat in much less grand conditions than we, but joining us in the evenings to watch films under the stars or to make up bridge fours, playing interminably in a smoky lounge. At Port Said the magic man, the goolie-goolie man, boarded the ship and travelled with us through the Suez Canal, with white chickens up his sleeves, making them and various rings and watches disappear and reappear, just as he had for forty years. But by 1969, when we returned from India, the Suez Canal was closed, the British businessmen and tea planters were leaving for ever and India had shifted the whole direction of her diplomacy and industrial development.

Looking back on it now, the journey was a constant wonder. We were young, just thirty, and amazed with the tremendous excitement of sailing slowly in a sort of time capsule to the Orient. There were breathtaking things to see – flying fish and shooting stars, the planet Jupiter over Africa, and as we sailed through the narrow passage of the Suez Canal, camels loping along beside the ship on the Sinai side, at the same level as the deck and almost close enough to touch. There was an immense storm over Arabia, the desert and hills visible for thirty miles and more, under the huge, prolonged flashes.

There were shocks too and the first of those came with our arrival at Port Said. We docked in the very early morning, and I awoke to feel flies walking over my face and to take in for the first time the smell of the Orient. We disembarked for the day into Port Said docks but the heat, the smell, the noise and the sheer aggression of the traders, soon forced us back to the safe haven of the ship. How feeble we were.

In fact the *Caledonia* was a tub, and had no air conditioning, but as we reached the Red Sea and the weather started to warm up, we slept out on the deck under the stars and wrote letters to our friends, so wet with perspiration that we feared they would never be deciphered. We thought it was all fantastic. In the fancy dress competition, got up very patriotically as the Lion and the Unicorn, we won a prize.

Aden brought further excitement – the troubles there were in full swing, the speaker of the legislative council had been shot a few days earlier by terrorists demanding independence and an explosion on shore greeted the ship as we sailed in. That didn't stop us going ashore to bargain for watches and a camera at duty free prices but all the time I felt an uneasy sensation in the small of my back, wondering if anyone had a rifle trained on it. In fact the biggest excitement at Aden was the *Caledonia*'s fouling her anchor – round and round we went in the bay all afternoon as the crew tried to unwind it. We wondered if we would ever get to India.

At Bombay we were met by a superior-seeming person from the Deputy High Commissioner's office, whose job it was to look after us and put us safely on the train for the twenty-four-hour journey to Delhi. I was taken aback by what seemed to me the immense luxury of his style of life – servants in cockaded hats and long sashes offering tea and whiskies in cut glass tumblers, in surroundings of opulent furnishings and oriental rugs. Having no experience of diplomatic life at all, I had never seen anything like it. Strangely contrasting with all this were his wife's complaints about their living conditions – the shortage of hair lacquer, problems with the servants and the inconveniences of her apartment. All her conversation was complaints. I wrote rather laconically back to my mother, 'People here are terribly fussy about their accommodation. I think it is all a pose to make people think they are used to something better at home. I bet most of them live in semis in Surbiton.'

We were further amazed on being presented with a hamper of provisions for the train journey. There was everything in there, whole chickens, pudding in a tin and the inevitable bottle of whisky, without which one seemed to be able to go nowhere in India. We were told that on no account were we to touch a morsel of food or drink offered to us on the train; that way, they said, lay instant death. Actually it was a wise warning to greenhorns like us, with our shipboard-cosseted stomachs. Quite a long time later, when we had been in India for some years and become much more cavalier, John landed himself with a nasty dose of worms through incautiously eating the food on the train.

The train journey to Delhi was a trip back into biblical times, enjoyed by us from the comfort of the leather-covered seats of the Air-Conditioned Class. Already we felt many social layers away from the people we saw walking along the platforms or squatting on the station benches, their sandals neatly arranged on the platform beneath each owner.

When we arrived in Delhi in the autumn of 1965 it was only eighteen years after Independence. Signs of British influence and past domination were everywhere. One of the guests at our 'welcome' lunch in one of the big bungalows in the High Commission compound was the last British Chief Justice of the Punjab, still in place, as was, at that time a British Chief Administrator in Madras, both having elected to stay in the Indian Civil Service at Independence in 1947. After lunch our prospective bank manager, the elegant Mr Wroe of the Chartered Bank, a regular sahib, took us out in his car into the countryside and stopped by the well-kept towpath of a large canal where there was a wooden building. He said nothing. We walked in. No key. It was as though time had stopped still. The darkwood furniture, with its chintz covers lay undisturbed. There were mildewed-looking English novels of the 1920s in a glass-fronted bookcase. A big fan hung from the ceiling, the string for the punka wallah to pull as he fanned the sahib, still dangling down. The lodge was one of ten or so on the 270-mile canal, in which canal superintendents had stayed each night on their tours of inspection. Perhaps they still did, for there was no dust. Mr Wroe meant it as a kind of elegy on the order of the Raj, and indeed it was a strangely impressive tribute to some such thing, and perhaps also to the honesty of the Indians, for there had been no vandalism or robbery.

In New Delhi, statues of British Governor-Generals still stood on their plinths at the intersections of the major roads, which were still called by British names. The largest and grandest colonial-style bungalows were lived in by British and American diplomats, businessmen and military officers and most of the bathrooms contained lavatories and wash basins by Shanks and Thomas Crapper, their brass pipes sometimes polished to a brilliant shine. The dignified Bearers in their splendid turbans and smartly pressed uniforms had been trained by the British and knew how to make a pink gin and how to cook jam roly-poly and bread-and-butter pudding. Any attempt to modernise their menus was met with gentle but firm resistance.

But India was changing fast and by the time we left, in 1969, that era with its recall of the Raj had ended. The British were out of favour. The statues were being pulled down and replaced by local heroes and the roads were being renamed. Mingled with a certain sadness at seeing the statue of King George V being pulled from beneath his canopy on Rajpath, there was a certain understanding among the British community of the justice of these proceedings – the British had simply stayed too long and won too much. Our boss, an old India hand, said that he had been told, on applying for the Indian Civil Service in 1937, that we had ten years and must then get out.

And so the Anglo-Indian community, some still clinging to their solar topees, left for Australia and Canada, able to take very little with them, their possessions often looted, the most pathetic victims of the prevailing anti-British feelings. Mrs Gandhi, the Minister of Information when we arrived, was the genius behind these events and became Prime Minister before we left. She was no friend of the British, nor for that matter the Americans; her sights were set on the Soviet Union and as the British left, colonies of Russians moved in.

At the time we arrived, Delhi was in an uneasy mood. The north east routes to Assam and Sikkim had been closed three years before in a brush war with China; the north west routes similarly in the war with Pakistan, which was just flickering out after the biggest tank battles since the Second World War. Delhi itself, and even more the towns and villages in the Himalayan foothills, were full of Tibetan refugees, selling rough metal artefacts, all of which purported to be antique silver and lapis lazuli and many of which undoubtedly were. Some of the windows in the government buildings were criss-crossed with sticky tape to prevent shattering during air raids – an eerie flashback to my war-time childhood. On our first visit to Agra to see the Taj Mahal, there was an alert. Sirens wailed and aeroplanes screamed overhead, something I never thought to hear again, though as far as we could see no bombs fell.

Shortly after our arrival, we were sent on a familiarisation course for newly arrived diplomats in Indian history and culture, at Delhi University. The course was dominated by Americans who had the largest representation in the country, apart from the Soviet Union whose diplomats did not attend the course (no doubt they had a separate one). I found it surprisingly hostile and uncomfortable. The Indian academics were noticeably anti-West and pro-Soviet and their presentation of Indian history did not defer at all to our feelings. We had been equipped by the High Commission with a paper of useful rejoinders. Our paper said: 'After the Amritsar massacre, General Dyer was court-marshalled and dismissed from the Army.' Sure enough, the Indian version was that he had been fêted at tea parties by Imperialist ladies.

Perhaps he had; it all depends what you chose to emphasise. Our particular difficulty, apart from our colonial past, stemmed from the fact that Mr Wilson was believed to have blamed India for the declaration of war with Pakistan. Actually, he had also criticised Pakistan, but the Indian press had not reported that. The Americans did not escape unscathed. They came under a lot of criticism at that time for their heavy bombing raids in Vietnam.

After the course was over, political and international affairs did not figure much in my thinking for some time, as I rapidly became submerged in the role of diplomatic wife. My first letters home were all about cocktail parties and dinners and Scottish dancing on Burns' Night, with sixteen haggis flown in by BOAC. I spent quite a lot of time at first improving our flat, but I did not think much of the Indian workmen sent round by the Ministry of Works detachment at the High Commission. They were all long-standing employees with large families whom nobody wanted to sack in spite of their incompetence. So I painted the walls myself, which amazed our white-uniformed, turbaned Bearer, Nunkhu Ram, who did not think that was at all a suitable occupation for the memsahib.

Every day Nunkhu Ram and I went through a wonderful ritual, the household accounts. He would list in an exercise book his purchases of the previous day and what they had cost. The trouble was, he wrote it all down in Hindi, because although he could speak some English, he could not write any, and he also used the old currency of annas and pice. I think there were four annas to the rupee and sixteen pice to the anna, but the mathematics involved was far too much for me and I just took his word for it and gave him what he suggested. I still have his account book, with his Hindi and my English translation beside it.

In December, as forecast in the Post Report, it started to get cold. Anxious not to 'expose shoulders covered in goose pimples', I had a fire lit in the grate in our sitting room but clouds of smoke billowed out so Nunkhu Ram summoned a chimney sweep. 'We had the chimney sweep today,' I wrote home. 'Two men came. One sat cross legged in the hearth, holding a piece of blue-and-white spotted material over the grate ostensibly to stop the soot flying all over the room, while the other went up on the roof and dropped down the chimney a heavy weight on a rope. They then hauled it up and dropped it down again, and finally in a stroke of genius, the man at the bottom untied the weight and tied to the rope a great bunch of leafy twigs, like a sort of green bouquet, which was hauled up by the man on the roof. Some soot came down so it must have been partially effective, but I think they would have done better with a brush.' The chimney went on smoking.

I also spent quite a lot of time at first making clothes, an odd thing to do in India, where the tailors are so good. I reported to my mother that I thought my clothes were as good as most people's, except for a lack of long dresses. However, by the time we had been there a year, I had given up painting and dressmaking and was bemoaning the fact that I was too busy, exactly the same phenomenon that I experienced after I had been retired for a year. I have obviously learned nothing in thirty years about how to relax. Maybe as a consequence of my father's work ethic, I did not then, and I don't now, feel entirely comfortable unless I am busy and playing a part in whatever is going on.

I started looking round for something to do not long after we arrived. I went one day with some of the High Commission wives who helped in an orphanage in Old Delhi, thinking to offer my services, but I am ashamed to say that I could not cope with it. I found the sight of the babies lying in rows in their cots, hardly ever changed or picked up, and the young children, many very traumatised and banging their heads and rocking, more than I could deal with. Instead I joined a scheme to teach English to some of the girls who taught the children in the village schools. I used to drive early in the morning several miles out of Delhi to Pipavit, a village of mud houses, where the small children were taught sitting on the earth floor of a compound shaded by trees. I loved those drives, before the sun was properly up, while it was still comparatively cool and the smell of wood smoke and dust hung in the air. The teachers were delighted to see us and the village women welcomed us and showed us their babies while the teachers interpreted as they told us about their lives and problems, which were many. My Hindi never reached conversational standard in spite of lessons from a well-intentioned gentleman who came to our flat each Tuesday evening – though I did learn that the word for 'today' is the same as the word for 'yesterday' and 'tomorrow'. I can also remember how to say in Hindi, 'Please get in my taxi, Memsahib,' though surely that ought not to have been my side of the conversation.

The village visiting came to an end when one of the teachers got married and the other left. We were invited to the wedding, which I found a profoundly sad affair. The girl who was getting married came from a very modest family and she was not particularly handsome, but she was charming, sensitive and intelligent. Her marriage was, of course, arranged, and I believe she had not seen her husband until he arrived with his friends at the wedding, riding on a white horse in traditional fashion. He was awful, presumably the best her parents could get for her. He was loud and vulgar, as well as late, which I gathered was a protest about some aspect of the arrangements, possibly the dowry. I felt desperately sorry for her. She must have thought he was as ghastly as I did. I never saw her again, but I have often thought about her since, and wondered how she got on.

I was also at various times teaching English to the children of the Sudanese Ambassador, coaching an English girl who was trying to get into Roedean, and teaching Latin to a ferociously intelligent American boy. In my spare time from all that, I helped out at the Servants' Clinic in the High Commission compound. I was effectively the dispenser. The doctor, a venerable old Sikh with a long white beard, would say, 'Twenty four green pills, third bottle along,' and I'd pop them in an envelope, or 'bottle linctus,' which meant I was to fill up a little bottle of some brown substance from the big one. Many of the children suffered from hideous sores which the doctor called 'monsoon sores', which I had to paint with gentian violet. It didn't seem to do very much good as they were always there again the following week with their 'monsoon sores' even bigger and looking more frightening than ever, having turned bright purple from the gentian violet. The clinic could get rather gruesome, but as far as I was concerned it was nothing like so awful as the orphanage.

Everyone we knew was, as we were, required to act as nanny to the teenage children of friends who came through Delhi on the hippie trail. In those mid-1960s years, the Beatles had discovered India and every young person with a claim to be 'with it' had to make the journey overland from Europe, and go up into the Himalayas to commune with a Maharishi in an Ashram. Worried parents would write to ask if we would lend their young a hand, and in due course the young would turn up in kaftans and beads, filthy, exhausted and suffering from a variety of stomach ailments, with hair-raising tales of weeks spent travelling on buses through Iran and camping in Afghanistan. We would get their clothes washed, take them to the doctor, and feed them on decent food until they seemed well enough to go on, when we would stuff them and their rucksacks into our car and drive them to New Delhi railway station, where we would watch them climb into the packed, cattle-truck-like third-class railway carriages for the next part of their journey, while we went back to our whisky sodas and air conditioning. For some of them it turned out to be a disastrous experience and I remember on a trip to Nepal, seeing some youngsters at Kathmandu airport, who were obviously completely out of their minds on drugs, being repatriated to Britain.

In spite of my sorties into the countryside, it was inevitably a very privileged life, largely insulated from anything other than the very top end of Indian society. Some of the wives who lived in the High Commission compound rarely, if ever, went out, regarding the world outside the walls as too strange and threatening to risk. Their lives were a round of bridge parties and shopping from the many salesmen who arrived offering jewellery, brass trays, carpets, papier-mâché boxes and shawls from Kashmir. Many, though, were much more adventurous, the principal joy for the better off being the thousand-mile trip to Goa for the Portuguese cooking, or the journey to Kashmir for a stay in a houseboat and, it was said, the delights of cheap ganga. Others, like ourselves, went off to scrabble round the sites of ancient Hindu or Buddhist temples, to the hill stations in the foothills of the Himalayas or to one of the game parks in the hope of seeing tiger.

The nearest we came to seeing a large wild animal was one evening in Corbett Park. We had gone at dusk with some friends to the edge of the forest, where a clearing sloped gently down to the river and where, we had been told, animals came to drink before nightfall. We climbed up a rickety ladder into a large tree, where a worm-eaten wooden platform was precariously balanced. We settled gingerly down on it, with our hip flasks for nourishment, and waited in silence for something interesting to happen. As darkness fell, we listened to the sounds of the forest preparing for night, the cry of peacocks, the grunting of wild pig and innumerable rustlings. Then right at the foot of our tree we heard a much louder rustling that was clearly being made by an animal of some significant size. The rustling stopped. We knew it was still there and I am sure it knew we were there. I held my breath. Quite frankly I was terrified. I knew big cats could climb trees and we were sitting there like tethered goats, well within the reach of whatever this was and completely unprotected.

But I need not have worried. Just as the suspense was becoming almost too much, we heard the sound of a car coming along the forest track beneath us. A cadillac with all its lights on pulled up beneath our tree and an American, smoking a large cigar, leaned out of the window and shouted up to us, 'You guys seen anything?' At that, a loud, angry snarl came from beneath our tree and whatever it was, and John swears he saw it was a panther, bounded off back into the forest. So we packed up and went back to our cabin, disappointed but for my part rather relieved.

The part of my life I enjoyed least was the diplomatic wife role. I could never take too seriously the rules of High Commission protocol, which to one not brought up in that world could seem decidedly arcane. I understood the logic of arriving five minutes early at the High Commissioner's house if he were entertaining, so as to help greet the guests, and also that one should not leave before the last guest had gone. All that seemed to me to have a purpose. But what was the logic of the rule that if you entertained the High Commissioner at your own house, you should make sure that he sat at the right hand end of the sofa? (I think it was the right-hand end, though it might have been the left, and I can't now remember whether that was from a position sitting on it, or looking at it.) I remember agonising over this when such a visit to our flat swam into prospect. How was I to achieve it? What if someone else grabbed the right-hand end? Was I to move them or would that be rude?

The High Commissioner at the time was John Freeman. From what I had seen of him, I could not imagine that he would care a fig about the protocol but John came home with an alarming tale. Accompanying John Freeman to a meeting in the ambassadorial Rolls, John had happened to get in to the car on the wrong side protocol-wise. The High Commissioner had barked, 'Offside is for me! If anyone throws a bomb, it's supposed to hit you first!' On reflection, maybe it wasn't the protocol that concerned him, just self-preservation. Anyway, much to my relief, after dinner I did manage to get him installed in the right place on the sofa. But disaster soon followed. Unhappily our downstairs neighbour, a rather grand Indian businessman, sent up to complain that the Rolls was blocking his exit. His chauffeur having disappeared, John Freeman had to go down and move it. By the time he returned, the seat of honour had been appropriated by an Indian lady who was blissfully unaware of the niceties of diplomatic protocol.

My great coup as a diplomatic wife was organising the Thrift Sale, a kind of up-market jumble sale, run every year by the Diplomatic Wives' Association and regarded in Delhi as something of a social occasion. The year I organised it it made more money than ever before, but I found it more stressful than running MI5.

Even the diplomatic life had its funny side. After Harold Wilson had messed up his relationship with India by saying the wrong thing over Kashmir, a major effort was made to improve relations and the Foreign Secretary, Michael Stewart, was persuaded to come out. A grand dinner was held at the High Commissioner's Residence, No. 2 King George's Avenue, known to all as 2KG, at which the guest of honour was the then Indian Foreign Secretary, Moraji Desai. Moraji was a very austere and religious man, not only a strict teetotaller but also eating only the most restricted vegetarian diet, and, so it was reported, drinking only the milk of one particular cow. He also regularly drank his own urine, and lived to be ninety-nine.

The dinner was regarded as a very important occasion and we were all rather tense. A secret bar had been set up in the High Commissioner's study and we had been told to indicate this discreetly to those of the guests who were unable to get through the evening without alcohol. Unfortunately, as the tension rose, some of the guests paid increasingly frequent visits to the secret bar, and pockets of hysteria began to break out. The hysteria was encouraged by Michael Stewart's Private Secretary, Donald Maitland (later, as Sir Donald Maitland, our boss, when he was Head of the UK Permanent Representation to the EEC). Unable to resist improving on a dodgy scene, Donald insisted on giving extremely funny imitations, only just beyond the ears of our Indian guests. Things got worse and just before dinner was served, the news went like wildfire round the dinner party that Moraji's cow, which had apparently been tethered in the garden, had broken loose and was savaging the High Commissioner's shrubbery.

After a delayed dinner had been consumed, Michael Stewart addressed the company at great length from his position on one of the sofas in the drawing room. When he concluded, there was a pause, which lengthened and lengthened. No reply came from Moraji. Nervous conversations broke out round the room to cover the silence. The High Commissioner (at this stage it was Sir Morrice James) eventually decided that Moraji was not going to reply and the signal was given to Lady James that the ladies could leave the room to go to the bathrooms upstairs. Whether or not that was the signal Moraji was waiting for no-one ever knew, but just as the ladies were halfway up the stairs, he started to speak. The long line of ladies paused, uncertain whether it would be more polite to return or to proceed, and we finally stood, frozen immobile on the stairs, while he delivered a very lengthy oration.

At the time of the devaluation of sterling against the dollar in 1968, the Indian government, whose monetary reserves were in sterling, was to be briefed by two senior officials, Mr Milner-Barry of the Treasury and Mr Stone of the Bank of England. Preceding these two dignified persons by some days came three immensely long top-secret telegrams, which presumably contained the brief for their meetings with the Indian government. John was the representative of the Treasury in the High Commission at that time and so the telegrams came to him, with the accompanying instruction that they were not to leave his sight until they could be handed to the visitors. As he had no intention of spending the next few days in the office, the only solution seemed to be that he should carry them around with him and so we procured some oilcloth from the High Commission hospital, wrapped the telegrams in it and taped them around his midriff with elastoplast until they were needed.

After a certain time the diplomatic life began to pall for me. Although I got some enjoyment out of the family atmosphere that came from living for the first time as part of a community, something that the Foreign Office does provide, with it went a sort of identity crisis. I loved living in India and there was lots to see and places to go but I was not used to being just identified in terms of my husband's job – a First Secretary wife – with nothing of my own that I had to do each day. Everyone who was working in the High Commission seemed to be doing interesting and important things and I felt I was really just frivolling around. I was wondering how to solve this conundrum when one day in the summer of 1967, as I was walking through the High Commission compound, someone tapped me on the shoulder and said, 'Psst . . . Do you want to be a spy?'

What actually happened was that one of the First Secretaries in the High Commission, who I knew did something secret, though I did not know exactly what as one was not encouraged to enquire about these things, asked me whether, if I had a little spare time on my hands, I might consider helping him out at the office. He was a baronet and a bachelor and lived a comfortable life in one of the more spacious High Commission houses in Golf Links Road, very near to our flat. He was best known for his excellent Sunday curry lunches, which usually went on well into the evening, and for driving round Delhi in a snazzy old Jaguar.

I went into the High Commission office the next day and he told me that he was the MI5 representative in India and he had more work on hand than he and his secretary could cope with. Would I be interested in working for him on a temporary basis? I thought I would be very interested, though I knew nothing at all about MI5 except what I had read several years earlier in the Denning Report on the Profumo case when I was working in the India Office Library. What was it all about? He gave me a thin paper-backed pamphlet to read, which was probably the only thing in print about MI5 in those days. In about five or six pages, it told me that MI5 was part of the defence forces of the realm, with the special responsibility to protect the country against serious threats to our national security, like espionage and subversion (terrorism had hardly been heard of in those days). Its mandate was a directive given by each incoming Home Secretary to the Director-General. He told me that, among its other duties, MI5 was responsible for offering advice, training and assistance to Commonwealth countries on their security and he was one of a number of Security Liaison Officers posted all over the Commonwealth.

He was also responsible for the security of the High Commission and its staff. Before I could work with him, he explained, I had to be positively vetted. I filled in a form, which asked me all about myself and my family. We talked it through and he sent everything off to London to be checked out.

I wrote home, 'They have offered me a job working in the secret part of the High Commission, for £5 a week which I think I will take. It will help to keep me out of gonk-making.' (Gonks were the Teletubbies of the 1960s and I was at that time on the Committee of the Toy Fair, which meant endless sewing afternoons making stuffed toys.) MI5 beat the gonks as far as I was concerned. I warned my parents, 'As this job is in the very hush-hush part of the office I have to be what they call "positively vetted". So if you see little men in bowler hats lurking outside the house don't be surprised. They will just be checking up on you. They will find my form very boring as I haven't done anything sinister at all.' John took it even more light-heartedly and wrote to my parents, 'I do hope you are leading sinless lives during this period of examination in connection with Stella's security clearance. The least sugges-tion of improper entanglements or any attempt on your part to communicate with the Red Chinese Embassy or to manu-facture atomic weapons in the garage could have the most far-reaching consequences; most importantly that Stella will not get the job and will be a perfect pest. You may judge their thoroughness in that I was rung up the other day and a husky mysterious voice enquired whether I or Stella had ever been incarcerated in a prison camp subject to Fascist or Communist influences.'

My baronet friend does not seem to have taken it much more seriously himself. He wrote back to Head Office, 'She and her husband frequently take a picnic lunch by the High Commission swimming pool,' as though that were a prime consideration in giving me the job, and added, 'I have won her in the face of stiff competition from other parts of the High Commission [the gonks, I suppose]. I consider she would be entirely suitable for the work even though she is only a two-finger typist.'

All my references must have checked out because a few weeks later I was in. I later learned that references had been taken up with my school and that my headmistress, obviously somewhat dubious about these prospective employers, had written: 'She is the kind of girl who does not shirk unpleasant jobs. She is reliable and discreet, or at least as reliable and discreet as most young ladies of her age.'

The MI5 offices in the High Commission were at the end of a corridor behind a security door. My first problem was learning how to work the combination lock. There was something about the Indian climate that combination locks did not like and they were perpetually sticking and refusing to open unless you hit them sharply in between each number. The men used their shoes, but the flip-flop sandals I wore did not have the same effect. When I got behind the security door, I discovered that there was another secret part of the High Commission that I did not know anything about, the office of the MI6 representative, which was cheek by jowl with ours. I knew him as a genial, rather low-profile character, with some sort of job in the political section, but notable mainly for his performances in character parts in the plays put on by the British High Commission Amateur Dramatic Society. I was amazed to find him there, beaming at me, behind the security door.

My MI5 job did not turn out to be particularly exciting. I was merely a clerk/typist, though, as my recruiter had observed, my typing qualifications were not of a high order. However it was thought more important that I should be a sound and reliable person (which as the wife of a First Secretary in the High Commission I was presumed to be) than that I should be especially good at the job I was there to do. For the most part, I stayed in the office while my boss went out to meetings and interesting-sounding assignations. I had to answer the phone and type the reports he sent back to London every few days in the diplomatic bags. In writing to my mother, I was rather scathing about the bag arrangements: 'Friday is an exceptionally busy day as the bag goes out to London and all the letters have to be got ready. We are so secret in our office, that not only do our letters have to go in the Diplomatic Bag, but we have to have our own bag-within-the-bag which has to be listed and stuck up and sealed personally by me with three great red sealing-wax seals on every corner, making 9 seals in all. It's a great and complicated business. Anyway, I now wait for repercussions from London. If I have sealed up the bag wrongly they tend to send cypher telegrams, telling us so, in theory in case spies have tampered with the mail, but in practice I suspect because they like drawing attention to someone else's mistakes.'

As far as I was concerned, all this work had come at an untimely moment. The High Commission Amateur Dramatic Society, in which I was a leading light, was putting on a play at the time and I needed to learn my part. The only consolation about the work was that I got paid by the day and 'each day ends with the delightful ceremony of paying Stella and I come away 25 rupees the richer'. My enthusiasm for amateur dramatics was obviously a sign that I was beginning to feel pretty comfortable and self-confident in the Delhi diplomatic world. I was learning that I could do a lot of things just as well, if not better than others. It was a far cry from my appearances in *St Joan* at school as the Executioner, when even though I did not have a speaking part, I found my time on stage so traumatic that I had to be provided with a stool to sit on, in case I fainted. I was probably the only executioner so weak that he has been unable to stand up. The play we were doing when I joined the MI5 office in Delhi was Georges Feydeau's farce *Hotel Paradiso*, in which I was playing the part of Marcelle. Most of the male members of the High Commission seemed to be growing beards and other face-fungus to fit their parts – artificial beards and moustaches tended to fall off in the heat. From my new position as a security officer I observed in a letter home, 'I should think the East Europeans, aware that beard-growing is the first sign of a character breakdown, are moving in their operatives in a big way.'

The amateur dramatics came back to haunt me twenty-five years later. When my appointment as Director-General of MI5 was announced in December 1991, it turned out that someone who had been in those plays had some connection with the *Daily Mail*. Pictures of me dressed up as Lady Julia Merton in *Lord Arthur Savile's Crime* appeared all over the front page of the newspaper under the headline 'Mistress of Disguise'.

It was the height of the Cold War when I joined as clerical assistant to the Security Liaison Officer in New Delhi. The battle for influence or control in India which had been being waged between Russia and Britain since the 19th century continued. In Delhi in the 1960s it had turned into a struggle between the Soviet Union and the West and the weapons were 'aid' and the troops were 'advisers'. The country was overrun with foreign advisers, military advisers, agricultural advisers, industrial advisers, economic advisers and every other kind of adviser you can imagine. As we toured around the country we kept falling over them. On one trip we made to Lucknow, entirely as tourists, to explore the ruined Residency where the British community had been besieged in 1857, we were astonished to be greeted as we drove up to our hotel by the best part of the local business community, who garlanded us with marigolds and swept us into the hotel on a cloud of bonhomie. Just as John was beginning to think up a suitable speech, our welcoming party faded away and attached itself instead to a pair of heavy-looking Russians who had driven up in a car behind us and for whom the marigolds were obviously intended. Our erstwhile hosts, clearly confused by the diplomatic number plates on our car into thinking we were the Russian commercial adviser whom they had invited on a goodwill visit, left us to find our own way to the gloomy room that had been allocated to us, which was made more gloomy when the light over the washbasin blew up in a rather sinister way as soon as we switched it on.

The Russians had more so-called advisers than anyone else, though the Americans came a close second. Very many of them were officers of the KGB or the GRU, the Russian military intelligence service or, of course, the CIA, and there was even the odd one from MI6. The Soviet Union's efforts were meeting with considerable success at that period. There were many influential communist and pro-communist politicians, including Mrs Gandhi herself. One state, Kerala, already had a communist government, and it was thought likely that more would follow.

One of the tasks of the MI5 office in the High Commission was identifying who were the intelligence officers on the opposite side, and monitoring any efforts they made to get alongside our colleagues. Everyone in the High Commission was supposed to treat all invitations from the Russians or East Europeans with great suspicion and report any social contacts. People did as they were asked, though some took it more seriously than others, but most people realised that the recruitment as a spy of a member of the British High Commission or of another Western embassy could have resulted in great damage to Western interests. We worked closely with the representatives of the security services of other friendly nations in India in a combined defensive effort.

The Russians had a great white palace of an embassy just down the road from the British High Commission, never visited in those days by Western diplomats. They astonished the whole Delhi diplomatic corps one day by inviting all First Secretaries and their wives in the various missions to a cocktail party. Whatever it was all about, it was not thought that much good was intended, but as no-one could think of any reason why we should not go, we dressed ourselves up and went along in a state of considerable excitement and some suspicion, expecting to be propositioned or to have our drinks spiked or our coats bugged when we put them in the cloakroom. The party itself took place in a huge ballroom, glittering with enormous glass chandeliers. Nothing obviously very remarkable happened, rather disappointingly as far as I was concerned, except that we were all plied with excellent Russian champagne and chatted up by charming Russian diplomats, who were also no doubt assessing us all for later cultivation. Whatever else went on that night, at the very least some good photographs of us all were obtained for their records.

Just before I joined the MI5 office, John and I were the subject of what I later recognised as a targeting operation. We got to know a young lecturer at Delhi University and his wife, and they invited us to their house for supper several times. We reciprocated. We found them interesting to talk to – they were very left-wing and they gave us a different angle on India and its problems. This went on for several months and we became quite friendly with them. Then one day when we went round to their flat for supper, they had, without warning us, also invited a Russian diplomat and his wife. The Russians were most amiable. Would John like to join a chess club? What about duck shooting – did we shoot? Could we possibly get him an invitation to see the film of the World Cup final which he understood had reached the High Commission? Would we come to their flat for supper? When on reporting back we found that he was a KGB officer and our friends from the university were communists, we could see where it was all leading, and we had to break off the contact.

Before we did so, what seems to have been a classic sting operation was tried on us. Our Indian friends tried to get us to import into India, through the diplomatic bag, some drugs which they said one of their children needed and which could not be obtained in India. It may have been true, but had we done as they asked, we would have been in breach of diplomatic regulations and of the Indian law and very vulnerable to pressure. The story was very convincing but thankfully we saw through it. I am glad we did or both of our careers might well have been scuppered. Of course, after that we had to end the relationship, which was a pity, as we had enjoyed our conversations. But that sort of thing was going on all the time in those Cold War days of the mid-6os.

One Cold War episode that really set the British High Commission by the ears was the arrival of a defector. All British posts have a detailed drill laid down for how to cope with such an eventuality. I wasn't really on the inside of this, being merely a clerk/typist, but it was clear to all that something exciting was happening and that things were not going according to plan. The complicated balancing act that has to be achieved in such circumstances is for you to keep the prospective defector safe from his own side, which may well have some inclination of what he is up to, while assuring yourself, as far as you can, that he is genuine and has something interesting to offer. At the same time, you have to check out with home that some department or agency is interested enough in him to be prepared to pay the substantial cost that will be incurred. All that, while simultaneously not alerting the host government to what is going on, and trying not to do anything that they will later regard as an abuse of the hospitality of their country.

Of course, the great moment always comes when it's least expected. On this occasion, when the time came to send a cypher telegram home to alert the Head Offices to what was happening, the cypher clerk could not be raised as she was in bed with her Sikh boyfriend and would not respond to phone or doorbell. I was not allowed to know how the cyphers worked as I was only locally engaged staff, and all I was aware of at the time were earnest and angry consultations going on in huddled groups at a cocktail party on the High Commission lawns which most of the diplomatic community was attending. Miraculously, it all got sorted out, and the defector and a minder were shipped safely out of Delhi.

I worked with the MI5 office in Delhi for a year or so, until the baronet went home at the end of his posting, and his successor thought he could manage without me. I moved to work briefly with the Delhi end of a rather curious and at the time very secret Foreign Office Department called the Information Research Department (IRD). Nobody ever explained to me what was going on there. I was merely told to carry out the rather basic task of stuffing envelopes with all sorts of printed material, which was sent out from London, and posting them off to a whole series of addresses. It was very important, I was told, to get the right stuff in the right envelopes – not everyone got everything – and the whole operation and in particular the names and addresses were very secret. It did not take much wit to grasp that what I was actually doing was sending out covert propaganda of various kinds to a series of contacts of all sorts, some journalists, some politicians, some academics, who I guessed had been recruited to use the material unattributably. I didn't have time to read it all as I packed each envelope, but from what I could see most of it was anti-communist in tone and some of it was quite personal stuff about individuals. The objective of IRD, as I now know, was to influence public opinion in different parts of the world by planting stories and articles hostile to our enemies and favouring the British position. Whether any of it had any effect I was not in a position to judge, though I did notice from time to time articles in the newspapers which seemed to have drawn on the stuff I had put in the envelopes.

I did not work for IRD for very long. It was a very boring job and by then we were almost at the end of our posting. But, before we left, there was one journey I really wanted to attempt, and that was to drive from Delhi to Kabul over the Khyber Pass. I had been reading Kipling's *Kim* and I wanted to see something of the area where the Great Game had begun. I thought the North-West Frontier and the Khyber Pass would turn out to be very exciting and romantic. And they did, not because of foreign spies disguised as Pathan tribesmen (though there may have been some of those there still in the 1960s), but for a much more mundane reason.

We set off in late September 1968 with a couple of friends. We drove in two cars, partly because we thought that would be safer and partly because as well as our luggage (which, along with spares for the car, tyres, tubes, and cans of petrol, included a hamper full of tinned food, a case of whisky, an ice box full of beer, three thermoses of Martini, an apple pie, a bedding roll, a large walking stick and a shovel), we had the entire costumes for a production of *Cinderella*, which was to be performed by the British Embassy at Kabul at Christmas. How times have changed.

The journey was eventful and at times frightening, as such a journey was bound to be. We eventually reached Peshawar without too many problems but just as we entered the town, everything began to go prematurely dark. An eclipse of the sun was in full swing and in the villages on the outskirts of Peshawar they could not understand what was happening. People stood in the middle of the dusty streets in a reddish haze, pointing at the sky in amazement. The general eeriness and the excitement of the crowds made our task of finding the Residence of the British High Commissioner, where we were to stay the night, much more difficult and we only found it after much driving round and round the crowded streets.

The Residence had long since been deserted by High Commissioners but was still kept up for occasional use by British official visitors. It was an old house with a big gate to which we had been given the key, which let us into a courtyard in which there was a great tree. As we were installing ourselves an ancient servant materialised and indicated that there was hot water and though he could not provide food, he had plates and cutlery. So after cold beer and hot baths in that order, we ate a supper from our supplies consisting of pâté, salmon mayonnaise and spam using silver cutlery off china plates bearing the Royal monogram. We slept the night in linen sheets, all for five rupees a head.

The following day, fortified by all this luxury, we were interviewed in an upper room downtown – the Afghan consulate – by a hookah-smoking official and several casually interested loungers, who after the closest scrutiny of our credentials eventually stamped our passports for Afghanistan and we set off to drive the twenty-five miles or so to the beginning of the Khyber Pass. All went well until we had just begun to climb and twist up the first steep part of the Pass. We were following a great lorry that was grinding up in first gear.

It was very hot and, before we had gone far, our engine started to boil and then the car lost all power and stopped. 'Disaster,' I thought, 'we will never see Afghanistan.' We waited and drank some of our supply of cold beer, interestedly watched by two village boys in turbans with antique-looking rifles slung across their backs. I remembered being told that it was not safe to stop on the Khyber Pass, but they were all smiles when we gave them the empty beer bottles. After about half an hour the engine had cooled a bit, so we sacrificed some of our drinking water to it, started it up again and with our fingers crossed, nursed it, coughing and choking up to a flattish bit of road on the top, after which there was a slight slope down to a frontier town called Landi Kotal where we hoped there might be a mechanic.

We asked at the petrol pump and the group of ancient tribesmen, sitting smoking on string beds, with their rifles on their shoulders and bandoliers of cartridges strapped across their chests, nodded wisely. One of them got into the car with John, leaving me with our two friends who had waited for us in the other car at the petrol pump. Off John drove into the dust and distance with this ferocious-looking character on board, while we stood there eating melons and watching the madly overloaded buses and lorries go by and never expecting to see him again. Those clapped-out old vehicles seemed to manage the hills with no trouble at all and I realised why. They had no bonnet over their engines, but instead they had a wooden platform at the front on which a man sat, and when they went uphill it was his duty continuously to pour water onto the engine from a great skin water carrier.

After we had observed the passing scene for a bit, we thought we should go and look for John, so we all piled into the other car and eventually found him at the mechanic's 'shop', a little wooden hut with a de-gutted twenty-five-year-old Dodge outside. He was sitting in the shade, drinking green tea from a china bowl and talking to the owner about the US President, Lyndon Johnson. I think he had tried to explain he was English not American, but had given up. The conversation went:

'He not good man. You like?'

'No.'

'He set man against man. You like?'

'No.'

The 'no' was John's contribution to the conversation. Meanwhile, a young man who looked exactly like Peter Sellers trying to look like a Pakistani mechanic, was slowly and resolutely taking our car to pieces, blowing through each piece and putting it in his pocket. I was sure the car would never move again and I was saying to John:

'That's twelve pieces he's got in his pocket, thirteen . . .' etc, etc.

There did not seem anything we could do except pray, so we all accepted the tea and talk (still about President Johnson), until after about an hour, Peter Sellers suddenly said, 'Ready. You trying,' and John and Peter Sellers drove off into the distance, trying. When they returned, miraculously all seemed well. So we took everyone's photograph, handed round Peek Frean's ginger nuts, paid what seemed a very small sum but seemed to please Peter Sellers, and set off.

We reached the frontier without any more problems, and the Pakistani frontier guards bowed us out of their territory with many diplomatic courtesies. On the Afghan side, most of the guards seemed to be having a siesta. The few who were on duty regarded us with Central Asian contempt through their Afghan eyes and wrote what seemed like pages of elegantly turned insults in our passports in spidery writing, from right to left (we never discovered what it all meant). Then on we roared into the afternoon, already slightly worried in case we should not reach Kabul by dusk. We had no desire to drive through those parts in the dark. In the end, we got there safely, and the next day we delivered the Cinderella costumes to the British Embassy. The hats for the ugly sisters were travelling in my hat box, a rather expensive leather creation which I used for my wedding and funeral hats and which I rather treasured. Unfortunately, when we left to drive back to Delhi, I forgot it, and I have often wondered what became of that hat box

*My parents on their wedding day
in 1929, 'in high hopes of
a prosperous future'.*

*In my pram in 1935.
'I seemed pretty well
set up.'*

*With my mother and my brother, Brian, on holiday
in Bournemouth in 1938.*

*'Night after night the German bombers came over
to try to flatten the Liverpool docks,' 1941.*

*5 Ilkley Road, Barrow, 1942. 'We stuck tape over the
windows and battened down
to see out the war.'*

*Unwelcome guests in Edinburgh, 1956: Bulganin and Khrushchev.* 'Bulge and Krush go home!'

*Graduation day, 1958.* 'A degree in English seemed to qualify one for nothing.'

*Visiting families who had interesting historical papers, 1961.*

*The India Office Library Reading Room, 1963. 'The old East India Company clock ticking loudly presided over everything.'*

*The Establishment Club, hotbed of early '60s satire. 'My cutlery drawer to this day contains some of the Club's knives and forks, which have gone round the world with me.'*

*The Denning Report, 1963. 'I waited in a queue to buy one hot off the press.'*

'The part I enjoyed least was the
diplomatic wife role.' I stand in line
to be received by the
President of India, 1968.

On the voyage to India, 1965. 'Got
up very patriotically as the lion and
the unicorn, we won a prize.'

I was playing Marcelle
in 'Hotel Paradiso', 1968.

'All this work came at an untimely
moment. I needed to learn
my part,' 1968.

*Walking up the garden path to my first job in MI5.*

*On the road to Kabul, 1968. 'John's cheque passed through half the camel and carpet bazaars of Central Asia.'*

*Our engine boiled and we lost all power and stopped. 'Disaster, I thought, we will never see Afghanistan!'*

'In 1909 two officers were plucked out of the armed services and told to form a Secret Service Bureau.'

Left: Mansfield Cumming.   Right: Vernon Kell.

 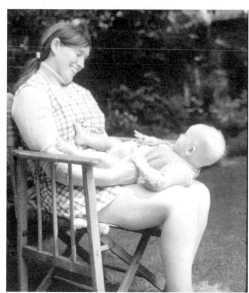

Left: 'With my wardrobe of exotic Indian clothes, I could not quite see how I was going to fit in,' 1969.
Right: 'My intention of returning to work after having a baby was incomprehensible to most of my male colleagues,' 1971.

*'By the time I worked on the Ring of Five we still did not know how they had been recruited or who had put who in touch with whom.'*

Burgess

Maclean

Philby

Blunt

Cairncross

through all the vicissitudes that Afghanistan has suffered since.

At the Embassy, we sought advice on which was the best bank to use to change our money into Afs. We were told, 'Don't on any account go to a bank. You'll get a much better rate of exchange in the bazaar.' We were directed to the shop of a barber, who also traded in transistor radios, as did everyone in that part of the world in those days. His shelves were piled high with huge PYE models and as they all seemed to be turned on at full volume, we had to shout to make ourselves heard. Our man was in the street outside his shop, using a cut-throat razor to shave around the beard of a wild-looking figure. Beside his client was propped a beautiful hand-crafted rifle, with a silver and carved wood stock. We shouted at our man that we wanted some Afs, would he prefer dollars or pounds? We could hardly believe our ears when he said, 'Give me a cheque.' So John wrote him a cheque on his Bank of Scotland, Dalkeith Branch, bank account and we took possession of a pile of exotic-looking currency.

Later, back at the Embassy, we were told that our cheque, in sterling on a British bank, was a very valuable commodity which would be traded on, as currency in its own right. This turned out to be true. More than a year later, the Dalkeith Branch of the Bank of Scotland returned John's cheque (as banks did in those days) and all over the back of it were strange scrawls in various hands. It had apparently passed through half the camel and carpet bazaars of Central Asia before returning home to Dalkeith.

It was in that bazaar, after we had changed our money, that I had an alarming experience. We were wandering around, admiring the brilliantly coloured spices in open sacks and the strange vegetables, when all of a sudden a nasty jagged stone landed near my feet. I looked up and saw a huddle of men on the other side of the market, one of whom had another stone in his hand, all ready to throw. They made it clear by gestures and shouting, that they wanted me out, and if I did not go, I was going to get the next stone pretty soon. So, without waiting to argue, we left. They clearly saw me as a half-clothed Western woman and an obscenity. I was not aware that I was wearing particularly revealing garments, but I certainly did have short sleeves and bare legs. The majority of women in Kabul at that time were not veiled though some did wear a yashmak and a few wore the full head-to-toe veil.

We finished our posting in Delhi and came home to England in February 1969. Again, we travelled by sea, but this time the journey took even longer than when we went out – five weeks instead of three – as the Suez Canal was closed and our ship had to go round the Cape. The ship, the *Victoria*, was an Italian vessel of the Lloyd Triestino Line, which sailed from Bombay to Venice. We stopped at Mombassa, Durban and Cape Town, but then there was a long stretch to Brindisi with nothing much to do. Boredom began to set in and most people on board, including the crew, seemed to spend most of the time drinking so that when we eventually reached the Straits of Gibraltar there was hardly a sober person on board. The Captain invited some of us up to the bridge after dinner as we sailed through the Straits. The radar screen was covered with bright blips, the chart was lying on a table with a pair of ladies' evening sandals on top of it, and the Captain and the owner of the sandals, a glamorous German lady, were nowhere to be seen. A solemn-faced sailor was at the wheel and I remember hoping that he at least was sober enough to navigate his way through.

We arrived in Venice just as the sun was rising on a cold February morning. The buildings floated out of the mist, all shadowy with golden highlights. It was a breathtaking reintroduction to Europe. We travelled on by train to London, and then as a banal end to our journey, took British Rail from Waterloo to Woking where we were renting a house from a High Commission colleague until we decided where we were to live permanently.

# 7

Both John and I returned from India in a very unsettled state. We had become used to an interesting and exciting life. We had travelled to fascinating places. We had been treated as people of significance, representing our country at a senior level in far-flung parts of the world. And here we were, living in Woking, in someone else's house, people of no significance at all – John a middle-ranking, moderately paid civil servant and me a suburban wife. It was not what we wanted.

I was quite a different person from the rather anxious, socially unconfident young woman who had set out. I had learned to deal with any social situation and my war-time hangover, the claustrophobia, had totally disappeared. But I had wanted to start a family while we were in India and this had not happened. With nothing much to do, cooped up in Woking from dawn to dusk and knowing nobody, I soon became quite depressed and obsessed with the baby I was not having. I remember the two of us going out in the garden in Woking in July 1969 and gazing at the moon on which Neil Armstrong and his colleagues had landed, and reflecting that lots of interesting things were happening in the world but everything interesting and exciting seemed now to be passing us by.

Before we left India, John's opposite number in the American Embassy, a US Treasury official called Sam Costanzo, had suggested to him that he should consider leaving the Civil Service to join him in a company called Comac. Comac was part of an American banking corporation, which had struck a deal with a British merchant bank to start a new lending institution in London. Almost as soon as we got back to

England, the Americans started to court John assiduously with the offer of a job in this institution. The boss of the outfit, a man called Parsons, came to London on several occasions. He was a loud, larger-than-life figure; one of those lean, enormously tall Americans, at least 6ft 6ins, to my recollection, wearing a button-down Brooks Brothers' shirt and loafers, who at that time at least, had the world at his feet. When he came to London he invariably stayed either at the Savoy or the Connaught, where, as far as I could see, he lived on well cooked mutton, washed down variously by champagne or first growth claret of the better vintages.

Once, we invited him to dinner in Woking. We had given careful instructions on how he should get there, by catching a train from Waterloo, and then ringing us up from the station, but he was not interested in any of that. On emerging from the Savoy Hotel he hailed a taxi and commanded the astonished driver to take him to Woking, where he turned up hours after he had been expected, describing the taxi's rate of progress as 'quaint'. What he thought of our domestic arrangements or the dried up meal I had waiting for him he did not say (at least in my hearing). On another occasion he invited John to dinner at the Connaught and amazed him by ordering a magnum of Château Mouton Rothschild, which the two of them consumed. I also experienced his hospitality once when I joined him and some others for dinner at Simpson's in the Strand. To go with our roast beef and Yorkshire pudding, he ordered a jeroboam of Krug. After our travels around the East, we thought we had seen a bit of the world, but nothing had prepared us for the lifestyle of corporate America let loose in London in the early 1970s.

While this courting was going on, we agreed that I would go back to work, as the best way of avoiding my sinking into total depression. I had no enthusiasm for returning to the archive profession, so I thought I would see whether there was any chance of joining MI5 as a permanent employee. I contacted my baronet friend, who put me in touch with the recruiters and I was invited in to the office in Great

Marlborough Street, just a step along the road from Dickens & Jones, which at the time housed the personnel department of MI5.

To understand what MI5 was like in the late 1960s and early 1970s, you need to know some of its history. Although the Elizabethan Sir Francis Walsingham is sometimes thought of as the first head of the Security Service, the true origins of MI5 lie in the period before the First World War, when a sort of spy mania developed in Britain. Newspapers were full of reports of German agents going round the country, measuring the bridges, inspecting railway tunnels and even counting the cows in the fields. Though this sounds hysterical, it was not quite as exaggerated as it may appear.

Quite early in the century, a fairly sophisticated German intelligence operation was already in place in Britain. As early as 1904, Germany had inserted into the country what we would now call 'illegals' – people with false identities, whose job it was to find out key strategic information, and communicate it covertly back to Germany. Many of them were set up as language teachers, near to the naval dockyards, where they had good access to both military and civilian staff who worked there. Ports and dockyards were a priority target for the Germans in those pre-war days, as they were later in the Second World War, and for both East and West in the Cold War.

By 1909, the Committee of Imperial Defence, under the Presidency of the Prime Minister, H.H. Asquith, was becoming concerned. When they asked what defences there were against all this activity, they were told that effectively there were none. So in a move which has a rather modern ring to it, they set up a Working Group to examine the German espionage threat, which proposed detailed arrangements for creating a Secret Service Bureau. Two officers were plucked out of the armed services and told to get on with it. One was Captain Vernon Kell of the South Staffordshire Regiment, who was at the time working on an intelligence desk in the Committee of Imperial Defence, and had made his reputation as a Chinese expert. The other, Captain Mansfield Cumming of the Royal Navy, was formerly Boom Defence Officer at Southampton.

Kell and Cumming were to undertake their task on behalf of the War Office and the Admiralty respectively and at first they worked jointly to set up the Bureau. But after a short time, they realised that in fact there were two angles to the job and if they were to beat the Germans at their own game, they needed to go at the task from both. One of them would try to find out what was going on in Britain, and try to stop it, and the other would start sending his own agents into Germany to find out what the strategy and the plans were, so they could be thwarted before they ever got off the ground. So Kell took the home end, responsibility for counter-espionage work within the British Isles, finding out what the spies were doing here in Britain, while Cumming, or 'C' as he came to be known, took responsibility for gathering information overseas – and MI5 and MI6 were born. The head of counter-espionage in MI5 was until quite recently known as 'K' after Kell and the Chief of MI6 is still known as 'C', after Cumming – not 'M' as James Bond afficionados think. 'M' was someone else.

Vernon Kell rapidly realised that he had taken on a very considerable task. There were at least a dozen German spies in place in 1909 and more coming in all the time, so he started to build up a staff of people to help him. One of them was a retired Metropolitan Police Superintendent called William Melville. He did most of the leg work, going round the country investigating the scores of reports of German spies at work in the country, and it was he who came to be known as 'M'. At first, Kell had just one rather squalid office near Victoria Station. John le Carré's *Tinker, Tailor, Soldier, Spy*, though it describes a much later period, contains a very good description of what it must have been like in those days, in the episode where Smiley and his police officer helper, Inspector Mendel, operate out of the seedy Hotel Islay in Sussex Gardens in Paddington.

Melville, 'M', developed his role into a fine art. He went

round the country adopting various cover identities, befriending suspect spies, drinking with them in pubs, and managing to win their confidence. He recruited their landladies to help him and took rooms across the corridors from his suspects. For one man he seems to have been everywhere at once. He and Kell and their tiny staff investigated at least thirty-six spies between 1909 and the outbreak of the war in 1914. They were helped by a real breakthrough in 1911, which demonstrates how unsophisticated the espionage business was in those days.

One of Kell's helpers was travelling one day on a train in Scotland when quite by chance he heard two men in the same compartment talking German, a language he understood. One was telling the other about a letter he had received from Potsdam asking questions about the British preparations for war. On investigation, the man who had received the letter turned out to be the German-born landlord of the Peacock Hotel in Leith, a Mr Holstein, and the letter, which he handed over, for he was loyal to Britain, was from German intelligence. The letter gave addresses in Potsdam to which Holstein was supposed to send his information. No intelligence service worth its salt would make such a mistake in tradecraft nowadays for Kell quickly got permission to intercept letters to those addresses – an early example of a postal interception operation – and so was able to identify a network of agents and their post boxes and cut-outs which German intelligence had set up all over the country.

As a result of that and other operations, Kell and his band of helpers had, by the outbreak of war, identified all Germany's spies in Britain. They were reading most of their communications and they knew practically everything they were up to. Then, just before the war broke out, Kell struck. In an operation which was designed, in his own words, 'to paralyse the German espionage effort in one powerful blow', he rounded them all up. On 4 August 1914, twenty-one people of German origin were arrested by the English and Scottish police on the same day, on receipt of a coded telegram from

Kell. Several of them were condemned to death, though a number were later reprieved. The first to be reprieved was a woman, which caused MI5 to protest strongly, on the grounds that once it became known to the Germans that Britain was lenient towards women, they would flood the country with them. Sherlock Holmes devotees will remember that the last Holmes story, *His Last Bow*, is about this sweep-up of German spies. Presumably, though the tale does not say so, Holmes is brought in to help, as MI5 were not up to dealing with the German master spy. The truth is, though, that Kell's tiny organisation was very effective.

The effect of Kell's strike on the German High Command was dramatic. We know this because the man responsible for the network in Britain, Gustav Steinhauer, later wrote a book about it called *The Kaiser's Master Spy*. He wrote that the Kaiser was dumbfounded when he heard that all his agents had been arrested and 'apparently unable to believe his ears, raved and stormed for the better part of two hours about the incompetence of his so-called intelligence officers, bellowing on . . . Am I surrounded by dolts? Why was I not told? Who is responsible?', and more in the same vein. So Kell, with his Bureau of only about ten people, had a successful start.

At the beginning of the war, the Bureau was 'mobilised' as part of the War Office and in January 1916 it became part of a new Directorate of Military Intelligence as MI5. During the First War, MI5's responsibilities increased to include the co-ordination of government policy towards aliens and other security measures. By the end of the First World War, Kell had acquired more than 800 staff, had responsibility for counter-espionage throughout the British Empire and had opened the first foreign links which now form such a vital part of security work. MI5 was there to stay.

As the years rolled on, the threats came from different sources. Between the wars, the world at first seemed a much more secure place and Kell let his staff numbers fall to only thirty people. At that time MI5 was not responsible for counteracting subversion or sabotage among the civilian population, That fell to the police to deal with. However, after the Bolshevik coup d'état in 1917, Kell and his colleagues began to work on threats of communist subversion within the armed services and of sabotage to military installations. In 1931, responsibility for assessing all threats to the national security of the United Kingdom, except from Irish terrorists and anarchists passed to MI5 and it was retitled 'The Security Service', which is its proper name today, though it is still known all over the world as MI5.

As Hitler rose to power in Germany, subversion and sabotage by fascists became a concern. But when the Second World War was declared in 1939, MI5 was not well prepared for its task. Staff numbers remained low and they had a large number of tasks to carry out, including counter-espionage, advising on enemy aliens and internment, vetting checks, advice on security measures, and dealing with reports from members of the public on suspicious activity. To make matters worse, in 1940, some of the records were destroyed when a bomb hit Wormwood Scrubs prison, to which they had been evacuated.

In 1941, the Director-General was given the resources to build up an organisation competent to deal with its task. The British government's policy of internment greatly helped by effectively depriving the Germans of all their agents in the country. When the German intelligence records were studied in 1945, at the end of the war, it was found that all the 200 or so German spies targeted against the UK during the war had been successfully identified and rounded up. Some were turned and used to supply false information to the Nazis about the Allies' military strategy. A particularly successful plan of this kind was known as the 'Double Cross' Operation, which contributed greatly to the success of the Allied forces' landing in Normandy on D-Day in June 1944 by feeding mis-information to the Germans about the date and place of the landing.

By 1945, no-one questioned the need for MI5. On the contrary, the threats to our national security were by then seen as so significant that the government thought it necessary formally to define their role and the Director-General was made directly accountable to the Prime Minister, who, as head of the government was personally responsible for the security of the state. It was not until 1952 that the then Prime Minister, Winston Churchill, partially delegated his responsibility for the Security Service to his Home Secretary, Sir David Maxwell Fyfe. Maxwell Fyfe issued a directive setting out the Service's tasks and defining the role of the Director-General. This directive, which was renewed by each incoming Home Secretary of whatever party, provided the basis for the Service's work until 1989, when the Security Service Act was passed.

Following the defeat of Nazi Germany, Western intelligence turned its attention to the activities of the Soviet Union and what was soon to become the Cold War. By then there were three British intelligence services each with its specific task: the Secret Intelligence Service or MI6, focusing, as it had since it was founded, on acquiring foreign intelligence primarily related to defence and foreign affairs; GCHQ whose responsibilities were the gathering of intelligence by technical means; and MI5, the domestic service, responsible for defending the country's national security against whatever threats arose. At the end of the war MI5 was given an expanded directive, which stressed its duty to provide advice and assistance on security matters to the colonies and the Commonwealth and also to friendly foreign governments. By the early 1950s, there were about 850 people in MI5, including forty or so Security Liaison Officers overseas. My baronet friend in Delhi, who had first recruited me, was of course one of these.

The main focus of MI5's work at the end of the war and for many years afterwards was communist subversion, coupled with espionage by the intelligence services of the Soviet bloc. The activities of the Communist Party of Great Britain (CPGB) had already been a matter of interest to MI5 for some time. From the Russian revolution right through the 1930s there

was much ideological sympathy among the British intelli-
gentsia for the Soviet Union. Though many people changed
their views at the beginning of the war when the Soviet Union
formed a non-aggression pact with Hitler, sympathy as well as
practical links increased from 1941, when we became allies
against Nazi Germany, and consequently the Communist
Party of Great Britain grew in numbers. The Party remained
large and influential after the Iron Curtain came down in
Europe and by 1948, there was such concern about the
potential for the leakage of vital information to the Soviet
Union through members of the Communist Party that the
Prime Minister, Attlee, announced that communists as well as
fascists would be excluded from work 'vital to the security of
the State'. This was to be achieved through the vetting system
which MI5 was charged to support and which I was to help to
implement in my first job in MI5.

# 8

When I arrived at MI5's offices in Great Marlborough Street on a June day in 1969, wearing a striped Indian silk suit with a mini skirt, and a little hat sitting on top of long hair done up in a bun, I had very little idea about the organisation I was seeking to join. Had I known a bit more about its early history, perhaps I would not have been quite so surprised by what seemed its old-fashioned and eccentric aspects. Because, even in 1969, the ethos had not changed very much from the days when a small group of military officers, all male of course and all close colleagues working in great secrecy, pitted their wits against the enemy.

In the personnel department, I was interviewed by a bouncy Welshman and a rather severe middle-aged lady, who was responsible for the female staff. It soon became clear to me that a strict sex discrimination policy was in place in MI5 and women were treated quite differently from men. They had only recently abandoned the dauntingly entitled post of The Lady Superintendent, whose job it was to supervise the welfare of all the female staff and to ensure that the proprieties were observed. No doubt this position dated from the days when only girls from 'good families' were employed, and their mothers and fathers were promised that they would be properly looked after.

All that the Welshman and his colleague were prepared to offer me, as a female, was a job at the equivalent of Civil Service Executive Officer. It did not matter that I had a degree, that I had worked for several years already in the public service, at a higher grade than they were offering, or that I was thirty-four years old. The policy was that men were recruited

as what were called 'officers' and women had their own career
structure, a second-class career, as 'assistant officers'. They
did all sorts of support work – collating, indexing, ensuring
the papers were filed in the right place and simple, straightforward enquiries, but not the sharp-end intelligence-
gathering operations. What the two recruiters were offering
me, that June day in 1969, was a post as 'Junior Assistant
Officer', the bottom rung of this rather humble ladder.

In adopting this policy towards women, MI5 differed
markedly from the mainstream Civil Service where women
had been accepted into the senior ranks since the early 1920s.
By the time I joined MI5, there had already been several
women Permanent Secretaries.

I often wonder why I took the job. In salary and responsibility terms it was clearly unattractive. Certainly my
motives were nothing like those they look for in recruits
nowadays. I did not feel a particular urge to serve my country,
though I was averagely patriotic, nor did I have a strong sense
of dangers to the state to be tackled or wrongs to be righted.
Apparently I told them that I liked the orderly collection of
information and research, but I added, rather ironically in
view of the way my life turned out, that I would certainly not
enjoy public speaking. But all that was probably what I
thought they wanted to hear. In fact, I was still romantically
dreaming about the Great Game, and my experiences in India
had reinforced the dream rather than destroyed it.

Nowadays, my recruiters should have tried to flush out that
attitude and if they had succeeded it would have rung alarm
bells. People with romantic illusions about spies dressed as
Pathan tribesmen would not be thought at all suitable as
recruits to MI5 in the serious 21st century.

The truth was that I hadn't seen enough of the dull side of
the work to be put off; I thought it would be interesting and
that I would get some amusement and fun out of it. I was also
curious to find out more. What did they really do in this
mysterious Head Office to which I had despatched so many
letters from India? But I was still taking quite a dilettante

attitude to my work. I saw this just as a job, something I might do for a time, something to keep me interested and amused, hopefully until I had a baby, but possibly until something else cropped up. I didn't look at it as a career and it never occurred to me to see if I could do better elsewhere. So when I was offered the job, I took it.

In July 1969 I started work in MI5's headquarters in Leconfield House at the Park Lane end of Curzon Street. Leconfield House is now the glitzy London headquarters of banks and property companies. In 1969, like many government offices in those days, it was dreadfully run down. The inside had not been painted for an age, the windows were dirty and everything about it was dark and gloomy. There was a canteen on the top floor. The most you could say about that was that it functioned. The lady in charge was one of those office 'characters', with whom everyone seems to be on good terms but whom they secretly despise. She would slop the food onto the plates with a huge spoon and a great splat, making it, if possible, even more unappetising than it looked in the container. Out of the grimy windows you could watch the rich and famous going in and out of the White Elephant Club and the other gambling dives on the other side of the road or driving up to the Bunny Club on the corner of Curzon Street. The contrast was acute. I thought the whole set-up was grim, and after one lunch there, I never went again.

The partitioning of Leconfield House had left some of the rooms without windows and the size and shape of cupboards, but I was put to work in a long narrow room with about ten or so other people, mostly women. This was the section where all new joiners, whether they were men (officers) or women (assistant officers) were put for a few months to be trained and it was presided over by a couple of training officers, two well-bred ladies 'of a certain age', from the twin-set-and-pearls brigade.

On my first day I was intrigued when at 12 noon, these two opened their desk drawers and produced exquisite cut glasses and bottles of some superior sherry, and partook of a rather elegant pre-lunch drink. I realised then that I had arrived in the land of eccentrics and that this promised to be a lot more entertaining than spending my days in Woking.

The job of the section was to identify as many members of the Communist Party of Great Britain as we could and, having identified them, to open files on them. The purpose of this activity was primarily to provide the raw material for the vetting system introduced by Clement Attlee's government in 1947. The rules of the vetting system were that access to official information vital to the security of the state, 'classified information' to use the term of art, should be denied to members of certain organisations regarded as 'subversive'. 'Subversion' was closely defined in the directive under which the Security Service worked in those days and that same definition applies today. It meant activities designed to undermine or overthrow parliamentary democracy, by political, violent or industrial means. So organisations such as the Communist Party, the various Trotskyist parties and fascist organisations, whose declared or covert purpose was to change the democratic system of government, were deemed to meet the criteria.

The assumption, which the government had adopted, was that members of such organisations could not automatically be assumed to be loyal to the country and so could not be trusted with the nation's secrets. Although people who were being considered for jobs with access to classified information were asked to fill in forms, declaring any membership of such organisations, it was assumed that they might not tell the truth. So MI5 had the responsibility of finding out, insofar as it could, who the members were, and keeping a record of them. If they applied for work giving them access to that sort of information, they would then be checked out with MI5 and the results would be taken into account in deciding whether they should get the job. This was a safeguard but of course it only went so far. A good number of ideological spies for the Soviet bloc either never joined the Communist Party or cut their overt links.

There were various sources of information to keep us up to date with the membership, some documentary, some human. The human sources were called 'agents' in the jargon. Unlike in the FBI, where 'agents' are the employees of the Bureau, in the British system 'agents' are never employees of the intelligence services, they are the people with access to the required information who are persuaded or paid to provide it. Getting used to the jargon was a big part of feeling one belonged to this strange world. All the agents had code words to disguise their identity, as did all the other sources of information. So, on first reading, any file was almost meaningless. It was not until one came to recognise the code words which explained the origin of the information, that one could interpret it and evaluate its reliability, vital of course to forming an assessment.

The meeting and controlling, or 'running' as it was called in the jargon, of the agents was regarded as a separate rather esoteric skill and was done in a different section. In those days, it went without saying that no females were allowed to work in the agent-running sections or to meet these human sources; we had to ask the male officers who 'controlled' them to find out the specific information we required. One very good source of information, which was readily available, was the *Morning Star*, the newspaper of the Communist Party of Great Britain, from a careful perusal of which we could learn a lot about who was where in the Communist Party and what they were doing. I am sure that the vast standing order for *Morning Stars* for Leconfield House kept that newspaper on its feet when it might otherwise have gone under. We and the Soviet Embassy were, I believe, its main large-scale supporters. Keeping up the circulation was always a problem for them and members were constantly being exhorted to spend time selling the paper on the street corner, thus conveniently drawing attention to themselves.

The key to the proper operation of the vetting system was precise identification and accurate recording in files. A security service lives by its records. The first and most important thing is to know precisely who the person is on whom you have a file. It may seem obvious, but it is sometimes not as straightforward as it sounds. The information on the file must be accurate, relevant and must clearly distinguish between what is hard fact and what is speculative or unconfirmed. If you do not know who the information in your files actually refers to and you do not know whether it is true or not, you are not likely to be very effective in any action you take on it. So accuracy, precision and the proper assessment of information are fundamental skills for a security service officer, and those were the skills we were learning in our training section, on a comparatively simple target. We were not responsible for taking decisions on the information we gathered, which involved making recommendations about whether people should be employed or not. That required sometimes quite difficult judgements about the interpretation and assessment of the information and was regarded as more skilled work, requiring far greater knowledge and experience than we novices had. The ultimate responsibility for deciding whether somebody got a job or not lay with the employing department, a decision they took in the light of MI5's assessment.

In that summer of 1969, I was learning the first principles of intelligence work and I must say that at that stage I found it pretty dull. Trainees were given responsibility for the rural branches of the Communist Party where membership was low and not much was going on. I got Sussex, where there were very few Party members and many of those were fairly ancient. Such revolutionary activity as there was in Sussex in those days was of a different kind and was centred on its new Basil Spence-designed university, where every form of protest from vague student revolutionary fervour to the full blown Trotskyism of Militant Tendency was to be found.

But as for the Sussex comrades, as far as I could see not much of interest was happening so, after I had found out what I was supposed to be doing, I whiled away the time reading Dornford Yates novels under the desk. I followed with enthusiasm the exploits of agreeable upper class people with names like Boy Pleydell, as they roared across Europe in their limousines to rescue beautiful ladies from the clutches of international villains. If the ladies in charge of training us had known what I was up to, they would have thought I was unsuitably frivolous.

As part of the early training, one spent a period working in the Registry. This was where all the Service's files were stored; where the new files, which we and other people working in the different parts of the Service asked for, were actually created and where names would be looked up in the indexes at the request of desk officers, when they needed to find out if a person had a file. All parts of the Registry, the file making, storing and the indexes, were staffed by female staff in those days. There were a number of very senior ladies, known as Registry Examiners. Their job was to preserve the purity of the files. They scrutinised the requests which desk officers made of the Registry, whether it was to make a file, or to put papers away in a nominated file, or whatever it might be. If anything that had been requested did not comply with the strict rules in force, they would send back what was known as a 'green note', drawing your attention to whatever error you had made. The arrival of the files one thought one had got rid of, covered in green notes, was a sort of ritual humiliation that one was required to suffer as an embryo desk officer. These ladies were known to the male desk officers, in a show of bravado, because they were secretly terrified of them, as 'The Registry Queens'.

The only men to be seen among the Registry staff were the Head of the Registry, and his two assistants. The Head of the Registry at that time was a Scotsman who rather reminded me of Mr Sargeant, the Chief Archivist in my Worcester days. He was a bully with a heart of gold. He hectored and shouted at his lady employees constantly, but they all seemed to love him. One of his great delights was making new joiners, particularly female joiners feel small. A favourite trick was to yell at new arrivals, 'Where is the Great Bed of Ware?' If you did not know the answer (and I didn't), then as far as he was concerned, he was one up and you were one down for life.

The entire Registry was paper-based for this was long before computerisation. The indexes were on cards in row upon row of brown wooden drawers, stored in a big room in the basement, which had no natural light. The files were all in great racks in basement rooms and overhead, through all the rooms, a railway system rumbled and rattled. This railway went through much of the building, carrying tin box-like containers into which the files were put to be transported to local registries in the sections which had asked for them. Even in those days the railway was getting rather decrepit, and from time to time a tin box fell off or flew open, causing alarm and occasionally injury to those underneath it.

In the parts where the railway did not penetrate there was a Lampson's tube, similar to the system I remember in shops in my youth, by which the counters used to send off your money to the cashier when you bought anything. In our system, you put your paper or whatever it was into a container and shoved it in a pipe and with a great sucking noise and a clatter, it disappeared – only to pop up in someone else's pipe seconds later.

The Registry 'ladies', as they were called, were under a draconian regime, particularly those who worked in the index. They were not allowed to take anything into or out of the room where they worked, certainly not their handbags; they were not allowed to eat at their desks, and there were innumerable other regulations, all designed to safeguard and preserve the purity of the index, which, together with the files, was the lifeblood of the Service.

We trainees were learning to be 'desk officers'. A desk officer, working in a team or group, carries out the main investigative and assessment work of the service on its different targets. The desk officers, who are nowadays usually graduates with good degrees, often recruited directly from university, can deploy, as appropriate to the investigation, various sources of secret intelligence against their targets.

Nowadays, training and development for desk officers is highly structured and sophisticated. When I joined, it was fairly haphazard. Indeed some of my older-established colleagues used to assert proudly that they had never been on a training course at all. We were advised to read *The British Road to Socialism*, the programme of the Communist Party of Great Britain, and the classic work, R. Carew Hunt's *The Theory and Practice of Communism* and we sat through occasional after-lunch lectures on Marxism-Leninism from a senior officer who had made a study of the subject; but the time of day and the boring delivery meant that all of us, including the lecturer, ended up more asleep than awake. Later, more relevant and sophisticated training courses were developed and those of my intake period were guinea pigs for an emerging training régime.

In those days, as a newcomer, you were not sure what you were allowed or expected to know and you were not encouraged to seek information. I was always quite inquisitive and I wanted to know what was going on, but I soon realised that people regarded you with suspicion if you asked too many questions, so I learned to keep quiet. Indeed, you were hardly sure whether you were even meant to know the name of the Director-General, and since you certainly never saw him or received any communication signed by him, you might just as well not have known. There was a joke going around the Service that you would know which was the Director-General because he was the one who always wore his dark glasses indoors so that he would not be recognised.

Outside the Service of course very little at all was to be said. It was impressed on those joining that they must be extremely cautious about confiding where they worked to anyone. Young people joining were told they should think whether it was even necessary to tell their parents who their employer was and a sharp distinction was made in those days between spouses, in whom you might confide, and boyfriends and girlfriends in whom you definitely might not.

I remember a circular came round setting out the position

with regard to fiancé(e)s, but I can't remember now which side of the fence they fell on. When I was Director-General I was told by a man who was retiring after a long career in the Service that he had never informed his wife where he worked. Even in Cold War days that would have been regarded as carrying things too far.

This almost obsessive secrecy was not unique to the British intelligence services during the Cold War. All intelligence services in East and West behaved in much the same way because of the well-founded fear of infiltration of one side by the other. That was indeed the top priority intelligence target for both sides and success in that objective could do immense harm.

In the late 1960s the top-priority intelligence target for both sides in the Cold War was the infiltration of the others' intelligence services. In the British intelligence community everyone was acutely aware of the notable Soviet successes in the not-far-distant past – the Cambridge spies, Philby, a member of MI6, Burgess and Maclean of the Foreign Office and, very recently uncovered and not at that time publicly known, Anthony Blunt, the Keeper of the Queen's Pictures and spy for the Soviet Union, who had worked in MI5 during the war. Their shadows hung heavily over us when I joined in 1969. Both sides responded in similar fashion, by cutting themselves off as much as possible from the outside world. But that had bad effects. In the Eastern Bloc it resulted in repressive organisations, which saw their own citizens as the main threat rather than what they existed to protect. In the West, it resulted in old-fashioned, inward-looking organisations, cut off from modernising influences and afraid and unwilling to change.

Information was, very properly, held tightly and there was a series of circles within circles. As a newcomer, you were in the very outer circle, but as you carried out your day-to-day tasks you became aware that there were lots of other circles of which you were not a member. From time to time, when I asked for a name to be looked up in the index, to see whether someone already had a file, the answer would come back that I must refer to someone else, as I was not on the relevant list for seeing whatever there was. You knew, when that happened, that either the person you had stumbled upon was an agent, a human source, whose identity was kept very closely guarded, or there was information on the file which revealed some other secret source of information or some operation which you were not allowed to know about.

This system was necessary, as some of the human sources whose identity it was protecting were at risk of imprisonment or death should their activities be revealed. And there was the ever-present fear that one of us might be a spy, a penetration agent for the Soviet bloc. But the difficulty lay in applying those rules sensibly. It was important not to make the principle of 'need to know' – that is that no-one should be told anything unless they could demonstrate a real operational need to know it – so important that the principle of communication was overlooked. And in those days in the '60s and '70s the balance was quite understandably weighted on the side of secrecy.

There were risks from this Cold War ethos. Firstly, there was a real danger of inefficiency, because information might be so squirreled away behind rings of secrecy that its existence was not known to those who needed it and investigations might be damaged as a result. Secondly, of course, extreme secrecy can lead to paranoia. What I did not know when I joined was that MI5 had recently almost torn itself apart because of this fear of infiltration. A faction, led by Peter Wright, had nearly brought the Service to a standstill by its conviction that there was penetration both at high and middle levels of the Service. They had become convinced, wrongly as was later established, that, amongst others, the then Director-General, Roger Hollis, was a Russian spy. Wright and James Angleton of the CIA fuelled each other's paranoia, which was reinforced by defectors from the Soviet Union, and convinced themselves that many Soviet-run moles had penetrated the CIA and British intelligence, and that Moscow was

manipulating the United States and Britain through dis-
information and propaganda. One has only to read Peter
Wright's book *Spycatcher* to understand the level which this
obsession reached.

As a newcomer, arriving fresh from the relaxed world of
India with my wardrobe of exotic Indian-made silk clothes
and sandals and a residual suntan, I felt like a real outsider. I
could not quite see how or where I was going to fit into this
very curious set-up. It was indeed, as the recruitment process
had made clear, unashamedly male-dominated. The men were
the 'officers' and the women were the 'other ranks' in military
parlance, and there were still quite strong military overtones.
The men were largely from a similar background. To me it
seemed that they all lived in Guildford and spent their spare
time gardening. Many had fought in the armed services during
the war; some had performed heroically and some, perhaps
not surprisingly, seemed drained by their experiences. I
remember one, who had been a Dambuster and had flown the
most dramatic and dangerous sorties when he had been very
young. He regularly withdrew into his office and locked the
door after lunch. I used to jump up and down in the corridor
to look over the smoked glass in the partition, to see what he
was doing, and he was invariably sound asleep. No-one
thought it appropriate to comment.

Many of the men had come in to MI5 from a first career in
the Colonial Service. They had come in in little groups as each
of the colonies had become independent, and there were
circles of friends known as the Malayan Mafia or the Sudan
Souls. They had come in as 'officers', broadly equivalent to
Principal in the old Administrative Class of the Home Civil
Service, but they were given no promise of progression
through a career. Most had a pension and a lump sum which
had enabled them to buy a house, so they were not on the
breadline. Though some did well and rose to senior positions,
others did not and, not surprisingly in the circumstances,
many of them lacked any motivation or drive and did not
exactly exert themselves.

Some of them, far from exerting themselves, seemed to do very little at all and there was a lot of heavy drinking. I remember one gentleman, who was supposed to be running agents against the Russian intelligence residency in London. He favoured rather loud tweed suits and a monocle. He would arrive in the office at about 10 and at about 11 would go out for what was termed 'breakfast'. He would return at 12 noon, smelling strongly of whisky to get ready to go out to 'meet an agent' for lunch. If he returned at all it would be at about 4pm, for a quiet snooze before getting ready to go home. Eventually, he collapsed in the lift returning from one of these sorties and was not seen again.

Maybe it was not as bad as I remember. I was very lowly in the hierarchy and from low down you often get a very partial view of what is going on. But I know the various drinking clubs around Soho were much frequented by the older MI5 officers in those days, because occasionally I went with them. These were the kind of places where drinks were available at all hours; you signed your name in a book as 'Mr Smith and two guests' and you could drink all day.

The women were a curiously mixed bunch. There were still some of the debs around, the generals' and admirals' daughters who had peopled MI5 as clerks and secretaries during and just after the war – recruited more for their obvious reliability, for whom they knew and who could vouch for them, than for their brains or education – though some of them were very bright women being seriously underemployed. But there were also beginning to come in women like me, with a good degree, some straight from university, some who had already had a career in some other profession. But, even so, not much regard was paid to your qualifications or ability if you were a woman.

The nearest the women got to the sharp end of things in those days was as support officers to the men who were running the agents. They would be asked to go and service the safe-house where the agent was met – making sure there was milk and coffee there and the place was clean and tidy, and very occasionally they might be allowed to go with their officer to meet a very reliable, long-standing agent on his birthday or some other special occasion.

This attitude to women seems incredible now, looked at from the standpoint of the 21st century. So much has changed in women's employment expectations since those days. But I don't think it ever occurred to my male colleagues that they were discriminating against us and in those days it was not really questioned inside the Service. And to be fair to them, even I, coming in from the outside, did not question it at first.

## 9

After a few months I escaped from the training section and the Sussex communists. Perhaps helped by my experience as an archivist, I had mastered the intricacies of the files without too much difficulty and I was chosen to go to a new section which was just starting up to focus on the situation in Northern Ireland. This must have been about October 1969.

The year 1969 had seen increasing violence in Northern Ireland and deepening divisions between the two communities. The Civil Rights Movement which had been gaining ground since the mid-1960s was in full flood; in April, the twenty-one-year-old Bernadette Devlin had been elected to Westminster as MP for mid-Ulster; and at about the same time there had been a series of bombings carried out by the extreme loyalist group the UVF. August brought the loyalist Apprentice Boys march in Londonderry which resulted in stone throwing and violence and then, as the police arrived in force, barricades, petrol bombs and the first use of CS gas in the UK, in what came to be known as the Battle of the Bogside. After forty-eight hours of continuous attacks British troops were sent in to help restore law and order in the Bogside but then violence broke out between the two communities in Belfast. The affairs of Northern Ireland, which for many years had hardly impinged on the government at Westminster, began to preoccupy it more and more and ministers and senior civil servants looked round for intelligence to help them understand and manage the situation.

At that time MI5 had practically no sources of information and very little intelligence was available. It is a feature of a democracy that a security service will *follow* a new security threat rather than foreseeing it. Of course, resource is devoted to assessing likely new threats but before an investigation can be mounted, using the full panoply of covert resources – interception of communications, covert surveillance and agent sources – it has to be demonstrable that a serious threat to national security exists. Stated baldly that sounds ineffective, and indeed it does sometimes mean that at the beginning of any new threat, intelligence lags behind and takes time to catch up. But it is important for the protection of individual rights and freedoms that the resources of the secret state are applied only when a serious threat exists. During my time in a senior position in MI5, we assessed on several occasions whether the level of the threat from serious organised crime, for example, or animal liberation extremism justified action by MI5 or whether such activities represented primarily a law-and-order issue properly left to the police to handle.

So the Irish section to which I was sent in autumn 1969 was a small affair. In fact at the Leconfield House end, it consisted at that time of one experienced lady assistant officer and myself. We were supporting a small group who had gone to Northern Ireland to work with the RUC and to assess what MI5 should do. My job was to try to create some order in the papers which began to be generated and to get them put on files so that they could be located and used. My boss and I very rapidly became almost submerged, trying to make sense of the information that began to come in. I looked back with some nostalgia to the underemployment of the training section, as I began to have to stay late into the evenings just to keep up with the flow of paper. My colleague had a habit of talking out loud all the time, telling herself what to do next and, as the days wore on and the pressure mounted, her instructions to herself became more and more manic. Anyone coming into the room was faced with two dishevelled-looking women, one chattering like a parrot and the other peering out squirrel-like from behind a tottering pile of paper. As far as I recall, the tottering pile did not at that stage contain much in the way of real intelligence. It was largely assessments of the situation on the ground, reports of meetings and newspaper cuttings but as is always the way with paper, once it had started coming in, it was very difficult to stop. Such were the beginnings of what was eventually to become a large and very successful intelligence operation against terrorism in Northern Ireland.

At the time I did not realise it, but looking back now it is clear that that period in 1969 marked the beginning of a big change for MI5. The emergence of a serious threat of terrorism on our own doorsteps, and the almost simultaneous development of what was to become so-called 'international' terrorism, marked the start of a significant shift of resources away from the traditional Cold War targets. With that came what was eventually to be a huge change in the way we worked and in the whole culture of the Service. But I did not stay in the new section more than a month or two, and it was many years before I was to return to the counter-terrorist field. When I did it was as the Director, responsible for our work against what had by then become the major security threat to the UK and to a large part of the world. I moved on because it was rapidly realised that more than one lady assistant officer and a raw recruit was needed to cope with everything that was beginning to happen in Northern Ireland. The section was expanded, more experienced staff were drafted in and I was sent off elsewhere.

I left dark and gloomy Leconfield House with no regrets at all, for a building in Grosvenor Street, one of the many offices around Mayfair which MI5 occupied at that time. Then began what turned out to be quite a long period working against what was still in those days very much the main enemy, the intelligence services of the Soviet Union.

What I was now to do was work which resulted directly from the defection of Burgess and Maclean in 1951 and Philby in 1963 and the assessment which had by then been made, that they had been recruited by the Russian intelligence service, the KGB, while they were undergraduates at Cambridge and directed into various parts of the public service. It was not known at that time how they had been talent-spotted, or who had done the recruiting. An extensive programme of interviews had been launched, of people who had been at various universities, not just Oxford and Cambridge, in the 1930s and '40s, some who had been in the university Communist Parties and some who had not, to see whether any leads emerged to indicate that there had been more serious penetration of the Civil Service than we knew. A team of four or five officers (male) was put together to do the interviews, supported by a number of assistant officers (female) to do background research and organise the papers. It was a big undertaking, and many interviews were done and long reports written, but ultimately nothing emerged to show that there was a more serious problem than we knew about.

After a few months of this I, with the wisdom of inexperience, had decided that we were not going to uncover more spy rings and that this was a bit of a side-show. I knew that in other parts of the Service, what I regarded as much more interesting things were going on. Real, current espionage was being investigated and I was eager to get my teeth stuck into it. However in April 1970 I learned that, unlikely though it seemed after so long, I was pregnant. I first realised that this was probable one beautiful spring day as I was sitting in Cambridge University Library, doing some research. Considering that I had wanted a baby for such a long time, the pregnancy came, as seems so often to happen, at the most inopportune moment.

In February that year, John and I had taken the plunge and had bought a house in Islington. Our time in Delhi had enabled us to save up some money and with that as a deposit we had been able to afford to buy a forty-three-year lease on a small terraced house in Canonbury Grove, just off Canonbury Road in Islington. It was a charming little Georgian terrace house with a beautiful view at the front over the gardens of the New River Walk, which were full of flowering trees in spring. But buying it was a risky enterprise for us as we could only just afford the deposit and the mortgage on our salaries. A lease was not a very sound investment, but we hoped that the BP Pension fund, the owners of the freehold, might sell it one day and that at that stage we would be able to afford to buy.

Restoration work was going on all over Islington in the early 1970s, as the young middle classes began to focus on it as a convenient and stylish place to live. The Victoria Line of the Underground had arrived and from Highbury and Islington Station one could get to Oxford Street in under twenty minutes. We could see that property prices were going to take off and we felt we must get into the market. But we had not bargained on my becoming pregnant almost immediately after we had moved in.

To make matters worse, things were not going well with John. After much anxious thought, and following a transfer to the Department of Employment, which he hated, he had succumbed to the wooing of Parsons and the Comac team and had joined them. What they had not told him was that immediately before he arrived, the deal with the City merchant bank, on the strength of which he had joined, was off. The collapse of that deal merely presaged worse problems for the enterprise and after a few months the company which had recruited him broke up. John was offered a job in one of the company's assets, a large bank in Detroit, but neither of us felt that would be a very wise move, particularly with me pregnant. So John left them and sought and got reinstatement in the Civil Service. Unfortunately, under the draconian pension rules then operating in the Civil Service, he effectively had to start again and lost his pension entitlement for the years he had already worked.

This was an anxious period. Knowing we had probably overstretched our finances, I worried inordinately about the house. Though some modernisation work had been done by our predecessors, it had some serious problems, in particular ferocious rising damp and a dangerous, old-fashioned central heating boiler. At the time we had no spare money to deal with any of this. Before we had the money, that central heating boiler had killed our two Burmese cats whom I had christened

Burgess and Maclean, though later, when our daughter Sophie was learning to speak, they had become known as Pussy Red and Pussy Blue from the colour of their collars. The boiler almost killed Sophie as well on the same occasion. The cats had been shut in the kitchen for the night and the baby was asleep in the room next door. The boiler's ventilation system, it later turned out, was almost totally useless and allowed its fumes to blow back into the kitchen. When I went into the kitchen first thing one morning, I discovered the room full of fumes and both the cats dead on the floor. I rushed into the bedroom next door, but mercifully the fumes had not got in there and Sophie was unharmed.

Another problem we had not foreseen came from the Council block at the back, whose walkways overlooked our garden. At the time we first moved in, the flat directly at the bottom of our garden was occupied by an Irish lady whose custom it was to come out on the balcony and prophesy at the top of her voice, wearing a nightgown, with her hair blowing in the wind, like some Irish Cassandra. When instead of prophesying, she started to let loose a stream of foul language, she was taken away by the social services as unable to look after herself.

Peace returned temporarily, until a family moved in with two children, Roy and Elaine. For a long time we did not see the children and we only knew their names because their father used to come out on the balcony, lean over and bellow in a huge voice, 'Roy, Eelaine. Come up 'ere or I'll belt the daylights out of yer.' Not surprisingly, Roy and Eelaine seemed reluctant to obey, and the bellowing went on for some time, several times a day. We imagined Roy and Eelaine as recalcitrant, knife-wielding teenagers in motorbike kit, and wondered if they were dangerous. But one day there was a knock on our door, and there outside was a very small girl in glasses with one lens covered with sticking plaster, holding by the hand an even smaller boy with muddy knees. They had come to get their ball, which had come over into our garden. In a moment of inspiration John said to them, 'Are you Roy and Eelaine?' They nodded. We never felt the same about Roy and Eelaine again.

I had worried a lot about how we were going to manage when the baby was born. It had never been my intention to be a working mother and I was extremely uneasy about the idea. In the early 1970s, it was still regarded as quite unusual for professional women to go straight back to work after having a baby. Those were the days when, in the Foreign Office, women diplomatic staff had to leave when they got married, let alone when they had babies. My mother was much against the idea of my going back to work. She was firmly of the view that a mother's place was with her baby, at least until the child was old enough to go to school.

She was not the only one – there were lots of people around to add to my sense of guilt by expressing their amazement that I should even consider such a course. Certainly this situation had not arisen before in MI5. I discussed the options with the personnel people in the office and it was made clear to me that if I wanted to come back even at my then grade, I would have to come back full time. And I would be expected to return after three months, if I wanted to be certain that there would be a job for me to come back to. There was no part-time work in those days, except for clerks and typists, and job-sharing had not been invented. It was taken for granted that intelligence staff worked full time or not at all. Inevitably, John's loss of years of pension affected my own attitude to my career. Although we always hoped that it would be restored, even right up to the time of his retirement, I felt that it was more important than ever for me to go on working to make sure that I had a pension in my own right.

I stayed in the group working on university research until November 1970, when I left to have Sophie, though with all this going on at home, the problems of the possible infiltration of the Civil Service by Russian spies seemed to pale into insignificance, as far as I was concerned. When I left to go on maternity leave, my boss wrote on my annual confidential report: 'She is a most acceptable, warm-hearted and engaging colleague', but then he spoiled the sentiment by adding 'even though she is an upholder of women's rights.' I don't think I was aggressively feminist, but my intention of returning to work after having the baby was incomprehensible to most of my male colleagues in those days and must have seemed like an advanced case of 'womens' lib', a phenomenon both scorned and feared by many men in 1970.

Sophie was born on 30 December 1970. Almost immediately I had to start planning how I was to manage to go back to work, though I certainly did not at all want to do so. I think I would have felt better about it all if I had been able to afford to have someone to live in the house and look after her but on my salary, and with our commitments, that was not possible. With a heavy heart, I started to investigate the prospect of day nurseries for babies, but in Islington at that time they were few and far between and places in them were limited to what were known in the jargon of the times as 'problem families'. Whatever they were, we obviously were not one of them. I did not know what to do next, but our local health visitor suggested the idea of a child minder who would look after our baby in their house. I had never heard of this – in those days it was not nearly as common as it is now — and did not at all like the sound of it. However, the health visitor put me in touch with the wife of a civilian police employee with a family of her own, who lived in the police flats in Canonbury, not far from our house. I was greatly cheered when I met her and found a friendly, sensible down-to-earth lady who it turned out also looked after the daughter of our doctor.

Nancy looked after Sophie from the time she was three months old until she was four-and-a-half. It was an arrangement that worked very well for the two of them and they developed a warm, happy relationship. For me it provided what I needed at the time, the comfort that my daughter was being well looked after in a secure and caring environment. But I was the one who suffered most from this arrangement and I found it at its most difficult when I first went back to work. I couldn't escape a sense of guilt every morning as I handed over my baby in her pram to Nancy at the gates of Canonbury School. When Sophie got a bit older, and knew what was going on, she used to cry and cling on when I left her in the morning, as children of that age will. I found it distressing, even though I knew that as soon as I had gone, she cheered up. All this is the currency of many people's lives nowadays and is not taken as at all unusual. But in the early 1970s, with lots of people ready to tell you it was wrong and that you were risking long-term damage to your child, it was tough. My mother always asserted that Sophie's rather anxious personality was caused by her early upbringing. I forbore to remind her that my own early childhood experiences had hardly been secure and that I was probably an even more anxious child as a result.

There is never going to be any perfect answer to the dilemma faced by mothers who opt to work full time, whatever their reason for doing so. Even today, though it is not regarded as the strange and unusual thing it was then, and though the support mechanisms are better organised, it is no easier. I am now watching one of my daughters trying to do what I did then, and manage work and a family. And twenty-five years on, it is no easier for her than it was for me. She is still trying to fit being a mother in around the edges of her working life, or to fit working round the edges of being a mother, depending on what the day brings, and my granddaughter is looked after in much the same hand-to-mouth way as she was.

The debate has moved on from stereotyping men's and women's roles as worker and homemaker, but we still define everyone in society in terms of what they 'do', i.e. their job, and we have not yet managed to come to grips with the relationship between work and home. Though it is much more socially acceptable now for the male parent to share what was traditionally 'the mother's role', that causes its own tensions. It can mean merely that both members of the partnership, instead of just one, are attempting the difficult task of balancing the

competing pulls of career and home and feeling dissatisfied
with their performance in both. Women are doing well at work
and society needs them to. Most neither can nor wish to return
to being segregated in their homes, as 'housewives'. The result
is that even nowadays most mothers, particularly when their
children are very young, are strongly pulled in two different
directions. Of course, it helps if one is strongly committed to
one's work or, to be brutal about it, if one is earning large sums
of money and can afford everything of the best in one's own
home, as nowadays some young people can.

I don't know what the answer to this conundrum is, and
neither does anyone else. When I hear of increasing 'family-
friendly' policies, more 'rights' for employees to maternity
leave, paternity leave, special leave during the early years of
their children's lives, I worry. Obviously, I would like things
to be easier for my daughters and their children than it was for
us when they were little and I want those women with the will
and the capacity to rise to the top in employment, to be able
to do so. But I don't want young women to become dis-
advantaged in one way because we have sought to give them
more advantages in another. I have seen enough of employers
in the public and private sector to know that those employees
who take all they are entitled to, even now, are less likely to
get on than those who do not. Getting to the top, for a woman
in particular, is still a question of having enormous energy,
determination and focus.

At that stage, I was neither strongly committed to MI5, nor
was I earning large sums of money. I went back to work solely
because I felt I had no option, though I would not have
admitted this at the time, and if asked I would have talked
about the importance of my career. But it was difficult. I
would call at Nancy's on my way home from work and collect
Sophie in her pram and later her pushchair. As soon as we got
home I would give her tea and a bath, aware that however
tired I was I must be lively and jolly as I was cramming all my
mothering into these few hours. Those were the days of terry-
towelling nappies, disposables were just coming into the

shops, and they had to be washed by hand every evening as at first we did not have a washing machine. Luckily, I had and still have a robust constitution and more energy than most people. And I certainly needed it. But in spite of that, my memories of those early years of Sophie's life are primarily of hard work and exhaustion and of relations between John and myself going into severe decline.

It was at this stage of my life that I began to acquire the skill, essential for a working mother, of compartmentalisation. You have to learn to divide your life up into boxes; not to worry about one thing when you are doing something else. It is not easy at first and for me it was not made any easier by concerned friends constantly asking, 'Don't you worry about your baby when you're at work?' I did at first, very much, but I soon realized that if I were to survive, I would have to learn to put her out of my mind while I was in the office. I did manage to do that in the end, but even years later when I had two children at school, if I drove past a school on my way to a meeting, just when all the children were coming out and being met by their mothers, I would feel a twinge of guilt that I was not there meeting mine and taking them home for tea. I have to admit, though, that however much I enjoyed doing that occasionally, I felt a sense of satisfaction and fulfilment that I also had something else interesting and even important to do.

There is another skill, related to compartmentalisation, which all successful working mothers have to develop to a fine art, which I began to learn at this stage, though I became much more skilled at it later. It is sometimes said that women are better than men at *doing* several things at once and I think that is probably true, but more than that, you have to develop the skill of *keeping your eye on* lots of different things at once. Without having time to focus on anything in much detail, you begin to recognise when something is getting out of place in the big picture. You are constantly reviewing things, whether at home or at work, then when you spot something getting out of line, you focus on it at the expense of other things until you have pushed it back into place. It's what successful senior managers do and hard-pressed working mothers, whatever level they have reached in their profession, do it too or they don't survive long.

## 10

When I returned to work in April 1971 there had been a few changes. Much less attention was being paid to what might have gone on at the universities in the 1930s and '40s. The effort had been redirected onto the re-examination of specific cases and the pursuit of any information which was still unexplored and might produce an undiscovered spy. The Director of Counter-espionage when I arrived back at work was Michael Hanley, a large, gruff, red-faced man, who had a reputation for being abrupt and having a fierce temper. This was perhaps not surprising considering that he had himself fallen prey to the paranoia of the 1960s and '70s and had been investigated as a possible KGB mole because he appeared to fit the description produced by a defector from the Eastern bloc. I was surprised to be called into his office to be to welcomed back to work and to the counter-espionage branch. His kindly interest was unusual in those days when personal contact between directors and junior staff was rare. He moved on very shortly afterwards to become Deputy Director-General and then in 1972, Director-General. It was he who when Director-General finally managed to get Peter Wright away from the counter-espionage field, and ultimately out of the Service altogether.

My section consisted, as usual, of a number of male officers supported by a collection of female assistant officers. I worked in an office with two men who had been friends in the Colonial Service. They fell firmly into the cynical camp and while they were together, not a great deal of useful work was done. They spent a lot of time in the office telling jokes about their colonial experiences, and took extremely long lunch hours. It was routine for them to return from lunch at about four in the afternoon (they had some 'arrangement' with a pub up the road), and then we all settled down to afternoon tea laced with whisky accompanied by peppermints in case the boss called them to a meeting. He rarely did and the days passed quite peacefully, with them occasionally going out to interview someone and me sitting at my desk writing summaries of files and sorting out papers. I used to go home to my baby daughter some evenings rather the worse for wear if the whisky tea had been too well laced. I suppose there was some plan in what we were doing and some strategic direction somewhere, but I certainly did not know what it was – perhaps I was too lowly to be told.

In and out of all this strode the extraordinary figure of Peter Wright. I believe he had at one time been regarded as an effective counter-espionage operator, but by the time I knew him well he was quite clearly a man with an obsession and was regarded by many of the newer arrivals in the Service and even by some of the older hands as quite mad and certainly dangerous. He had briefly been made the Assistant Director of the section I was working in, but according to rumour, he had been so bad at giving any direction or leadership that he had been 'promoted' to be a special adviser to the Director.

Counter-espionage work is not a glamorous business, however it has been presented by the spy-story writers. It is hard work. It is all about painstaking and rigorous analysis, the detailed following up of snippets of information and perseverance in the face of disappointment. A bit of luck helps of course. But it is not the quick jumping to conclusions and the twisting of the facts to meet the theory which Peter Wright went in for in those days. He was in fact by then everything which a counter-espionage officer should not be. He was self-important, he had an over-developed imagination and an obsessive personality which had turned to paranoia. And above all he was lazy. By this time his theories of high-level penetration of MI5, which had resulted in his ruthless pursuit of the former Director-General Roger Hollis, were very largely discredited. But he had established a very comfortable corner for himself.

It is hard to explain why he was allowed to stay for so long. As Special Adviser he had the right to pick up anything he liked and drop it when he tired of it. He used to wander around, finding out what everyone was doing, taking cases off people, going off and doing interviews which he never wrote up, and then moving on to something else, while refusing to release files for others to work on. He always implied that he knew more about everything than anyone else, but that what he knew was so secret that he could not possibly tell you what it was. That gave him the right to disagree with everything anyone else thought without challenge. He spent a lot of his time in those days leaning on the bar in the Great Marlborough Street office talking and talking endlessly to whoever would talk to him. That bar and bars in other office premises became the subject of earnest and long-running debate later after excessive drinking was focused on as a major threat to security. The debate was between those who thought in-house bars were inappropriate and those who thought it was better for staff to be encouraged to meet and socialise securely on office premises, where any extreme behaviour would be noticed, rather than in nearby pubs.

Everything with Peter Wright was expressed in nods and winks, designed to make him seem important and all-knowing. I remember sitting through one or two of the lectures he gave occasionally to the newer staff on the subject of the KGB. He was not a good lecturer – he had a monotonous voice and a lisp. He spoke with great conviction about the KGB, about their cunning, their operational effectiveness and their successes. But though I was quite junior, I found him completely unconvincing. We called him the 'KGB Illegal', because, with his appearance and his lisp we could imagine that he was really a KGB officer himself, living under a false identity, perhaps like Gordon Lonsdale, the 'Canadian businessman' who ran the Portland spy ring in the '60s and was really the KGB officer, Molody. Maybe, we thought, he had been sent into MI5 to confuse everyone. It was all a joke of course, but as things turned out it was strangely prophetic. Though he did not turn out to be a spy, he caused almost as much trouble then and later as if he had been.

I worked in this section for more than three years and after some time I was asked to accompany the officer I was working with when he went out to do interviews. By then we knew a great deal about Cambridge in the 1930s, but we still did not know exactly how the recruitments of the Ring of Five were done – who put who in touch with whom – and we were still trying to satisfy ourselves that there were no more university-recruited spies who had not yet been discovered. It was all a long time ago by then of course. Everyone relevant was getting old and whatever they once knew they had conveniently forgotten and were not prepared to try to remember and there was no sanction we could apply to make them change their mind.

We went to Cambridge one day to interview a don who had tutored Philby and had, we thought, played some part, exactly what is probably still not known, in putting him in touch with the Russians. It was a strange occasion. The old man, sitting in a high-backed chair in a dark old college room, was immensely courteous and gave us tea from china cups, but not surprisingly he had no interest in casting his mind back to the 1930s in order to help us and volunteered nothing. He must have wondered why it had taken us so long to come.

It was during this period that my colleague and I re-interviewed John Cairncross, who wrote about the experience in his autobiography, *The Enigma Spy*. He had been exposed as a spy for the KGB by Anthony Blunt and had been interviewed by, amongst others, Peter Wright, to whom he had made some limited admissions. At the time we re-interviewed him he was working for the Food and Agriculture Organisation in Rome and was allowed entry into this country only if he made himself available for interview by us. We met him in the evenings after his day's work, in some gloomy rooms in the old Ministry of Defence, which were kept specifically for our use. I remember him as a thin, grey, stooping figure, coming in out of a dark night, always wearing a mackintosh. He describes me in his book as 'a personable young lady in trousers'.

Those interviews were part of the push to establish the whole truth of the pre-war KGB university recruitments. Cairncross seemed to take pleasure in trying to turn our conversations into intellectual sparring matches and was quite determined to do everything he could to tell us no more than he had already admitted, which was nothing like the full story. In his book, which he wrote just before he died, he admits only to that much. But we had good reason at that time to believe that his espionage involvement was greater than he had admitted, and since then Oleg Gordievsky, the defector from the KGB, has stated that Cairncross was indeed the Fifth Man and was in contact with his KGB controllers for many years.

While I was working on counter-espionage, things were beginning to change inside the Service. The supply of ex-Colonial Service officers was drying up and new sources of recruits had to be found. In those days, recruitment to MI5 was still broadly by a tap on the shoulder from a friend or contact, the method by which I had been recruited. There were a number of contacts in various places with their ears to the ground, actively looking for the 'right sort' of men to come in as officers. Men with previous work experience in some walk of life were much preferred; they were thought to be more mature and therefore likely to make better intelligence officers.

In the mid-1970s, it was decided actively to seek out men in industry and commerce who, after working there for a few years, might be looking for a change and, as an experiment, also to try bringing in some young men straight from university as officers. I had already started to feel disgruntled about my second-class status. By then, I knew enough about the Service and the people in it to know that I was just as capable as many of the men, if not more, and I resented being given less responsible work to do and above all being paid less than they were. I couldn't stand working for people who were less competent than I was.

The last straw for me came one day when a nice young man arrived in my section to share my office. He had just come down from university, with a BA in something or another and he was about twenty-three. He had been recruited as an officer. There was I, having been in the Service already for three or four years, having previously had a career in another profession, aged thirty-seven or thirty-eight and still only an assistant officer. I thought carefully about what I should do. I knew that open protest was not likely to be successful. If one got a reputation as a revolutionary, one would be regarded as suspect and written off. So I waited until it was the time for my annual interview with my personnel officer and I took the opportunity to ask what was the reason that prevented me from being an officer.

The poor man was completely taken aback. I felt rather like Oliver Twist when he asked for more. The personnel officer was an ex-Army officer with a moustache and a pipe clamped firmly between his lips, given to wearing very hairy tweed suits and khaki braces. I do not think it had ever occurred to him that a woman might want to become an officer in MI5. He certainly had no idea that I was nurturing a grievance. After all, no doubt the women he knew stayed at home and did the flowers, so why was this woman, who had already broken all known conventions by returning to work with a baby, now demanding to be treated as if she were a man? He muttered about all the things one could not do as a woman, which made one less than wholly useful.

Indeed in those days there was a long list of taboos. As I have mentioned before, it was taken for granted that women could not work in agent-running sections, recruiting and running human sources of information. The theory was, and of course it had never been tested, that no KGB officer or foreign intelligence officer of any kind would take direction from a woman. Moreover, the theory went, you certainly could not put a woman to make direct contact with someone from an Arab country, because the cultural differences were too extreme for that to work. Nor was the Irish terrorist target suitable work for a woman. Again the cultural differences were too great, and in any case it was dangerous, and dangerous work was not for women. It was even said that women could not work in sections where they would have to deal a lot with the police, as policemen would not take women seriously as colleagues.

All this sounds quite bizarre from the standpoint of the present day. We take it for granted nowadays that women are often particularly good at so-called inter-personal skills, which is what agent-running and sharp-end intelligence work is all about. Presumably that's why there are so many women in personnel and human relations departments in the commercial world. But in those days these *ex cathedra* statements had never been questioned and there was no experience to show whether they were right or wrong. It was too much to expect my colleague of the tweed suit and khaki braces to have the imagination to look at things differently and take a risk.

But word of my remarkable demands filtered out, and there were other men around who were sufficiently open-minded to think that perhaps I had the qualities that made a good intelligence officer, in spite of my sex, and that if I got too fed up, I would probably leave. So, in 1973, I was at last promoted to be an officer and my salary took a healthy lurch upwards, enabling us to do some of the work on the house, which was by then badly needed.

What was it that I had and they had seen that made me a success in this rather unusual career? I have heard it said that women make particularly good intelligence officers, both spies and counter-spies. Some say that it is because they have orderly minds, some say that it is because they are discreet, some say it is because they are psychologically tough, and better than men at keeping their own counsel. I think all that is pretty much nonsense. In an intelligence organisation, just as in any other organisation, you need people of varied qualities and talents, and you find them among both men and women. It is vital to have balance and common sense and an ability to relate what you are doing to ordinary life.

Intelligence work inevitably takes up much of your time and affects your private life, but it is important to have something to go home to, so you can keep it in proportion. Again, in so far as women are very frequently managing work and family in a more intense way than men, they may be better able to keep that balance. Patience and persistence are also virtues in an intelligence officer, which are frequently seen as more feminine than masculine attributes. But this cannot be carried too far. The so-called 'masculine' qualities of dynamism and self-confidence are equally important. And a sense of humour is essential, and that is found in both sexes.

So what had I got? I don't think my mind is particularly orderly. I certainly don't think in a very orderly way. If I am faced with a problem, I either immediately know what my answer is, or I pick at it, rushing towards it and then retreating, constantly reviewing the information I have, until I've sorted it out to my satisfaction. I do dislike unsolved puzzles and ambiguities of all kinds, including in personal situations. Where others might let things alone, I can't resist trying to sort them out, and that is why I tend often to seek to change the status quo. And I am a very practical person. I don't like sitting around theorising. Above all, I like to get on with things, to get things done. So sorting out muddles and getting facts or information in order is what I really enjoy. Maybe that is what drew me to the archives profession in the first place. I used to love being faced with an old muniment room or an attic full of papers and parchments and finding out what was there and sorting it all out. It was exciting: you never knew what treasure you were going to find. But I also enjoy finding out what makes people tick. I have rather a cool, detached and analytical approach to people, which is helpful in the sort of relationships you have to develop in intelligence work. Also, of course, I have had the children to go home to and to help me keep my feet firmly on the ground.

How much of all that was apparent to my colleagues when they first recognised that I might make a decent MI5 officer, I don't know. Not much, I would guess. They probably saw a determined female, with an unusual amount of energy and the ability to get things done, whom it was quite difficult to ignore.

That promotion was actually no great shakes. After all, 'officer' equated to Principal in the Civil Service, a rank fast-stream civil servants expected in those days to reach when they were about twenty-eight. But in terms of *my* career, it was much more significant than it sounds. What it meant was that I had crossed the barrier between being a permanent 'assistant' and being someone whose career was taken seriously. My promotion did not mark the opening of the flood gates; it was not followed immediately by a great surge upwards of female graduates. It took a revolution, albeit a discreetly conducted revolution to achieve that. Not long after I had been promoted, some of the other women graduate assistant officers sent a round robin to the Director of Personnel, complaining about the discriminatory policy that MI5 was operating. Sex discrimination was just getting onto the political agenda, and someone's father was a lawyer, who had advised them that they might have a case against the Service. I can't imagine that in those days anyone would have thought seriously of taking legal action, but things got quite heated. The men in charge were genuinely surprised at the strength of feeling and sufficiently concerned that so many of their good female staff, essential to the running of the Service, appeared to be disgruntled, that the policy was changed. A number of female assistant officers were promoted and other women began to be recruited directly as officers, just as the men were. As usual in crises, some not very sensible decisions were taken, and some of those who were promoted and recruited were probably not up to the job, but neither were some of the men. It took much longer for the taboos on what the women could do to be removed.

My promotion meant that I was allowed out to do interviews on my own and one of those I interviewed at that period was a rather grand old lady, who had been the Head of Personnel in a large company, but was by then retired. She had been a friend of the Philby family and had known since the beginning the important fact, which Kim Philby had successfully disguised, that he had been a communist since the early 1930s. In the 1960s, she had revealed for the first time that he had made what she had interpreted as an attempt to recruit her as a Soviet agent. Peter Wright had interviewed her about all this several years earlier, but it was quite clear that she knew a great deal more about Philby and his activities than she had ever revealed, and we thought it possible that she even knew how he had been recruited as a Soviet agent in the first place; that was something we desperately wanted to know. I called on her in her flat in Mayfair, in 1974. Though she must have been in her late sixties by then, she was a formidable figure. I was pregnant by then with my second daughter, and she, used to controlling the personnel of a large company, thought she could have people like me on toast. Unfortunately, in this case she could, as I could offer no inducement to persuade her to talk and, very wisely, whatever she knew, she kept her own counsel.

It was also in 1974 that I went to Paris to interview someone who was living in France, whom, again, we thought might have some useful knowledge of that period. Or at least I thought I had gone to interview someone. Our French opposite numbers, a largely police service, were, at the time, very considerably behind us in the equality stakes. Finding that I was obviously pregnant, they insisted that I sit behind a screen, so I could not be seen by the person being interviewed, presumably in case he should be embarrassed by my condition. So there I was in their offices, which in those days were like a 19th-century French hotel, something out of a Maigret novel, all dusty bare wooden floors, tall double doors and shutters at the windows, a disembodied voice behind a screen. History does not relate what the poor man being interviewed thought, but as far as I remember he did not tell us anything interesting, not surprisingly in the circumstances.

Why did we rake over this period for so long? It has to be seen in the context of the Cold War, which was still at its height. There was a strong feeling that not enough was known about the KGB's activities against this country in the '30s and '40s and a real dread that there might be other highly placed spies, still operating, who had not yet come to attention. It was felt to be important to do all that could reasonably be done to flush out any there were. The best and most successful spies are the quiet, apparently boring and dull people who go on doing the same thing in an unostentatious way year after year, and the best counter-espionage officers are those who match them for perseverance. Ultimately of course it took defectors and, finally, the end of the Cold War to get anything like a full account of what had been going on. But when we did get that, it was clear that MI5's counter-espionage work had been well focused and there were few British names that emerged that had not already crossed our sights and been investigated and negated.

The criticism that can be levied at that period was that thoroughness tended to generate a certain dilatoriness, a lack of prioritisation and of the urgency and direction that I would expect nowadays. The Soviet Union had achieved a very considerable intelligence coup in recruiting some of the brightest of our undergraduates between the wars. Their recruits did great damage to the West before they fell under suspicion and the consequent investigations and the leads they generated tied up a good deal of the resources of British and US counter-espionage for many years.

## 11

Changes for women were not the only changes taking place in MI5 in the 1970s. The new requirement to tackle terrorism, which started early in the decade, was beginning to bring about what were to be profound changes in culture and methods of working. But I did not realise any of this until later, because by the middle of 1974, John had been offered another posting abroad. This time he was to go to be Counsellor (Social and Regional Affairs) in the UK Representation to the EEC in Brussels, as part of the British team which was to 'renegotiate' the Treaty of Rome. My second baby was due in November, and I decided to stay on in London when he left for Brussels in July and continue working until October and then go out to join him.

With my new officer status secured, and a rather firmer grip on the career ladder, I was not anxious to leave and throw away what I had worked hard to achieve. Having got the bit between my teeth by then, I hoped that the Service might be prepared to offer me some work while we were in Brussels so that I could continue my career. Several possibilities occurred to me. There were security adviser posts in the EEC and in NATO, which were often filled by MI5 officers, or maybe I could be seconded to work for another department in Brussels for the duration. I went off to see my personnel officer, this time a somewhat more open-minded man than before, to put these ideas to him. But even he was amazed that I should be thinking of such a thing. He told me firmly that those security posts were for experienced officers (I took him to mean men) and I would not be regarded as suitable. As for secondment to another department, he did not think that was a sensible idea.

I went away, firmly put in my place. Yet again I was asking for too much, and the imagination of those in charge could not or would not stretch to include what I wanted. I was told that I could have up to two years special leave to accompany John on his posting abroad. My pension would be frozen and I could pick up where I left off when, and if, I returned. I really do not think they expected to see me again.

Though I was anxious not to lose my position on the career ladder, I was not sorry to be leaving London. The previous winter had been particularly grim. We were having modernisation work done on the house, including an improved central heating system and a much needed damp course, which meant that we had had to evacuate the kitchen and live in the bedrooms, cooking on a camping stove. All this was made worse by the fact that the lights kept going out at irregular times, as Mr Heath slugged it out with the unions and the country struggled with the three-day week. At the office we were all issued with candles, which we stuck in our in-trays, and with a printed warning not to use the lifts.

Of course, as I now know, the industrial disruption in 1973 and 1974 meant far more than candles in the in-tray to some of my colleagues working in a different part of the Service, though the operation of the 'need-to-know' rule meant that, at the time, the rest of us knew nothing of what they were doing. The Communist Party of Great Britain then, as later when I was involved at the time of the second great miners' strike, had a large so-called 'industrial department', which was focused on achieving influence at executive level in the key unions, with the objective of controlling their policies. My colleagues then, as I later, had the difficult task of deciding what aspects of the industrial unrest were properly their concern and should be investigated, assessed and reported to ministers and what were not. Making these distinctions is not straightforward and lays open to suspicion and criticism those who are responsible for deciding them.

I left London behind with no regrets. By that time the IRA had launched a bombing campaign on the mainland which had come close to home with bombs in high-profile locations including Oxford Street and it was difficult to avoid a feeling that civilised life was coming to an end. The renegotiation in Brussels, in which John was involved, was by that time in full swing and the referendum on Britain's membership of the EEC was due the following June. A 'No' vote would probably have meant that we would have returned straight home. As it was, we stayed in Brussels, thankfully somewhat insulated from strikes, bombs and the inflation which began to rage its way upwards in Britain.

Sophie and I left London to live in Brussels at the beginning of November 1974, accompanied by the eighteen-year-old daughter of a colleague of mine in the Service, who was to be our *au pair*. I remember the journey well. I was eight-and-a-half months pregnant, driving a desperately overloaded Sunbeam Rapier car. We were travelling on the Dover to Zeebrugge ferry. As we were waiting on the dockside to board the ferry, all of a sudden smoke and a strong smell of burning filled the car. We grabbed Sophie out of the back, where she was sitting on a pile of luggage and I yelled to a policeman that we were on fire. I thought the car was about to blow up at any minute, and he greatly annoyed me by pausing to call into his radio, 'Car on fire on Dock No. 2,' before coming over to help us.

When he arrived he discovered that I had rested our lunch basket on top of the cigar lighter, which in those cars was between the two front passenger seats. Being held down it had overheated and started to melt the surrounding plastic. With a comforting calm and what seemed to me great presence of mind, he pulled it out with his gloved hands and threw it in a convenient puddle, and the fire subsided. By this time a crowd had gathered; it was a dramatic departure from the UK.

I went backwards and forwards with the children on that ferry many times during those two years in Brussels and something always seemed to go wrong. On one occasion another car I was driving, a Rover we had bought new to take out with us, refused to start when the ferry arrived in Belgium. We had to be ignominiously pushed off the boat and I found myself in Zeebrugge docks at 10 o'clock at night with a useless car, a small child and a baby, with no milk for the baby, all the shops shut and very little money. I had never liked that car ever since the gear lever came off in my hand one day when I was driving home with four children from a visit to Antwerp Zoo.

I had intended merely to spend long enough in Brussels to get established in the house and then to return to London to have the baby at University College Hospital where Sophie had been born. That is not how it worked out. We had been there about ten days when our heavy baggage arrived by road. With typical impatience, I decided to unpack it all by myself, having given the *au pair* a couple of days off to visit a relative in Holland. After a day spent leaning into tea chests and lifting things out and unwrapping them, by the early evening it was becoming apparent that all was not as it should be with the baby. I had no idea where John was. Having only just arrived in the country, and not expecting to need the services of a hospital, I did not know where it was, or even how to get hold of a doctor. I had not met any of the other wives in UKREP and was really quite isolated. It got to about 4 a.m. I was having regular contractions and just beginning to panic and tell myself that I must get up and do something about the situation, when John arrived home.

He had been at a meeting of COREPER, the Committee of Permanent Representatives to the European Community, which had been preparing for the first ever European Summit, the meeting of European Prime Ministers to take place in Paris. After the meeting was over, and like all such meetings in those days it had gone on well into the night, John had gone off with Ewen Fergusson, at the time the Head of Chancery at UKREP, to prepare a telegram to the Foreign Office, reporting the conclusions of the meeting. But they had been unable to get it done because Ewen's secretary, who was to type it up, had lost her cat, and was in tears and inconsolable. She had to be cajoled to come in to the office to take dictation, and that took a long time.

That cat, a nasty brute called Milly, eventually came to us when its owner went home. She was a cat of advanced murderous tendencies, and used to spend the night killing small furry animals whose corpses she laid out by the front door for our inspection in the morning. Worse, she discovered that on the undeveloped land next to our garden there were baby rabbits and moles and she took to bringing them in alive during dinner parties and biting off their heads under the dining-room table.

Having arrived home at last, John was able to get hold of a doctor, and at 7 a.m. we drove through a cold, grey, wet November morning to the Edith Cavell Institute, with Sophie who had been dragged out of her bed to go with us. There Harriet was born, three weeks early. The nuns, who were the nurses at the Institute, thought I was a most feckless mother. I had no clothes for the baby. When Sophie was born in hospital in Britain, it was customary for new babies to wear hospital clothes until they left to go home. In Belgium, as I learned, you go into hospital with a full layette of baby clothes. John had to go out as soon as the shops opened and buy a hideously expensive wardrobe of exquisite baby clothes from a fashionable Brussels store next to the hospital.

Even when the baby had some clothes, the nuns went on disapproving of me. As soon as it became known among the UKREP wives that a new wife had appeared on the scene and not only had she slipped through their well oiled welcoming net, but she had had a baby as well, I was inundated with visitors. There was a Foreign Office wives' system in operation, which was supposed to pick up each new arrival and welcome her into the bosom of the family. I think it had missed me, probably because I had already been over to Brussels earlier in the summer, while I was still working, for a holiday and to sussout the living arrangements. On that occasion I had been amazed to receive a telephone call from an aggressively cheerful lady who said, 'Hello, Stella. I am your welcoming wife,' and offered to take me shopping. I was rather taken aback, as I saw myself as a career woman on her summer holidays not someone in need of welcoming, and I was rather dismissive. However, pinned down in my hospital bed, I was much more vulnerable to this approach, which of course was kindly meant. But I felt very exposed as more and more people, none of whom I knew, poked their heads round the door of my room and came in clutching presents, usually something for the baby and a bottle of champagne for me. After a bit, I began to enter into the spirit of things and my room became like a party. The nuns did not think it at all proper that a new mother should be entertaining so freely from her hospital bed and knocking back champagne with quite such gay abandon and they warned me solemnly about the likely effect on my blood pressure. I was glad to escape from their clutches, and I am sure they were relieved to see me go. I got home quite exhausted by the relentless socialising.

I enjoyed having the opportunity to be at home with both my daughters for a time, but that was the only thing I did enjoy about Brussels. Once again I had that sense of loss of identity and exclusion from everything that is interesting that you get, or used to get, as a diplomatic wife in a foreign posting. Those mid-1970s years were the beginning of the end for the Foreign Office's traditional attitude to its wives. The custom had been that Her Majesty's Government paid for one employee, but acquired the services of two. The wives of diplomats were expected to devote their energies to furthering the interests of the Post and it was made clear that their success or otherwise in doing this would influence the course of their husband's future career. In return, they had a bigger house to live in and an overall standard of living that was more splendid than they had at home, which might or might not have been what they wanted. They also had, in some places, some difficult living conditions to cope with for themselves and their children.

Things had changed a little from when I had last been a diplomatic wife in India in the late 1960s. By the mid-70s wives were allowed to work in the country in which they were posted, provided the Head of Mission and the country concerned did not object. But it was not common, and wives were still expected to spend a lot of their time on entertaining and charity and other good works. There was a lot of entertaining to be done in Brussels in the mid-70s. Because it was so near London, ministers, politicians of all shapes and sizes, businessmen, trades unionists and civil servants streamed in, and it seemed to be expected that some sort of hospitality would be laid on for them all. Employing a cook for all these occasions was too expensive, and most of us did quite a lot of the cooking ourselves.

Looking back, I seem to have been forever standing in my kitchen, listening to the planes coming very low over the house to land at Zaventem airport, curling brandy snaps round the handle of a wooden spoon. I was not the only wife who felt she was being used as an unpaid cook and a lot of muttering went on, though alongside it went a lot of competition and the standard of cuisine to be found at most British diplomatic tables was excellent. It did all rather come to a head though, before the start of the British Presidency in the first half of 1977. Months earlier we wives had all been called together by Lady Maitland, the wife of the Permanent Representative to the EEC, our boss, and told that it was expected that during the Presidency we would feed our guests traditional British dishes. For those who did not know what these were, a recipe list was available.

Most of us had by then become rather expert at continental European cookery, using some of the wonderful ingredients available at supermarkets like Rob in Brussels, and we did not much relish having to revert to roast beef and Yorkshire pudding. I recruited my mother, who happened to be staying with us, to cook apple pie for one particular dinner party during that period. I had never learned how to make pastry as well as she could.

For me being in Brussels was a disorientating sensation. I had by then come to regard myself as a career woman, and here I was, definitely classified as 'a wife', though I had graduated from a First Secretary wife (as in Delhi) to a Counsellor wife. I suppose it is rather ironic that though I spent nearly two years at the heart of the European Community during a very important period for Britain, my most abiding memory is how to make brandy snaps. Living in Brussels was nothing like as exciting as Delhi had been. It was not like living in the capital city of any other country; I, at least, had no real sense of what country I was in. For one thing, I hardly ever met a Belgian to talk to socially. All the people who came to our house were either British or other Europeans, very rarely Belgians. The only exception to this was when, very briefly, Sophie went to a Flemish primary school in the commune.

We lived in Wezembeek, at the time a small Flemish village built around a church, with a few modern houses on its outskirts, one of which was our home. There was a fashionable theory going around among the wives that it was good for small children to go to non-English-language schools; they would quickly pick up the language concerned, the theory went, and become deeply cosmopolitan, and that would be a good thing in later life. That is certainly not how it worked for Sophie. At just about four, she was already a nervous child – 'genetic,' I would say; 'early upbringing,' my mother would counter – but whatever the reason, she was. Coming to Brussels was exciting for her, and having me around at home was great and she loved it when the new baby arrived. Then she was put into a school where she could not understand a word anyone said to her. It was not a good experience. She did indeed learn a collection of Flemish words, and sang along with the best in a performance of some, to me, totally incomprehensible song at the school parents' day. She was adept at interpreting 'Vicky the Viking' on Flemish TV in the evenings, but she hated that school and as it was her first school, I think it coloured her attitude to institutions for the rest of her life – and she very soon forgot the Flemish.

I look back on my time in Brussels with no pleasure at all,

in fact I have tried for the most part to block it out from my memory altogether. John and I had drifted far apart by then, so I was glad when it came time for me to return to London and take up my career again. He stayed on in Brussels to finish his posting.

## 12

My first task on returning to London in July 1976 was to find a nanny. I was determined that, with two children and me on my own, we would have someone living in with us. So I acquired a copy of *The Lady*, the magazine I have always turned to in times of domestic crisis (though never at any other time), put in an advertisement and waited to see what turned up. Choosing domestic help has always seemed to me much more difficult than any other personnel decision. My first choice seemed a delightful young woman. She had all the right references; her previous employer spoke very highly of her, though perhaps I should have taken more notice of the fact that she had employed her to look after horses not children. She came and worked, apparently satisfactorily, for three or four days and then suddenly disappeared with no explanation. When I found a half-smoked joint rolled up in some towels put out for the washing, I was rather glad she had gone, though as by then I had gone back to work, it was extremely awkward to be left stranded. I was even more glad when I went round to the address she had given me to try to get the door key back, and found it was a squat in Dalston, where a very shifty-looking man with dreadlocks, peering at me through a crack in the door, denied all knowledge of her. We never saw her or the door key again.

We had more luck the second time and Jane stayed with us until Harriet went to school. But she was only the first of a long succession of nannies and *au pair*s whose lives became intertwined with ours over the next few years.

Dealing with nannies I first met the phenomenon, which I later encountered at work when I began to be in charge of groups of people, of the way people remorselessly unburden their anxieties onto the one in charge as soon as they get the chance. As the one in charge, it is your responsibility to be always positive, cheerful and supportive. As soon as I opened the door in the evening, the *au pair*s in particular would tell me all the disasters that had happened during the day. My only defence was to develop the habit, which I kept until I retired, of ringing up home before I left work, so that I had a chance to get used to whatever had happened and I knew that when I arrived at the front door there would be no nasty surprises. I might even have thought of a solution to the problem, but at least I could ensure the kettle was on or the gin and tonic poured out, so that things would start to look better. On the other hand, I rarely ring home when I am abroad. Male colleagues are always telephoning home and reporting on what the weather is doing, or how their football team is faring. I never want to know what's going on, because I know I can't do anything about it, and if there is a major disaster I know someone will tell me about it before long.

One evening, when I made my telephone call before leaving work, I was told that a swarm of bees had invaded the house and what were they to do? I had no answer to that one except to advise them to go to my sister-in-law who lived round the corner. I did consult a colleague at work who knew about bees and I tried ringing around various Bee numbers that I found in the Yellow Pages before I left work, but I could not arouse anyone's interest. When I arrived, there were indeed bees everywhere, crawling up the insides of the windows, walking down the stairs, all over the beds. I hoovered them all up in the vacuum cleaner, which was probably quite the wrong thing to do, but it did eventually solve the problem.

On another occasion the house was burgled while the children were being collected from school. They had all arrived home to find they couldn't open the door, because the burglars had climbed in and out of an upstairs window at the back and had put the bolts on the front door so they would not be disturbed at their burgling. I got back to find a confused huddle of assorted adults and children at the front door, unable to understand why they couldn't get in.

We were frequently burgled during that period. It was one of the prices you paid for living in Islington, and our locks and bolts got ever more complicated. Once, after the days of nannies and *au pairs*, when Sophie was just old enough to look after herself and Harriet during the holidays, the telephone rang on my desk at work. It was Sophie who whispered, 'Mum. I think there's a burglar in the house.' She had been sitting in her bedroom on the top floor painting a picture, having left the door into the garden open, when she had looked up and seen a large young man in the doorway clutching my jewellery box (not much left in it to steal by then). Thankfully, when he saw her he rushed off down the stairs, muttering, 'Sorry, wrong house,' but they were afraid he was still there. In those days I was not well known and had no special security and those were the sort of telephone calls that put some strain on the working mother's principle of compartmentalisation. I rang up the police from the office and by the time I had rushed home the excitement was all over.

Exactly the same sort of unburdening that the nannies and *au pairs* practised used to happen at work, for example when I got back after being away on leave. On my first day back, each of the section heads would come in to tell me what had been going on and as the morning wore on, I felt that I had sunk further and further down in my chair as one after the other unburdened their problems and worries onto me, and they would go out looking taller than when they came in.

When I went back to work, in the summer of 1976, after being away for nearly two years, things seemed to be changing. More young people had been recruited, there were more women officers and the place seemed to have a livelier feel to it. By this stage I was committed to working. It looked as though I was likely to be dependent on myself alone in my old age, as John's pension situation was no nearer resolution, so I thought that I'd better knuckle down and get myself as good a career as I could manage. It did now seem possible that there might be a decent career for me in MI5, the way things were going.

On my return I was put into a section which was working to counter the activities of the Soviet intelligence officers and their Warsaw Pact allies in the UK – the 'residencies', as the groups of intelligence officers living here in various guises were called. As an officer, I was in charge of a small team of people responsible for a group of East European residencies. Another team across the corridor dealt with the rest of the East Europeans and in a long room round the corner a much larger team was looking at the Soviet residencies. My team was a mixed bunch, all women, one was the daughter of a diplomat, one had a degree in astronomy and one had left school at sixteen and had worked her way up after joining as a clerk. We worked in yet another run-down building, now demolished, at the corner of Warren Street and Euston Road. In its day it had been at the cutting edge of design, we were told, in that the heating came from pipes in the ceilings. Perhaps because hot air rises, the heating never seemed to work. I spent the winter of 1976–7 and the following one, working there wrapped in a blanket and clutching a hot water bottle to keep warm.

In the 1960s, the Soviet Union and their East European allies had been allowed to build up their diplomatic and commercial representation in London practically unchecked. Among all those people had been a large number of officers of their civilian and military intelligence services, present in Britain for the sole purpose of spying on us and our allies and spreading propaganda and disruption. In April 1971, the government, acting on advice from MI5 and the Foreign Office, had expelled from the country 105 Soviet intelligence officers in what was known as Operation Foot, which effectively damaged the Soviet intelligence operation in this country for some time. In the five years or so since Operation Foot, Soviet intelligence officers had begun to creep back into some of their old positions in the embassy and the trade delegation, and into some new ones in other Soviet organisations too. The Warsaw

Pact countries' intelligence services were also well represented in London under various covers.

The year 1976 was the height of the Cold War and a very serious effort was being made by the Soviet bloc to acquire information of all kinds to advantage them against the West. There were some 12,000 KGB officers in the First Chief Directorate, the foreign intelligence-gathering part of the KGB, when Gorbachev became General Secretary of the Communist Party of the Soviet Union, and very many of them were posted abroad. In the UK they were looking to acquire information of all kinds, military, economic, political, scientific and technical. They targeted not only people who were ideologically committed to communism, for there were less of those than there had been since the Hungarian revolution; they were also on the look-out for people who were disaffected for various reasons or who were just plain venal. This massive intelligence assault on the West had its successes, not surprisingly. It has been estimated, for example, that about 150 Soviet weapons systems depended on technology stolen from the West. The Soviet and East European intelligence officers were also trying to subvert Western democracies by funding and directing national communist parties to try to gain influence in legitimate protest groups like the unions or CND, in the hope that those parties would thus achieve influence beyond anything they could get legitimately through the ballot box.

To support us in our job of trying to deal with the residencies, we had the backing of a number of policies which the government had put in place. The first was the 'exclusions' policy which meant that any visa applicant who was firmly identified as an intelligence officer would be refused a visa. Not surprisingly, our colleagues in the Foreign Office scrutinised our identifications very closely indeed, as a visa refusal by us nearly always met with a tit-for-tat response from the other side. In gloomy moments I, as a desk officer, sometimes wondered who the true enemy was, the Foreign Office or the Soviet Union.

Many hostile intelligence officers were negated in this way before they ever arrived, but, of course we did not manage to identify, still less to exclude, them all and when each new official arrived in the country, our job was to study them to establish whether they were genuinely what they claimed to be or intelligence officers under cover. We watched the Soviet and East European embassies very closely indeed; we interviewed as many of their contacts as we could to find out what was going on; we ran double agents against them; we fed them false information ('chicken feed'), and we tried, with various ruses, to recruit them to the Western side.

If this all sounds rather like a John le Carré novel, it's not surprising. In many ways his account of those days is fairly accurate. Foreign intelligence officers *were* leaving packets of money in hollow trees on Hampstead Heath or, more frequently, in the Home Counties, for their agents, in exchange for secret documents left behind loose bricks in walls; they *were* communicating with them by making chalk marks on lamp posts or by leaving empty drinks cans on the top of walls, just as he describes. But though that period has been much fictionalised, it would be totally wrong to write it off, as some people do, as spies playing games. When our defences failed, the consequences for the West were serious. The loss of American submarine technology to the Soviet Union through the activities of the Walker family in America cost millions of dollars. The activities of Philby in an earlier age and Aldrich Ames, the CIA officer, more recently, cost lives as well as information.

But serious though all this was, it did have its lighter side. It was well known that the Moscow spy masters took information much more seriously if it was stamped 'secret', so we found ways to feed them false 'secret' documents which we hoped would mislead them. We watched as some of the intelligence officers, the military ones in particular, spent much of their time in libraries, copying out reams of publicly available information from technical and scientific journals. We speculated that they sent it back to Moscow stamped

'Secret', no doubt claiming that it had been obtained at great risk and expense from a delicately placed source.

Though some of these intelligence officers were engaged on serious and damaging espionage, the tasks which others appeared to have been given seemed a strange use of all the covert skills which were put into them, though to their own countries no doubt their tasks were very important. There was one East European intelligence officer, for example, whose main aim appeared to be to acquire the technology for fast-chilled foods. He went to a lot of trouble to get alongside people who worked in the right sort of companies and was prepared to pay considerable sums for the information. Inevitably he came to be known as the chicken tikka spy. But although those activities were clearly not threatening to national security, they were a potentially serious threat to the companies concerned. That, and the fact that our chicken tikka spy might well be doing other things we did not know about, and even if he wasn't then, if left to himself he might, was enough for us to want him out of the country and he was duly asked to leave.

Our counter-espionage efforts in the UK over that period were effective, though by no means every attack on our national security was detected and prevented. We heard from various sources that though London remained a very popular posting for hostile intelligence officers, because of the sheer pleasure of living there, the UK was known as a most difficult place in which to do their business. When Oleg Gordievsky defected from the Soviet intelligence residency in London, we learned that our identifications of the intelligence personnel in the UK had been consistently accurate over the years and our operations therefore well directed.

More difficult was the task of detecting the attack on our security from hostile intelligence officers in other countries. The challenge was to ensure that the UK did not present a soft target in countries where there were large British communities and a comparatively weak security regime. A number of successful recruitment attempts and some offers of assistance were made abroad and Berlin, in particular, with its large Western civilian and military presence cheek by jowl with an even larger Soviet presence, was a constant cause of concern. Geoffrey Prime, the GCHQ employee, volunteered to the KGB when he was serving in the RAF in Berlin and was encouraged to join GCHQ from which, undetected, he supplied secret information to his controllers, left in dead letter boxes in southern England.

Running in parallel with my section, where we were identifying and disrupting, was the agent-running section, whose responsibility it was to try to *recruit* the foreign intelligence officers in the UK, or those with close access to them, to work for us as long term 'agents'. This was the sharp-end activity, and of course, in the spirit of the times, it was still entirely staffed by men, except for the support workers. The section was jointly staffed by MI5 and MI6 officers and was a valuable place for the two cultures to meet and learn to understand each other. It was of great value to a young MI6 officer to learn how a sophisticated security service worked so that he would understand what he was up against when he went out undercover to his foreign postings. For the MI5 officers, there was much to be learned from their MI6 colleagues about the techniques of agent-running and the behaviour of intelligence officers under cover. Much imagination was expended in thinking of ways to get alongside the targets, who were mostly fairly well protected inside their embassies. Many a bizarre scheme was dreamed up to strike up an acquaintance with them. Nothing you read in a spy story is more unlikely than some of the things that went on in those days. If ever I see a jogger in the park apparently spraining his ankle or a dog suddenly keel over and look sick, I look carefully at the scene to see if I can make out a likely target there and detect at work the successors of those agent-running officers of the 1970s.

Much of this fevered activity was unsuccessful because the other side very frequently saw us coming, but now and again there were successes, and a defector or an agent in place in the KGB residency was invaluable.

It is a mistake to ridicule all this activity, as some have done now the Cold War is over. The intelligence services of the Soviet bloc presented a serious threat to our national security at a time when the world was divided into two armed camps. If we had gone to war, the advantage would have lain with the side with the best intelligence. I for one felt that I was helping to preserve democracy against the forces of totalitarianism.

# 13

John returned from Brussels in November 1977. By then I had managed largely on my own for more than a year and it was questionable whether it was worth trying to keep our marriage alive. Rightly or wrongly we decided to try and in early summer 1978 we sold our house in Canonbury Grove and bought a much larger, half-modernised Victorian villa in Alwyne Place in Canonbury, already by then a rather fashionable part of Islington. On the fanlight over the front door the name 'Spion Kop' was painted, in authentic-looking Victorian script. However it wasn't in the least authentic. It had been put there by the previous owner, Kenneth Griffith, the actor and television producer, from whose wife we bought the house. Kenneth Griffith had produced an anti-establishment television series on the South African war at the time he was living in the house. Spion Kop was the name of a hill in KwaZulu/Natal on which hundreds of British lives had been lost at a battle on 24 January 1900. Later the name was adopted for the home end of the Liverpool football ground, the Kop, frequented at that time by those who lived to tell the tale. We resented living behind its name and always intended to paint it out, or change it for something else, but it was one of the many things we never got round to doing. In some ways I suppose 'spy hill' was a rather suitable name for the house I lived in.

We were able to afford the house only because a controlled tenant lived in the basement, so the market value of the house was less than it would have been with full vacant possession. Our tenant was an old lady, who paid us £1 a week for her flat, including central heating. Quite frankly, in buying the house we had gambled that she would not last long and that proved to be the case. After a year or so she moved to a home for the elderly and we were able to let her flat at a market rent, which together with my increased salary made our finances look a lot healthier.

The Alwyne Place house was full of character and space and light and it was a pity that we were not all able to be happier there. Its ground floor rooms were high ceilinged, the fireplaces were intact and the tall windows still had their shutters. All the wood, including the front door had been stripped and those floors which were not stripped floorboards were covered with cork tiles – it was all very Islington 1970s. The ceilings had their original high-Victorian cornices and one of the first things we did was to steam all the accumulated paint of years out of them so that the design was visible again – a terrible, long-winded job, which we undertook ourselves. I marvel, looking back, at the things I casually took on in those days. I remember that I was always exhausted, and after one Christmas, while we were trying to do some ambitious DIY job, I fell over a railing onto our ice-covered basement steps while trying to hurl our large Christmas tree into the garden and almost killed myself. It was the sort of accident you only have when you are too exhausted to behave sensibly.

I was rushed off to Hoxton Hospital, now long since closed in one or another NHS rationalisation, with a fractured skull and a huge bruise, which quickly turned into a haematoma, on my thigh. I was still attached to a bottle draining off the fluid from the haematoma three weeks later when I went to Washington for talks with the CIA and the FBI about East European espionage. My doctor was not at all keen for me to go, but my main concern was what to wear that would conceal the bottle without making it look as if I were pregnant. I thought the Americans would be more enlightened than the French about these things, but I did not want to repeat my experience with French colleagues in Paris when I had to be hidden behind a screen because I really was pregnant.

By the time we had got the house into reasonable order, I

began to think seriously about trying to move on in my career. Until then I had regarded my life and career as an adjunct to John's; I had assumed that where I got to in life would be dependent on his success. And so the various roles I had played, the diplomatic wife, the reluctant working mother, had followed the course of his career but I had not found them at all satisfactory or fulfilling. By this time I had grown out of my early insecurity; I felt much more self confident and I wanted to explore what I could achieve for myself.

At this stage it did not occur to me to look for another job. I was focused on trying to break through the glass ceiling of the job I had and that involved persuading the men in charge to let me try my hand at agent-running, despite the fact that no woman in MI5 had ever done that work. The first response I got from my bosses was a delaying tactic. They sent me on the newly created agent-running course. This was designed to teach some of the skills thought necessary for recruiting and running the human sources of information, but being new it was rather experimental. As it turned out, I found it most uncomfortable, and it almost put me off wanting to do that sort of work for good. Perhaps that was their aim.

The first thing the students on the course had to do was to go to a given pub, strike up a conversation with anyone there and try to find out all about his private life. I say 'his' because when I got to my designated pub, somewhere near Victoria, there was no-one in the bar except men. You obviously had to be prepared to give some sort of fictional cover story about yourself in case the person was inquisitive, and I had prepared a suitable tale. What you were not told was that while you were doing this, someone from the course would arrive at the pub and recognise you, address you by your real name and do his best to disconcert you and blow your cover story. The test lay both in how much you could learn about your target and also how well you were able to keep up your cover story in the face of this unexpected disruption. For a female, of course, faced with a bar full of males, this was particularly difficult. Those customers in my bar who were not already in a group or a twosome, were a sleazy-looking bunch – the sort of people I would not normally have gone anywhere near. The man I accosted and started to chat up was just beginning to show a worrying degree of interest – he clearly assumed I was a woman of easy virtue – when my so-called 'friend' strode in to disrupt me. I treated him as a saviour rather than a nuisance, which was not quite what was intended. Of course I didn't dare protest that this was not really a very sensible exercise for women, for fear women would have been written off for all time from undertaking this sort of work. And when I did eventually become an agent-runner, I always took care to find suitable surroundings where I would not stand out.

In its early, primitive form that course was attempting to test and teach a vital skill of an agent-running officer, the ability to relate to and get on with anyone, whoever they are. It was also aiming to teach the ability to merge into the background, to be unmemorable, which is another important skill. Unfortunately, because like everything else in those days it was geared to men, that part did not work for me and I stuck out in that pub like a sore thumb. Afterwards, those courses became a lot more sophisticated, and for those who were training to do agent-running in dangerous circumstances such as in Northern Ireland or the Middle East, a lot tougher too. But these were early days for any form of training, and especially for training women.

Eventually, when both the Director of the Counter-espionage Branch and the Assistant Director in charge of the agent section were less conservative and more open minded than others had been, the barriers fell. I was posted to the 'joint section' as it was called, trying to recruit human sources of information on some of the Warsaw Pact countries. I was delighted with this. My first case was a regular visitor from one of those countries. On one of his visits, he contacted a policeman in a small coastal town and said that on his next visit he wanted to meet someone from the intelligence service as he had information of value to give. The case came to my desk. We monitored the movements of his ship around the world and next time he was due to put in at a UK port, I set off all primed and ready to meet him and find out what he had to say.

The plan was that the policeman would make the first contact and would lead our man to where my interpreter and I were waiting. We would then drive off to a quiet pub, which we had already reconnoitred, where we could hear what he had to tell us. I was very excited about this operation, even though I knew that whatever the man had to say, it was hardly likely to be the crown jewels in intelligence terms or anything that would alter the course of the Cold War. But that did not matter to me. This was the great breakthrough; women were on the way up.

At the time I hardly thought about something which has troubled me much more since, the ethical dilemma of intelligence work. How far are you justified in persuading or encouraging someone to put their liberty or, much more, their life at risk to give you information? The answer, of course, lies in proportionality and in professionalism. The level of harm you are seeking to prevent should be in proportion to the risk to the source. And you should not let people put their lives into your hands unless you are confident of your own professionalism and that there is an acceptable chance of being able to protect them if things go wrong.

None of that was in the forefront of my mind that day in the excitement of the moment. But the excitement was soon to be swallowed up by mortification. While my police colleague and our man made the first contact, I stood back, lurking, in what I hoped was a casual but purposeful way. I could see the police officer pointing me out. But I could also see our man's face when he saw the representative of British intelligence who was waiting to talk to him. It fell; he shook his head and the policeman came back to report that our friend was not prepared to talk to a woman. My future career flashed before my eyes – a wasteland of boring desk work. I wondered if all the taboos about what women could not do had been right after all. Having come so far, I was not going to take no for an answer and I sent the policeman back to negotiate. After some diplomacy on his part, and the realisation on our contact's part that I was the best thing on offer that day, indeed the only thing on offer, he agreed to talk. We drove off to our chosen pub and no more strange quartet can ever have drunk in this rural saloon bar – the lady MI5 officer, the rather scholarly interpreter, the young police officer and the visitor from Eastern Europe, seeking to establish the value of the information he had to trade. Strange to say, once we got talking, things went quite well, and an odd rapport was established among the ill-assorted group. The contact continued for some time and produced some useful information but by far the most important thing about it for me was that it saw the breaching of a major barrier to the progress of all the women in MI5 and the beginning of a real cultural change.

I stayed in the agent section until the spring of 1983 and for my last two years there I became the deputy head of the section, working under an MI6 officer who was the section leader. During that time we mounted a number of operations against the Soviet bloc intelligence officers in the UK. Some were recruitment operations, aimed at those whom we thought, from careful observation, might be venal, disgruntled or in some way vulnerable or susceptible to such an approach. The difficulty was to get close enough to them, without them or the security team at their embassies, whose job it was to guard them, seeing us coming. If they did, the prey would withdraw where we could not reach them. The Sovbloc officials needed to be out and about making contact with British people, either to do their jobs if they were genuine trade or diplomatic officials, or to gather their intelligence, if they were intelligence officers. But the security people were acutely aware of the risk that in being out and about, their charges might come across us. Those security officials knew that a good many of their people were disgruntled with life behind the Iron Curtain, and might well be attracted by what we had on offer, if we could get close enough to make our pitch and they had the nerve to accept it. It was a battle of wits.

We adopted all sorts of covers, carefully designed to achieve the objective of getting alongside and cultivating the chosen target, until the moment came to drop the cover and make the pitch. Some of my colleagues specialised in cover stories which required the adoption of particularly flashy lifestyles, involving expensive sports cars and flats in stylish parts of town. Later on, such extravagances would have foundered on the need for sharp budgeting, but in those days things were more relaxed.

My own cover stories were rather more modest, but in the course of 'living my cover', to use the term of art, I had to spend nights in a flat I had rented under a cover name and on other occasions in a hotel. It was a rather odd feeling to know that only a few miles away the girls were going to bed in our house, while I, as somebody totally different from their mother, was sleeping in a flat they had never seen.

Once the two parts of my life came together in a way that was unprofessional but unavoidable. There was a sudden transport strike. One of the girls was by then at a school on the other side of London from our Islington home. She travelled there by tube. The only way she could get home, on the day of the strike, was to be picked up. But John was away and the *au pair* had to collect the other girl from the other side of London. Inevitably, as always seemed to happen in those days, I had a meeting arranged with a contact, which I did not feel able to cancel. The flat I was using to meet this particular person was, by lucky chance, very near the school. So I told my daughter how to get there by walking from the school, gave her the key and a cover story to use in case anyone should ask what she was doing and told her to let herself in and wait. When I arrived I made her some supper and shut her in the bedroom to do her homework while I had my meeting. We both spent the night there and I walked with her to school in the morning. She was eleven at the time. By then she knew that I did something secret for the government but heaven knows what she really thought was going on, and nowadays all she will say about those sort of experiences is that they made her independent.

It is impossible totally to compartmentalise your life, however hard you try. On another occasion I was due to meet an agent who was considering defecting. The meeting was, of course, to be in conditions of strict secrecy, because he would have been at great risk if it had become known to his own authorities that he were in touch with British intelligence. I had agreed to meet him in a safe house in the Barbican and just before I set off to go there, the telephone rang. It was the nanny, to say that my younger daughter, Harriet, had gone into convulsions; she had rung for an ambulance to take them to St Bartholomew's hospital. Would I meet them there? This was a real dilemma. If I did not turn up at the safe house, my contact would be left standing in the street, exposed and vulnerable, though, being a sensible man with a fall-back plan, he would go away and come back later – but far worse, he might think I had let him down, which I did not want him to do. In the end I managed to do both by going via the safe house to St Bartholomew's, where delays in NHS Accident and Emergency, even in those days, ensured that Harriet and the nanny were still waiting to see a doctor. I had to borrow money from the would-be defector, though, to pay for all the taxis involved in this complicated bit of manoeuvring, as I had not had time to go to the bank that morning. Whether the apparent scarcity of funds available to British intelligence influenced his decision or not, I don't know. But he did eventually decide not to make the jump across.

I was amused not long ago to see a distinguished financial journalist doing the same balancing act. She broke off a conversation with the chairman of a company to take a call from her daughter, who had just come back from the doctor, to discuss with her whether or not she should go to school that day. Then, having resolved that, she got back without a flicker to the conversation in hand. I recognised the problem, though I suspect that mobile phones have made it worse rather than better than it was in my day.

I was working odd and unpredictable hours in the agent section for much of the time we lived in Spion Kop. The ground floor rooms of the house had been knocked through to form one huge area. In the kitchen at the back, overlooking the garden, was an Aga around which the dramas of the family were played out. In succession a nanny, three German *au pair*s and a French *au pair* looked after the girls and cooked on the Aga – or tried to, as all the foreign girls found it a deep mystery. When I did see them, the children complained mightily about the strange meals served up to them.

My frequent absences on operations and the stressful nature of the work and all the things we were trying to do to the large house ourselves, without having enough money to pay anyone to do it for us, did nothing to bring John and me closer together, in fact quite the opposite. John had by then moved to be Director-General of the Health and Safety Executive, which was not a job he had particularly wanted. When we were together we were both tired, cross and seemed to be continuously arguing. I still have a tragic little note written by one of the girls from those days and left on the stairs for me to find when I came home late one evening. It reads 'Mum. pleas dont argew with dad'. I kept it to remind me what effect our problems were having on them. Not that it made it any easier.

To do well at agent recruitment you needed a fairly well-developed imagination and good amateur dramatic skills. But none of it was any good unless you could also make a convincing recruitment pitch to your target when the moment came to drop your cover and emerge as a member of British intelligence. The skill was to be able simultaneously to explain the deceit you had been practising on your target and to inspire his confidence in you, all in a very short time before he panicked and left. After all, you were effectively asking him to put his life and liberty and the well-being of his family in your hands. Many of our targets saw us coming before the recruitment pitch was made, but not all, and if only one of those operations worked, the intelligence that it could provide was worth the effort. In any case this activity kept our targets on their toes and made life more difficult for the hostile intelligence officers who were themselves trying to recruit

British citizens and others in this country with access to the information they wanted.

One way of trying to find out what our opponents were doing in this country, what their intelligence targets were and their methods of operation, was to run long-term double-agent operations. This involved playing back against them some of those people they thought they had recruited. Soviet bloc intelligence officers in London in the '70s and '80s were prone to try to recruit members of the ethnic minority communities as agents, working on the usually mistaken assumption that they would not be loyal to this country. In fact a number of them reported the approaches, and with considerable courage and the expenditure of much time and nervous energy, agreed to be played back as double agents, sometimes putting themselves at serious risk by travelling behind the Iron Curtain for training sessions and faithfully reporting what they learned – all this for very small recompense. I worked very closely with several of these people and the following case is typical though for reasons which will be obvious it is not one specific case but an amalgam of several. The agent was of African origin and had a comparatively humble job, which gave him no access to any information of value. He was being cultivated by an East European intelligence service for some undefined purpose, possibly to be activated as an agent in place in time of war. Periodically he was taken to training sessions in a safe house behind the Iron Curtain, where he was kept incommunicado for several days, cooped up with one or two training officers, and taught how to communicate by short wave radio and how to decypher coded messages and reply by post, using special paper and secret ink. He found his excursions behind the Iron Curtain terrifying, as he was in constant fear that his 'controllers' would discover that he was a double agent and was reporting to British intelligence.

One of his most alarming experiences came as he was returning home to the UK after one such session. His controllers, with what seemed to me scant regard for tradecraft, had given him a pile of dollars as payment. He had put these in his wallet, not really thinking anything about the risk of carrying such a sum around. If he thought about it at all, he assumed that he was under the protection of whatever organisation his controllers worked for, and that at the London end, if there was any difficulty, I would sort it out. On that evening, the authorities at the airport seemed to be taking an inordinately long time to get everyone on board the plane. They seemed to be examining everyone's luggage with enormous care. At first he was irritated by the slow-moving queue, but as he got near to the front and saw what was happening, he began to get nervous.

When it was his turn, they unpacked his suitcase, and examined everything, though to his relief they did not ask him to turn out his pockets. Eventually he got on board, and sat down in his seat with a sigh of relief to try to calm down. Everything seemed to be just about ready for take off when some men in uniform appeared at the front and started calling out names and taking people off the plane. Terrified lest they should call him, he took the bundle of notes out of his pocket and shoved it in the sick bag in the pocket in front of his seat – and they did call him. He was taken off the plane and made to turn out his pockets and the contents of his wallet were scrutinised. Nothing incriminating was found and he was allowed back on the plane, to find the money was still in place in the sick bag. Finally the plane took off, with him by that time a nervous wreck, reaching with trembling hand for the drinks trolley.

What that was all about, we never knew. Perhaps one part of the system was trying to embarrass the other, or, possibly more likely, it had nothing at all to do with him and was just a coincidence. But bravely, and in spite of everything, he stuck with it, solely out of patriotism and a sense of public service, for he made no money out of it. He handed in the money he was given, and we gave him in return very little beyond his expenses. As a result of the actions of him and others like him, we learned a great deal that was useful about the methods and targets of our opponents, which made our protective measures much more effective.

I met my agents all over the country, to fit in with their lives, and to give them as little need as possible to make up complicated stories to cover our meetings. I can remember sitting with my African friend in a hotel bedroom in Huddersfield, helping him with his secret writing, in May 1982, during the Falklands War. The television was on, broadcasting the gloomy tones of Ian Macdonald, the Ministry of Defence press spokesman, telling us of the sinking of HMS *Sheffield*.

Writing about this now, several years after the Cold War has ended, it sounds like another era. But in this post-Cold War world spying and counter-espionage still goes on and always will, though the targets are different and for the most part the intensity is less. In times of war and peace governments will always seek other countries' information to give them an advantage in international situations. When the state is in danger internally, from terrorism for example, intelligence information is a vital tool in dealing with the threat. Though those who do this sort of work almost invariably enjoy it; they also take it very seriously. It is not a game. It is always testing and sometimes it is frightening too. For the spouses and the children who are at home wondering where their nearest and dearest are, as they work all hours of the day and night, without ever saying precisely what they are doing, it is far from a joke. For those who were carrying out the same sort of operations against terrorists then, and even more later as the threat increased, it was utterly serious.

The inclusion of women in the agent sections in MI5 during the late '70s was a big cultural change. It came because of quiet pressure and the logic of a situation which found by then a number of competent and well-educated women in the Service, on whom it in large part depended and who naturally wanted to do the sharp-end work. Not surprisingly, many were good at the role and particularly good at running the agents. Agent-running is the process which begins once a person has been recruited to give information, and has agreed to remain where they are, working on a long-term basis, covertly from inside whatever organisation they belong to. Controlling or running these people is very much a full-time job. It involves directing the agent, explaining to him precisely what information is required and trying to move him gradually into the place where he has optimum access, while at the same time guarding his security and preventing him from drawing attention to himself. In many cases it also involves being confidant, adviser and friend to the agent, who will not be able to talk to anyone else about the stressful and often dangerous role he has agreed to perform. Agent-runners frequently find themselves becoming financial advisers, marriage guidance counsellors and psychiatrists, ready at all times of the day or night to respond if there is a crisis.

It was not until the early 1990s that women were involved to recruit and run agents against terrorist targets. The idea persisted that the culture of Arab countries and even of Ireland would make it difficult for women to recruit and run male agents from those societies. There was also some paternalism left in the Service right through the '80s and the men then in charge sincerely believed that the most dangerous work was not suitable for women.

After I had been in the Sovbloc agent section for about three years or so, and was again wanting to move on, I pressed to be sent to do similar work against the Provisional IRA. My Director at the time was Cecil Shipp, whom I had first come across in my first year in MI5 when he was in charge of the group investigating the ramifications of the 1930s Cambridge spy ring. In the interim Cecil had been in Washington as liaison officer to the CIA and the FBI and had established a reputation as an interrogator and a counter-espionage expert.

Like all the best counter-espionage officers, Cecil was a details man. He did not feel comfortable, even as Director, unless he knew everything that was going on; not for him the delegation of the operations to the desk officers while he got on with the strategy. He wanted to see the papers and make his own mind up, then he would call you in to discuss what you were doing while puffing clouds of cigarette smoke over you and the files. This detailed approach could slow things up, particularly later when he became Deputy Director-General and files would be incarcerated in his cupboard for days while action ground to a halt.

He was the man who had been open minded enough to post me as the first woman in the agent section and I had a lot to thank him for. But for me to run agents against terrorists in Northern Ireland was a step too far even for him. He told me firmly, 'A family needs its mother,' and who is to say he was wrong? My daughters would certainly have agreed with him if they had been asked.

Nowadays these considerations do not apply only to women; everyone's circumstances as well as their qualifications would be taken into account before they were asked to do dangerous work. Women are working very successfully in all areas of the Service, even the most dangerous, and are proving, as most people would expect nowadays, to have a valuable contribution to make.

# 14

Of course I did become involved in counter-terrorist work eventually. Considering that within a few years terrorism was to rise to become far and away the major threat to the security of this country, it was inevitable that I would. But as things turned out it was not until I had reached a much more senior position.

My next move was in a different direction. In 1983, after about three years as deputy head of the Soviet bloc agent section, I began to pick up vibes that I was about to move on again. My boss had been told not to tell me where my next job was to be until I had been formally told by Cecil. But he was an MI6 officer and MI6 officers have their methods. One day he brought the conversation round to moves and then pointedly opened the office telephone directory at the relevant page. The open page was for a section I knew almost nothing at all about and I spent the next few days trying to learn what I could. What I picked up, I found disappointing. It seemed that I was going to a rather quiet backwater, involved in monitoring subversive influence in particularly sensitive parts of society. I did not know what that involved, but I gathered that the present Assistant Director was retiring, and nothing of much interest had happened there for quite some time.

When I was summoned by Cecil to be told formally of my move, I tried to look both surprised and enthusiastic. I was indeed delighted to be promoted Assistant Director, the first significant management level in the Service, which only one other woman had reached. But I was disappointed that it was not a more exciting job, and yet again I had a sense that they were being extremely cautious and that I was being tested in a way a man would not have been.

My promotion to Assistant Director brought some financial relief into our lives, and it also meant that my working hours were considerably less erratic. I led a section of some forty people, which was comparatively large. Sections varied in size depending on what they were doing. Agent sections tended to be comparatively small, because the work they were doing required close supervision. If their cases were not carefully and sensibly handled they could go quite dramatically wrong, and result in diplomatic protests and significant political embarrassment, if nothing worse. There were also ethical issues involved, which required careful handling, and not infrequently important legal issues too, particularly in running agents inside terrorist organisations.

My new post was as Assistant Director of one of the sections in the counter-subversion branch. It involved moving away from the centre of things in Gower Street to Curzon Street House, the bunker-like building next door to the Lansdowne Club, at the other end of the street from gloomy old Leconfield House where I had begun my career. Curzon Street House is yet another of the buildings we occupied in those days which has now been replaced by elegant offices. Our building had two claims to fame – the first, possibly apocryphal, that it had been specially reinforced for use by the Royal family in time of war, the second, true, that it had been the Ministry of Education when Mrs Thatcher as Minister of Education achieved notoriety as 'Thatcher the milk snatcher'. I know this because on one of her visits to the building she broke away from socialising with the staff after a briefing to stalk the corridors, clutching her glass of whisky, looking for her old office. I did not know whether to be proud or mortified when it was found to be the one I was then occupying.

My new section did indeed turn out to be a bit of a backwater and during my first few weeks at my new desk, the telephone never rang, and no-one came into my office to see me. It was a huge change from the agent section, which had been bustling with lots of comings and goings and constant operations and excitements. However, this period of calm did not last very long; after I had prowled around a bit to see what was happening, I soon realised that there was a lot to do. As it turned out, this period presented some of the most intellectually challenging problems of my career and also proved to be one of the busiest and most interesting.

My time working in counter-subversion spanned a period of very considerable political upheaval – the miners' strike, the Greenham Common protests, the height of CND, the growth of Militant Tendency and its activities in Liverpool and a Socialist Workers' Party very active in universities. Most of the subversive activity, as distinct from the political protest, which was going on at that time came from communists, acting, at least at the centre, on advice and support from the Soviet Embassy, and from the Trotskyist organisations. It was, by design, focused on particularly sensitive areas of society, local authorities, education, the unions, peace movements and in the case of Militant Tendency, the Labour Party. These were the areas where the democratic system was judged, by those who wanted to destroy it, to be most vulnerable and where also any interference or monitoring by the secret state was likely to be regarded as most unacceptable. My colleagues and I had the difficult task of deciding what, if any, of this activity should be of proper concern to the Security Service, in fulfilling its function of defending democracy.

MI5's work against subversion in the 1980s was based on the definition of subversion which had been given in Parliament in the 1970s. It is the same definition which was later incorporated into the Security Service Act of 1989, the Act of Parliament under which MI5 now operates. Subversion is defined as actions which are 'intended to overthrow or undermine parliamentary democracy by political, industrial or violent means'. The concept of subversion is thus focused on hostility to the democratic process itself; it has never included political dissent. We worked to the principle that the activities of organisations or individuals with subversive intent was of concern to us; the right to set up and join pressure groups and to protest was not. It was a distinction which the then Home

Secretary Douglas Hurd made plain in Parliament at the end of the '80s, at the time of the debate on the Security Service Bill. He said :

There is no power in the Bill to enable the Security Service to take any interest in any person or organisation or any activity or enterprise which presents no threat to the security of the nation as a whole. It does not matter if such people have views on the structure or organisation of Parliament or if they are involved in seeking to change industrial practices in this country or to negotiate a better deal if they are members of trade unions, or if they seek to challenge or change the Government's policies relating to defence, employment, foreign policy or anything else. The narrow party political interests of the Government of the day have no part to play in deciding on the necessary involvement of the Security Service. Its sole criterion in relation to a subversive threat is whether there is a deliberate intention to undermine parliamentary democracy and whether that presents a real threat to the security of the nation.

We gave a great deal of careful thought to this distinction, and to establishing what we should and should not investigate and report on. I was fortunate that some of the clearest thinkers in the Service, men and women with integrity and open minds, came to join me in that section, because these were not easy issues and some of the judgements made by our predecessors had not been sufficiently rigorous.

Given all that, I don't find it particularly surprising that this period of my career has been represented by certain commentators in various exposés as deeply murky and suspicious. I have been accused variously of seeking to undermine democratic institutions, in particular CND, and even of conspiring to have murdered Hilda Murrell, an old lady peace campaigner, who was found dead in the countryside in mysterious circumstances, a death which as far as I know is now thought to be connected with an ordinary burglary. MI5 does not kill people.

It is an established fact that the anti-nuclear movement, in its own right an entirely legitimate protest movement, was of great interest to the Soviet Union. As part of its subversive activities in the West, the Soviet Union sought covertly to encourage anti-nuclear, ban the bomb and other such protest in many Western countries, as a way of weakening the defences of their enemies. Of course that does not mean that everyone who joined CND was part of a subversive plot. But Soviet officials encouraged Western communist parties, like the Communist Party of Great Britain, to try to infiltrate CND at key strategic levels by getting their members elected as officers. The idea was that they could then direct the activities of the organisation to suit their own long-term objectives. Our job, and what we were doing, was to monitor those activities, not to investigate CND, which on its own was of no interest to us. The allegation that we investigated CND has been denied on countless occasions, including by ministers in Parliament but I have come to accept that no-one who firmly believes the allegation will ever cease to believe it whatever is said.

In similar vein, the 1984 miners' strike was supported by a very large number of members of the NUM but it was directed by a triumvirate who had declared that they were using the strike to try to bring down the elected government of Mrs Thatcher and it was actively supported by the Communist Party. What was it legitimate for us to do about that? We quickly decided that the activities of picket lines and miners' wives' support groups were not our concern, even though they were of great concern to the police who had to deal with the law-and-order aspects of the strike; accusations that we were running agents or telephone interceptions to get advance warning of picket movements are wrong. We in MI5 limited our investigations to the activities of those who were using the strike for subversive purposes.

The reports we issued to Whitehall during that time were

most carefully scrutinised to ensure that they referred only to matters properly within our remit. Nevertheless, they were treated as most particularly sensitive documents, which were supposed to be returned for destruction after they had been read. I remember the panic, exacerbated by the general hysteria of those days, when a minister at the Department of Energy lost one. People were sent down to Thames House, where his office was, to search down the sides of the chairs and sofas, but when he casually remarked that he thought it might have blown away when he was reading it in his garden, we gave up and waited for the furore to start when it turned up. As far as I know it has never been seen again. When MI5 moved into Thames House and the whole place was gutted, I wondered whether the report would turn up behind the panelling, but it never did.

One of the more bizarre theories that was around at that time was that John as Director-General of the Health and Safety Executive and I were working together on behalf of Mrs Thatcher to break the NUM's strike and destroy the union. During the mid-80s, the Health and Safety Commission was trying to replace the old and out-dated regulations governing mining safety. John, as head of the Health and Safety Executive, was seen as the front man pushing through the changes in the law. Change was much opposed by the NUM, which wanted the old regulations, one of which entailed certain manning levels, to remain in place. During the closing days of the NUM strike, NACODS, the union of mining deputies, tried to use this particular regulation to force the closure of the pits in Nottinghamshire which were standing out against the strike and continuing to work.

The level of the conspiracy theory only became clear to me in 1988. At a certain point in the contentious discussions over the new mining regulations, John happened to be travelling on a train with one of the mining union leaders. Suddenly, leaning across the carriage, John's companion said to him, 'They know your wife is high up in MI5.'

Piecing all this together it seems likely that certain people in the NUM, knowing I was working on counter-subversion, thought that John with his regulatory reform and I with, as they thought, my spies in the unions were part of a concerted plot to destroy them. Again, I don't suppose that any amount of denials, mine or others', will ever alter the minds of those who believe it, and there is little more other than denying it that can be said. The fact was that far from plotting joint strategies or sharing working secrets, John and I were barely speaking to each other in those days, and were effectively living separate lives.

The charge that MI5 was then, or at any other time, subject to political direction is unfounded. We certainly did not work as tools of Mrs Thatcher in her battle to break the miners' strike and destroy the NUM. In all my time in MI5, at the various levels at which I worked, I am aware of only two occasions when the government of the day enquired whether it would be possible for the Service to investigate something. The miners' strike was not one of them. In neither case did those with the authority at the time think that what was being sought was within the Service's remit and it was not done. No Director-General as far as I am aware ever hesitated to resist an inappropriate suggestion or was ever penalised for it.

I had a strange flashback to those days recently. For some years I have been non-executive Chairman of the Institute of Cancer Research, an academic research body affiliated to London University. The Institute is a charity but it works very closely with the Royal Marsden Hospital, which is an NHS Trust, and it has been the custom for the Chairman of the Institute to sit on the Board of the Marsden Trust, in order to assist the close working of the two organisations. When I was asked to join the Board of the Marsden by the former Chairman, Marmaduke Hussey, I filled in the necessary papers from the Department of Health. There was then a very prolonged silence. Enquiries were made, and I was told that the Secretary of State, Frank Dobson, disapproved of my appointment, apparently saying that he did not want a former spook in the NHS. If this was true, he must later have been persuaded that I was not a threat to the NHS and I joined the board.

Though I can't be sure, I should not be at all surprised if that episode does not have its origins in the time of the miners' strike. As I guess does another. In about 1993, John was invited to address a meeting on safety in hospitals, which was also attended by several union leaders and by Frank Dobson. Mr Dobson did not shake John's hand when introduced before the meeting and later in his speech attacked his supposed attitudes quite bitterly for, as he put it, being totally careless of the safety and welfare of coal miners. John deeply resented that charge, knowing it to be quite unfounded. His grandfather and great-grandfather had been coal miners, his father had spent his life in the mining industry, and he had a deep sympathy for those who worked in it.

My colleagues and I in the counter-subversion section spent a good deal of time thinking through what we should and should not be doing, as the files record. I believe we got it right, though it would be foolish to claim that no mistake was ever made. But we did not have sole responsibility for those decisions. It has long been a principle of investigation in MI5 that the more intrusive the form of investigation, the higher the authority must be which authorises it. This period in the 1980s was before the Acts of Parliament were passed which have now brought both external scrutiny to bear on the Service's work and avenues for the public to lodge complaints. However, even in those days, to tap a telephone, it was necessary to have a warrant signed by a Secretary of State, usually the Home Secretary. The process of obtaining such a warrant meant that each case was scrutinised internally through the management chain up to the Deputy Director-General, then it moved on to the Home Office where it was examined by officials and finally by the Home Secretary himself before the warrant was signed. All the Home Secretaries I knew took that responsibility very seriously indeed.

After the Interception of Communications Act was passed

in 1985, putting the process of telephone and mail interception on a statutory footing, an additional scrutiny was introduced in the form of a Commissioner (always a senior judge) who was responsible for reviewing retrospectively the issue of interception warrants. The Act also provided for a tribunal to investigate any complaints from the public about the interception of telephones or the mail. The Interception of Communications Act gave us our first experience of having to present our intelligence case to senior lawyers, something with which we became much more familiar during the '90s, when the additional Acts of Parliament which now govern the Service's work were brought in. A formal and rather stately process was created, which involved taking tea in china cups in the Deputy Director-General's office, while explaining to a patrician figure (the first Commissioner was Lord Bridge of Harwich) the sometimes rather squalid activities in which our targets were engaged.

My team was also responsible for what was known as the 'General Election exercise'. At each general election it was the responsibility of the Director-General to provide for the incoming Prime Minister any serious security information available on Members of Parliament of his own party, so that he could take it into account in forming his Cabinet. It was a cardinal principle of this work that information about members of one party was not made available to the other. Although the number of MPs on whom there was serious security information was minimal, completing the exercise itself was a huge chore. Most of it had to be done in the period between the election being declared and election day. It was often quite difficult to get full identifying particulars for all the parliamentary candidates because the exercise was regarded as particularly sensitive, because of the ease with which it could be misrepresented, and we were not allowed to seek any help from the parties themselves. As we did not know who was going to be elected in each constituency, let alone which party would win the election, much of the final preparation had to be done at the last minute. A further problem was the definition of what information was and was not sufficiently serious to get a person included in the exercise. Final decisions on all this were taken at the top of the Service and not entirely surprisingly our bosses did not always agree with the assessments we had made.

I well remember the election of 1983. We had worked night and day to get everything prepared and beautifully typed, ready to go down to the Cabinet Office. I took it all in to be approved, first by my Director and then by the Director-General. Those were the days before we had word processors, and though we did have typewriters which worked off disks, so that alterations could be easily made to text, the Director-General of the day had decreed that this exercise was far too sensitive for disks to be used. I suppose he was afraid we might lose them. Unfortunately for me, both the Director, David Ranson, and the Director-General, John Jones, had in their day held the post I was then occupying, so they had very firm views on how things should be done. Firstly David wanted wholesale amendments, so everything had to be re-typed and then John Jones wanted other things changed, so it all had to be re-done again.

In parallel with the difficult issues of what we should and should not be doing, I was personally trying to work out my own style of management, with no training or advice. There were not many examples of good practice around to copy as far as I could see. Those were the days when the 'need to know' principle reigned supreme – the policy, essential in an intelligence organisation which held people's lives in its hands, should be not to disseminate sensitive information unnecessarily. But it had become more of a policy of telling no-one anything unless they had a demonstrable need to know – the antithesis of communication. This was not a style with which I felt very comfortable, as my natural instinct was to consult my senior colleagues, ask their advice and run my section like a team. Having no experience to go on, I applied the same principles I used on the nannies and *au pair*s. One of the first things I did was to buy a very large tea pot and to institute a regular weekly tea meeting. Perhaps it was an unconscious flashback to my days working for Mr Sargeant in the Worcestershire County Archives. At least that meant that we all met each other regularly each week and all of us knew what was going on. We progressed naturally from that to formulating some strategic view of what ought to be going on and working out how we were going to ensure that it did. It all sounds very primitive stuff in these management-obsessed days of the 21st century, but in MI5 in the early 1980s these were novel ideas.

I also had to address that most difficult of arts for a manager, the art of delegation. How do you ensure that you know enough of what is going on to be truly in charge, while leaving the detail of the work in its appropriate place, at the front line? Like everyone I have had to learn this by trial and error throughout my career. It has been interesting to me, since I left MI5, to see others, in commercial companies for example, grappling with the same problem and not necessarily getting it right. And sometimes not grappling with it at all, so that decisions are taken at the wrong level and no-one knows what they are responsible for or where their authority begins and ends.

I found delegation at its most difficult when, later in my career, I became Director of Counter-terrorism. It sometimes seemed to me then that my role was to sit at my desk and worry, while everyone else was out on the street in difficult and sometimes dangerous circumstances getting on with the work. The truth, of course, is that my job was to make sure that the policies, the planning, the people, the training and the resources were right, and then leave them to get on with the operations, being there and ready to handle the political fall-out whether things went right or wrong.

It was during my time in the counter-subversion branch that I began to get quite well known in Whitehall, which was essential if you were going to get anywhere in MI5. I used to go down to the Cabinet Office to talk things through with Robert Armstrong, then Secretary to the Cabinet, in appearance at least a truly mandarin-like figure, sitting in the panelled office with chintz-covered sofa which has become familiar to afficionados of *Yes Minister* as Sir Humphrey's lair. I don't recall him ever volunteering much comment, though he was closely interested in everything that was going on, but I suspect his warmth towards the Service may have waned a little when later on he was called on to be the face of the British government in the *Spycatcher* trial in Australia. Those were the days when the leaders of MI5 were not particularly well known to ministers or to senior civil servants. They still took the view that the less said in Whitehall the better. It was misguided of course, because it meant that Whitehall tended to regard us with suspicion and we could not rely on their support when it was needed – as it soon came to be.

## 15

The early '80s were a time of crisis for me personally, both at work and at home. At work, in spite of my promotion I felt out of sorts with my employment. MI5 still seemed to me a male-dominated, old-fashioned organisation, which was going to take years to change. I regarded the senior management as remote and out of touch with the staff. They were not seen around as much as I thought they should be but sat in their offices, and the rest of us, even at my middle management level, only heard from them when they had something to complain about. I did not think they were at all influential in Whitehall and they did not spend any time, as far as I could see, making sure that what the Service did and why and how it did it was sufficiently well understood, either in Whitehall or more widely in the country at large. When issues connected with the Service were raised in Whitehall or in the press they took an unnecessarily defensive line. I was not the only one who felt like this and I suppose it was inevitable that something would give in that situation. And it did. In fact, during the early 1980s, crisis seemed to follow crisis.

But before the crises started, I had decided that nothing was going to change in the foreseeable future, and I was fed up with it. So, just about the time I was promoted, I decided to look for another job and I applied for the post of Headmistress of a major girls' boarding school, Roedean. Filling out the application form presented me with quite a difficulty. Those were the days when one was not supposed to admit one worked for MI5.

There were various formulae provided for use, if one applied for a job. But they were so downbeat and grey as almost to ensure that no prospective employer would even consider one's application. I seem to remember you were supposed to talk about 'research' and the 'management of information'. I didn't follow the formula, but said I worked for the Security Service. I remember going for an interview with the Governors at a house in Mayfair, just round the corner from our Curzon Street offices. I think they were very puzzled about my application; the more so because due to some postal delay, my references arrived at the same time as I did, and they were reading them out of the corners of their eyes while talking to me. Anyway, whatever they thought about my current occupation (and we had a very circuitous conversation about it as they didn't know what they could ask and I wasn't too sure what I should say) they clearly, and not surprisingly, thought that my lack of any teaching experience made me unsuitable for the job and I didn't get it. I was rather surprised to find out a few years later that a copy of my application had been given to a journalist.

Meanwhile, at home, things were not improving and I decided that the best solution for John and me would be to separate. It is impossible to say at this stage whether if I had not worked, or if I had had a less stressful job, things would have turned out differently. Marriage breakdown is certainly quite a common feature of the intelligence services – whether it is more or less than in other professions I am not qualified to say. As it turned out, we never took the next step to divorce, and years later we became friendly again, though by then we had learned that we got on much better living apart than together. In the summer of 1984 we put Spion Kop on the market and I found a much smaller house in the parallel road, Alwyne Villas. In December 1984 I moved there with the girls.

The house, which was early Victorian, had just been restored in a very stark, scraped-out way, with everything painted white. At first I liked that – it felt simple and uncluttered, which was exactly what I wanted after the emotional disturbance of splitting up and the chaos of dividing one large household into two. But after a bit, I found myself inexorably home-making, painting the sitting room and wallpapering the bedroom. How I fitted it all in I can't now imagine. I can recall evenings spent reading *Lord of the Flies* with one daughter, while sticking a wallpaper frieze round the dining room and simultaneously advising the other daughter on a project on Islington in the 18th century. There was a new garden to make, and that all somehow got done. I would have been amazed, at the time we moved, to know that only seven years later this house was to appear in all the national newspapers as the home of the Director-General of MI5, and that we were going to have to leave it, in conditions of great secrecy, because staying there had become too dangerous.

Actually, we did have a bit of a forerunner not long after we moved in. One evening when we had just finished supper, there was a ring at the door. One of my daughters opened it, without checking by looking through the spyhole, as they had been warned to do. A man on the doorstep asked if I lived there. 'Mum, someone for you,' she yelled, leaving the door open. I went to see who it was, and as soon as I appeared at the door, there was a flash from the front garden. Just for a split second I wondered if it was a gunshot, but I realised almost at once it was a camera and slammed the door shut.

It was a journalist and photographer from the *New Statesman*. They had chosen to do a series of 'exposés' of MI5 officers, on the pretext that we were engaged in improper investigations into political figures. This involved taking snatched photographs and publishing them with a few lines of highly speculative text. Those were the days when no hard information was available, and we never in any circumstances corrected what was written about us.

The journalists and I shouted at each other through the letter box for a few minutes, as they asked me for an interview and I told them to go away. The girls were amazed and we all found it quite a frightening experience. We were to become a lot more used to this sort of thing a few years later. I'm not exactly sure how they got hold of my name in the first place, but once they had it they had acquired our new address quite easily. John had given Spion Kop as his address in his *Who's Who* entry some time before, never thinking at that time that there was any reason to keep it secret. I thought I had taken care to leave no trail when we moved to our new house, but by an unfortunate coincidence, we had sold Spion Kop to the family of a girl who was in the same class at school as my younger daughter. When the *New Statesman* turned up at their front door and asked for me, they quite unsuspectingly told them that I had moved to the next street and gave them our new address.

The *New Statesman*'s efforts to photograph me at my front door were clearly not a success. I must have slammed the door too quickly. So a few days later they came back and covertly photographed me in the street as I walked up the road to catch the tube to work. The resulting rather blurred photograph of me wearing a black and white houndstooth coat and carrying my sandwiches for lunch in a small Jaeger carrier bag appeared in the magazine. I'm sure the *New Statesman* did not know how valuable that photograph was later to become. When my appointment as Director-General was announced at Christmas 1991, it was the only publicly available photograph and appeared in many newspapers in this country and abroad. They must have made a mint out of it. The Jaeger carrier bag started many years of obsessive interest in the media about where I bought my clothes.

Fundamental change in any organisation only comes through crisis. It is the way the crisis is managed which determines whether the organisation goes on to prosper or whether it goes under. In MI5 during the '80s, we suffered two major crises and one smaller one. Those crises, which at the time seemed to be major blows, had far-reaching and ultimately beneficial effects on MI5's internal culture as well as its external position. Because on the whole they were well handled, they had the effect of pushing us into the modern world much more quickly than would have been the case without them. The first of the shocks struck shortly after I became an Assistant Director.

In 1983, an officer in the Counter-espionage branch, Michael Bettaney, was detected passing sensitive counter-espionage documents to the Russian Embassy in London and offering his services to them as a spy in place in MI5. Bettaney worked in the section where I had previously operated, investigating the activities of the Soviet intelligence residencies in London. He was therefore very well placed to know exactly what monitoring systems were in place and how best to avoid them. And he did successfully evade detection as he delivered his documents. However, two things scuppered his efforts to be a second Philby or Anthony Blunt. Firstly, the security officer at the Embassy was so suspicious of British intelligence that he did not believe that Bettaney's offer was real. He thought it was a coat-trail operation, designed to catch him or one of his colleagues out in spying, so we could expel them. So he did not respond effectively to Bettaney's approach. The second thing which neither he nor Bettaney knew was that MI6 had an agent inside the KGB residency in the Soviet Embassy in London, Oleg Gordievsky, who was in a position to report what was going on. So Bettaney never had a chance.

I did not know the ins and outs of all this at the time. I was not one of those who was aware of Gordievsky's position, nor did I know how Bettaney had been detected. Even though I had been in the agent section when Gordievsky was posted to London, already a recruited MI6 agent, I was not brought into the close circle of those who knew about it. It had already been decided that I was moving very shortly to the Counter-subversion Branch and I therefore had no 'need-to-know'. This case demonstrated the importance of the need-to-know principle, when it worked as it should. Had Michael Bettaney been part of the circle of knowledge, he might never have been caught, because he would have done his volunteering in a different way or, disastrous for Gordievsky, he might have told the Soviet Embassy of his recruitment. It was only when 'need-to-know' was used as an excuse for bad management and lack of communication that it was damaging.

So I knew nothing about Gordievsky's position or the

investigation and interrogation of Michael Bettaney until it was announced to a startled Service that he had been arrested for espionage. This was breathtaking news. As a section head I had to manage the shock of a number of people in my section who had known him well and liked him and could not believe what had happened.

We were still reeling from the Bettaney affair when the second crisis struck. A member of my section, a woman called Cathy Massiter, resigned and both appeared on television and gave interviews to the newspapers asserting that she had been asked to do inappropriate investigations, including spying on CND and the unions. She was the first of the so-called 'whistle blowers', an activity which became rather the fashion during the '90s, and not just in the intelligence world. But then, in the mid-80s, it came as a massive shock to everyone in MI5, so unused were we in those days to any form of public exposure or to any member of the Service breaking cover. It is difficult to convey now, from the standpoint of the 21st century, how amazing and shocking this event seemed to us then. We had been brought up to accept that not only did you not talk in public about the work you did, but more than that, you did not even tell anyone that you worked for MI5. And here was this erstwhile colleague, someone we all knew well, talking about her work on nationwide TV and what's more giving an interpretation of it which to us seemed distorted and un-recognisable. It was breathtaking.

The inevitable review took place after Cathy Massiter's allegations. It was decided that there would be advantage in having an outsider to the intelligence services, to whom any member of those services could talk in confidence if they had anxieties about the propriety of their work, or any other problem which they did not feel able to discuss with their line management. So the Staff Counsellor was born, a post filled up to now by a retired Permanent Secretary. The existence of someone in that position is a useful outlet. Though not many people have wanted to use it over the years since it was created, enough people have for it to have proved its worth.

The fact that such a post existed when David Shayler and Richard Tomlinson decided to go to the press with their allegations, saying that they were doing so as a matter of conscience, raises strong doubts for me about their real motivation. The Staff Counsellor post, put in place in 1987, formed one plank of what later became a complex network of external scrutinies over the way the intelligence services do their work

One of the problems of working in a secret organisation is maintaining a normal life outside one's work. Making and keeping friends, even the sort of loose circles of friends and neighbours which most people have, is not straightforward when you are required to keep your employment secret. By the 1980s, the obsessive secrecy of the old days had gone. But we were still supposed to disguise where we worked, and to avoid conversations which might drift into details about work. Of course that's much easier said than done, particularly for young people, and many of us got round the problem by making friends with each other and having quite restricted circles of close friends outside work. I can remember many occasions when I have avoided going to drinks parties with neighbours and people I didn't know well, because I couldn't face the inevitable question, 'What do you do?' and having to pretend that I bought boots for the Army or whatever story occurred to me at the time. Luckily, I never had much time to feel lonely as a single parent, which was probably just as well. If I had wanted to find a new man, I certainly would not have felt able to advertise in the lonely hearts columns or go to a marriage bureau. In one way it was a great release for me when my name was made public when I became Director-General, at least everyone then knew what I did, though that brought with it a different set of problems, as I shall explain later.

Personal problems did, of course, occur in the closed organisations of those days, with limited official and personal contacts with the outside world, and a management which was remote from the staff. It is easy for confused loyalties to develop and for loyalty to friends and colleagues to seem more important than loyalty to the organisation. Michael Bettaney had been behaving inappropriately for some time. He had been drinking excessively and behaving in ways which should have sounded loud warning bells that all was not well. Though some of those who had seen his behaviour alerted the personnel department, it was not thought necessary to move him from his counter-espionage work. It was not surprising that the subsequent enquiry by the Security Commission, the body of the great and the good which exists to report on the circumstances surrounding any prosecution under the Official Secrets Act, and to make recommendations, commented adversely on MI5's management practices and style. They noted and criticised the closed culture, the remote management, the things with which we, working in the organisation, had felt discontented. So, in 1985, following the retirement of the then Director-General, a new Director-General was appointed who was not a career member of the Service.

Sir Antony Duff, a Foreign Office official, a former Ambassador and a war hero from his time in submarines, was familiar with the intelligence world. He had already been Chairman of the Joint Intelligence Committee and Intelligence Co-ordinator. The Prime Minister, Mrs Thatcher, who persuaded him to take on the job when he was on the point of retirement, asked him in particular to address the criticisms the Security Commission had made about the management of the Service.

It is hardly surprising that management had become an issue. None of those who had the responsibility in those days had any training or relevant experience. What's more, because of the closed and secretive culture of the time, they were isolated from contact with thinking that was going on elsewhere. Running a secret organisation such as MI5, within the constraints of the public service, presents some of the most difficult management issues there are. It is not a Civil Service department, responsible for creating policy and limiting risks. It is an operational organisation, where people are expected and required to take risks, sometimes risks with their own or others' safety. They must be able and prepared to take personal initiatives and quick decisions, often out on the street, in circumstances where they cannot seek guidance from anyone else and frequently on the basis of inadequate information. But in doing so it is vital that they work always and only in a context of strict adherence to the law and to the operational rules.

Many operations are extremely delicate, either politically or because a life-threatening situation exists. So staff have to be managed in smallish groups, both for security and so that the work can be properly supervised. But it is vital not to over-supervise, to ensure that decisions are delegated to the appropriate level, so that staff will not lose their initiative.

The motivation for people to work in this way is not money. Unlike major companies in the commercial sector, MI5 does not set out to offer top quartile executive pay with bonuses and share options. Motivation is complex. It comes from a combination of the intrinsic interest and excitement of the work itself (whether it is a painstaking espionage investigation or a fast-moving counter-terrorist operation) and a sense of the importance of the job to be done. There is also a strong sense of loyalty to the organisation, to colleagues and to the country, however that is defined and however unfashionable that may sound. It is a delicate balance to create and maintain.

Every organisation has to cope with the problems of confidentiality but in MI5 this issue exists in an extreme form. Everyone, even the most lowly member of staff, has some secret information in their head, or available to them, which could cause damage if leaked. So rigorous and intrusive security checks are required, not only when staff join in the first place, but regularly throughout their career. But at the same time it is important to avoid any sense of mutual suspicion. On the contrary, what must be generated is mutual trust and loyalty, because the success of any operation depends on teams working closely together, and people's lives may be in the hands of their colleagues.

It is vital to balance the 'need to know' against the need for people to be properly informed, especially at a time of organisational upheaval, when staff need to understand and support change.

Excellent personnel management skills are required to handle any inadequate performance and to try to avoid disgruntlement. Some mistakes will inevitably be made in recruitment, as they are in every organisation. When things don't work out, proceed with great care, because anyone who feels hard-done-by can at least guarantee to get their story on the front page of the tabloids, even if they don't decide to become a spy for the country's enemies. Unlike in the commercial sector, those who fail cannot be given a large sum of money to go quietly.

Then there are the families to think about. What reinforcement and reassurance is adequate and appropriate for the spouses and families of agent-runners, for example, who may be away from home erratically and at short notice, doing things and taking risks which their families will not know in detail or fully understand?

At best, a strong communal loyalty develops in organisations like this, and that is a great strength. It comes out at its strongest at times such as in June 1994, when the helicopter carrying MI5 officers and colleagues from the Army and the RUC crashed on the Mull of Kintyre. A huge sense of family loss was felt by everyone concerned.

Sir Antony Duff went about his complicated task with gusto. He had to regenerate the morale of a depressed and demotivated organisation. He had the support of practically everyone, but in particular of those who were already anxious for reform. I certainly welcomed his arrival, though he himself did not at first sight appear to me to be the model of a modern manager. He was already sixty-five when he arrived, a patrician figure, with an ambassadorial style and public school manners. But importantly he was open-minded and prepared to listen. One of the first things he did was to tour around all parts of the Service, asking the staff at all levels what they thought was wrong and what ideas they had for change. This went down extremely well and the fact that he was well plugged in to Whitehall and had the ear of the Cabinet Secretary and the Prime Minister were just what we wanted. For me though he had one big downside, for which I never really forgave him. He addressed me as 'dear'. I found this deeply patronising and thought it meant that he did not take me seriously.

However, he clearly took me more seriously than I thought, because in 1985, following the unexpectedly early retirement of the Director of Counter-subversion, I was made acting Director responsible for all the counter-subversion sections. This included an agent section similar to the counter-espionage agent section in which I had worked earlier.

This elevation was a trial run and lasted only a few months. There was someone else thought to have more of a claim to a Director's post, and when he was available, I was demoted again and put in charge of recruiting and staff security. I was not too upset by this because I was told that I would be a substantive Director before too long. In truth, such elevation was more than I had ever expected.

## 16

When I joined MI5 in the late 1960s recruiting was an entirely covert affair, dependent on a haphazard system of talent spotting. Since 1997, advertisements for staff have appeared in newspapers and journals. When I was briefly responsible for recruiting, in the mid-1980s, we were half way between the two positions. It had been recognised by then that the tap-on-the-shoulder system of recruiting posed a real danger of cloning, of recruiting only people in the same mould as each other, but we were still not ready to be completely open. Such a fundamental change in positioning had to wait until a whole series of events brought about a change in the entire relationship of MI5 to the world outside it.

In my short time in recruiting I realised for the first time what a complicated task we had set ourselves, unable as we were to call fully on the advice and resources of the recruitment industry. As well as intelligence officers, usually generalist graduates, we needed experts in various fields, communicators, photographers, linguists, lawyers and many more, but only in comparatively small numbers. We also needed surveillance officers, not an employment category widely found outside the intelligence world. They fall into two types: the 'mobiles', those who are out on the streets in cars or on foot, covertly following targets around, for whom the main qualities are alertness, stamina, the ability to merge into the background, to drive with flair and to cope with inactivity followed by periods of extreme activity; and the 'statics', those who spend their days, and often nights, sitting in observation posts in houses, flats, factories or whatever, watching the comings and goings in a target premises opposite and recording what is going on. They are very different jobs, but accuracy and the ability to keep awake during the boring bits are vital to both; accurate movement information can make the difference between success and failure in an operation.

Identifying selection procedures for the surveillance officers was a challenge and I am sure that we should have taken more external advice than we did. To the final selection panels, which I chaired, came a cross-section of British society. Our static candidates ranged from an ex-policeman to a jazz trumpeter, a zoo attendant and a member of the aristocracy; judging which of them would do that particular job well was testing.

In the mid-80s most candidates were still identified covertly. A number of talent spotters in different parts of the recruitment business were on the lookout, particularly for likely graduates. If any crossed their sights, they would ask them discreetly if they would consider a job in a non-mainstream government department and those who showed interest were sent to us for a preliminary interview. This covert system was not a great success; some of our contacts disliked appearing to be part of the secret state and produced not a single candidate, others entered into what they thought was the spirit of the thing and introduced quite unsuitable James Bond lookalikes. Occasionally, a good candidate was surfaced by this route but it was haphazard.

Another method adopted in those days for identifying likely intelligence officers was the syphoning off of some applicants for the Home Civil Service. One or two were approached with the suggestion that they might consider 'another government department'. It was not until 1996, when, as part of the new openness initiatives, MI5 began to produce recruiting literature under its own name, that it became one of the government departments from which candidates for the Civil Service could choose. Not surprisingly, a large percentage put MI5 first, to the chagrin of mainstream departments.

It was to avoid cloning that the Service had, some time before this, decided to use what was then called the Civil

Service Selection Board (CSSB) to help in the selection of graduates. The difficulty came in trying to produce selection tests which would detect reliably whether a candidate had that rather odd mix of qualities and talents we were looking for. It is recorded somewhere in the records that when Vernon Kell first created MI5 in 1909, a key criterion for recruitment for men was the ability to make notes on their shirtcuff while riding on horseback. For women it was less demanding. Kell's only known utterance on the subject of qualifications for women is, 'I like my girls to have good legs.'

By the time I was involved in recruiting, we were looking for people with a quite rare mix of talents. For our cadre intelligence officers we wanted people with a good brain, good analytical skills, the ability to sort out information and put it in order and to express themselves well orally and on paper. But coupled with that they needed to be self-starting, with a warm personality and the ability to persuade. And we needed people who would be good on their feet in difficult and possibly dangerous operational situations, where they could not seek advice. We also wanted common sense, balance and integrity. It's quite a tall order.

We were constantly refining our graduate selection tests to try to identify the qualities we were seeking, but ultimately we had to accept that some of these things are difficult to detect reliably in people of only twenty-one or twenty-two whose personalities are unlikely to be fully developed. We didn't always get the recruiting right, who does? For a time we recruited too many people with intellectual skills, but not enough practical skills, and that resulted in a crisis when we were overweighted with excellent assessment abilities but had too few people capable of gathering the raw material, the intelligence, to assess. Occasionally we recruited people who simply lacked the necessary judgement and common sense. The problem for secret organisations is that getting recruitment wrong can have more far-reaching effects than in other fields.

I had been only a year in recruiting, when, in December

1986, I was promoted to be Director of Counter-espionage, a position known in those days as 'K'. Nearly eighty years on, I had become the modern manifestation of Brigadier Vernon Kell, the founder of MI5. Though my promotion was seen as a breakthrough for women – I was the first to have reached this level – some of the men regarded my elevation as a step too far and I heard tell of mutterings about it in the men's toilets. By that stage in the Service's development there were so many women around that most people regarded it as inevitable that they would begin to rise to senior positions.

My counter-espionage credentials were good; I had worked in both the investigative and agent side of the business for a good number of years, and my management credentials were good too, having been Assistant Director in two quite different sections, and an acting Director for several months. Had I allowed myself to brood on these things, I would have felt that I had been asked to prove myself for longer and more thoroughly than any man, but I didn't. I just felt pleased and satisfied to have made it. I also felt that the post of Director of Counter-espionage was one of the best jobs in the world.

In 1986, the intelligence services of the Warsaw Pact were still aggressively targeting the West. Though our efforts over the years, and the exclusion and expulsion policies which successive governments had operated, had made the UK a very difficult place for them to work, they had not given up, far from it, and inevitably from time to time they had successes.

One of the more unexpected things I had to do as Director of Counter-espionage was to give evidence in the trial of an 'illegal', a man who had come to this country under a false identity in order to collect information. Such people are the most difficult of all spies to identify. They rarely have any contact with the embassy of the country they work for, or with the intelligence officers there, who, it is assumed, will be closely watched and so might unwittingly draw attention to the illegal. This man had been successfully identified and investigated by our staff acting in close collaboration with the police. We were able to arrest him *in flagrante* as he was sitting in the kitchen of his flat listening to his regular short wave radio broadcast from his controllers at home. I was present in court as the 'expert witness' to give evidence on the significance of his activities.

Those were the days when MI5 officers appeared in court very rarely indeed and it was a disorientating experience for one whose career so far had been spent, as mine had, in an environment where one said nothing outside about one's work. It was to become a much more common experience for MI5 officers in the years which followed, as more and more work was done in close cooperation with the police in countering terrorism. For my evidence, the press and the public were excluded from the court and the judge accepted that, in order to protect my identity, I could wear what was described as a 'light disguise'. So I appeared at the Old Bailey feeling ridiculous and looking rather like Agatha Christie's Miss Marple, with (for me) strangely curly hair, make-up which made me look ten years older, and clothes which were quite unlike my normal style. I was gratified that the defendant was convicted and amused when, a few months later, I met the judge at a dinner party and he did not recognise me.

My time as Director of Counter-espionage was very largely dominated by the third of the 1980s crises to hit MI5. In 1987, Peter Wright, that strange and untrustworthy figure of my early days, wrote his book, *Spycatcher*. Or it is probably more accurate to say that he told everything he could remember or had ever noted down to a journalist, who wrote it up in the most saleable way he could. The book went out of its way to mention every sensitive operation that Peter Wright had ever known about and to name every codeword he could recall. *Spycatcher* was a book designed to cause the maximum amount of harm and embarrassment to an organisation which Peter Wright wrongly thought had cheated him of his due.

Whistleblowing revelations, purporting to disclose something seriously wrong in an organisation, tend to reveal far more about the whistleblower than about the organisation which is having the whistle blown on it. These so-called 'revelations' have been, in my experience, invariably partial, one-sided and as such ultimately misleading accounts of what are usually much more complex situations than they present. I believe that such revelations are very often motivated by a grudge against the organisation as a whole, or some of the people within it, who in the whistleblower's view have failed them in some way. Often the whistleblower has been denied the advancement in their career which they thought was their due, or it is a question of money, as with Peter Wright, who thought his pension had been unfairly calculated. (In fact, his pension entitlement had been reviewed several times both inside the Service and by an external adviser and he was given exactly what he was due.) Whistleblowing is likely to be very damaging to any public organisation, or to a company – it is not restricted to the public sector – but it is particularly damaging to the intelligence services about which conspiracy theories already abound. For the organisation concerned, the claims made are usually impossible to disprove in circumstances where all the relevant information is unlikely to be able to be revealed. The whistleblower is inevitably seized on with alacrity by the press, to whom he or she represents good, exciting headlines. The one question rarely asked is 'Did you try to do something about it before going public?'

Peter Wright's case is a graphic illustration of the difficulty of dealing with disgruntled employees of secret organisations, and the potential costs and problems. There is rarely a perfect solution, except of course the impossible one of never making a mistake in recruiting people in the first place or in managing them when they are in. In retrospect, it is very possible that huge expense and embarrassment for HMG might have been avoided if a little more flexibility in the matter of Peter Wright's pension had been shown at the time. Business is freer to adapt to circumstances, in effect to buy people off, but the public service, bound as it is by the rules of public expenditure, accountability and precedent, does not have the same level of flexibility.

The prospect of the publication of Peter Wright's book sent the intelligence community and Whitehall into a spin. The fear was not only of what he himself might reveal but also that if he were not prevented, many members of the intelligence community from then on would blow the gaff on all the nation's secrets. It's the same fear that still exists today when anyone wishes to publish a book, as I know from my own experience. Though nowadays some attempt is made to distinguish between books which do damage and those which do not, every effort is still made by the Whitehall machine to prevent anyone who has been an insider writing anything about their life. In Peter Wright's case it was decided to pursue the book through every possible legal channel, whether there was any hope of success or not. I thought at the time it was the wrong thing to do and as it turned out the huge furore merely drew attention to it and resulted in far higher sales than would otherwise have been achieved for a book which many people found disappointingly dull. His second book in the same vein passed almost unnoticed and neither book at the end of the day did any great damage to MI5's ability to do its work.

The drama was finally enacted in Australia. The Cabinet Secretary, Sir Robert Armstrong, was sent out as the chief witness to defend the Government's case in the court in Sydney. At home we had teams of people scrabbling through files, trying to find out what exactly were the facts of various long-gone operations and events, so that Robert Armstrong could give as accurate evidence as possible. Although the Cabinet Secretary is the most senior Whitehall official and very close to the intelligence services, being the accounting officer for the money voted to them by Parliament, he is not responsible for their operations. Robert Armstrong had no first-hand information about the operations which Peter Wright described and in having to answer questions about them, even with the briefing material provided for him, he was put in a very difficult if not impossible position. His appearances in the court provided Malcolm Turnbull, Peter Wright's defence counsel, with the opportunity to make a very senior representative of the British establishment look ridiculous.

There was one allegation in Peter Wright's book which aroused considerable interest and caused the most anxiety, the so-called 'Wilson Plot'. This was Peter Wright's assertion that a group of thirty MI5 officers, of which he was one, plotted to get rid of the Wilson government, because they suspected Wilson of being excessively sympathetic to the Soviet Union. Because this allegation, if it had been true, would have meant that the service whose role it is to defend our democratic system had sought to act against the democratically elected government, it was taken immensely seriously not least within MI5. Sir Antony Duff, the Director-General of the day, who was not an MI5 insider and had no personal knowledge of the Service's activities in the period concerned, was determined that the story should be thoroughly investigated. Extensive interviews were conducted with those who had known Peter Wright and were still working; white-haired gentlemen were dug out of their retirement all over the country and asked to cast their minds back but though much reminiscing went on, no-one could recall anything that sounded like what Peter Wright was claiming had happened. Files were trawled through with the same result. Finally, a detailed report was written for Whitehall and ministers felt sufficiently confident to state publicly that no such plot had ever existed. Peter Wright later withdrew the allegation, admitting, in a *Panorama* programme in 1988, that what the book said about the so-called 'plot' was not true. However, as is always the way of these things, his retraction went almost unnoticed, and the untrue allegation stuck in some circles and remains in currency to this day.

When, much later, I was Director-General, I decided I would try once and for all to knock on the head the Wilson plot allegation. I asked some of the old grandees of the Labour Party, most of whom had at one stage been Home Secretary, to come in to Thames House to talk about it. It was clear to me then that the conviction in that generation of the Labour

Party that there was some kind of a plot against them, organised by the intelligence services, runs deep. Though I tried my best to convince them that they were wrong, I knew at the end of the exercise that further efforts would be fruitless. The fact that Harold Wilson himself said, at the time he left office, that he was convinced that MI5 was spying on him, meant that through loyalty to him, if for no other reason, it was difficult for his former colleagues to accept that there was nothing in it. But one of those former colleagues did go so far as to remark to me that if Wilson had really believed that, it was very strange that he never mentioned it at the time to any of his political colleagues so that the first time they knew about it was when, like everyone else, they read what he had said about it to the *Observer*. I am now convinced that those who believe there was a plot want to believe it, and nothing anyone can say will change their minds.

Of course, those former Home Secretaries date back to the time when there was a great deal less close communication between the intelligence services and ministers and their Civil Service advisers than there is now. It seems to me, looking back on it, that the fault for that distance lay on both sides, and it was not a party political issue. I think that the then heads of the intelligence services probably felt that they could not trust civil servants and ministers to understand the issues and to take a balanced view of what the intelligence services were seeking to do. So they kept their distance. Ministers, for their part, may well have thought that although the intelligence services were essential, they were a potential embarrassment to the government and the less they knew about them the better. The fear was that if they knew too much they might be accused of being responsible for something awkward and difficult to explain. Or perhaps they feared that knowledge might in some way compromise their political independence. Whatever it was, I am sure that some of them had little confidence in the intelligence services' competence or probity and thought it was safer to remain largely in ignorance.

Both sides were wrong. It seems to me that ministers in

those days were avoiding their responsibilities, and heads of the services were reducing the effectiveness of their organisations by keeping their heads down and keeping their distance, rather than explaining more of what they were about and trying to correct misconceptions. Old former Home Secretaries who pop up now saying they never really knew what MI5 was up to in their day and had the most acute suspicions of it, should ask themselves why they didn't do more to find out. After all, it was their responsibility.

Several former Home Secretaries appeared not long ago in a television programme called *How to be Home Secretary*. Their replies to questions about what it was like being responsible for MI5 illustrated this attitude perfectly. Roy Jenkins, who was Home Secretary from 1965 to '67 and again from 1974 to '76, said that he thought that MI5 used secrecy to run rings round successive Home Secretaries. He added: 'I didn't form a high regard for how they discharged their duties. They were secretive *vis à vis* government. Living one's life in a spy-bound world gives people a distorted view of life.' Merlyn Rees, who was Home Secretary from 1976 to '77, said that he did not know what MI5 was up to. But more recent Home Secretaries, speaking on the same programme, were much easier with the relationship. Both Douglas Hurd and Michael Howard said that they felt they knew what they needed to know. Jack Straw sounded totally relaxed about the relationship. He was not at all in awe of the secret state and said it was not as big a deal as people imagined. He described himself as having got down into 'the engine room of the business'. In my view the modern closer relationship between Home Secretaries and MI5 benefits everyone including, very importantly, the democratic process itself.

The closeness of the relationship between the government of the day and the security service should be limited only by the need to ensure that the service is not and does not appear to be the tool of the government. In my experience the limits were well understood and existed long before the relationship was embodied in legislation at the end of the 1980s. Lord

Denning's 1963 Report on the Profumo case, to which I have already referred, explains in fascinating narrative form what a Director-General should take into account in considering what he should or should not report to ministers. As Lord Denning explains, 'The operations of the Security Service are to be used for one purpose and one purpose only, the defence of the realm. They are not to be used to pry into any man's private conduct or business affairs, or even into his political opinions except in so far as they are subversive.' Denning supports the Director-General of the day for not reporting on or investigating John Profumo's links with Christine Keeler and the Russian Military Attache, Ivanov (an intelligence officer), once he was satisfied that action had been taken to negate the Russian's activities. The only criticism he makes is that the conduct of Mr Profumo, in having an affair with a call girl, disclosed a character defect, which pointed to his being a security risk in that the girl might try to blackmail him or bring pressure to bear on him to disclose secret information.

The Denning Report is to this day the guide for Director-Generals if they are ever in doubt as to whether they should tell the Prime Minister anything they might know about the behaviour of his colleagues. It is not the responsibility of the Director-General of MI5 to seek to protect the government of the day from political embarrassment; that is the job of the Whips. The DG should only pass on anything about behaviour if it could adversely affect security in any way, including perhaps, laying open to blackmail a minister in a department where he has access to state secrets. That responsibility is one reason why the Director-General of MI5 has the right of direct access to the Prime Minister, without going through the Home Secretary. The other reason of course is that the Prime Minister has ultimate responsibility for the security of the state and needs to know about serious threats; information of that sort would always be known to the Home Secretary as well. The Prime Minister would expect to see the DG regularly for a briefing on the security situation, but the knowledge that there is another possible reason why the Director-General might be talking to the Prime Minister can cause anxiety in some quarters. John Major liked to conduct meetings in the summer sitting in the garden at No. 10, which is overlooked by many windows. News travels fast on the Whitehall grapevine and towards the end of my time as Director-General, when John Major was governing with a very small majority and political nerves started to fray with allegations of sleaze ten a penny, I would often find myself rung up after such a meeting by someone who had seen us talking and was eager to try to get some hint of what we had been talking about.

## 17

The much more relaxed and open relationship which exists nowadays between ministers and MI5 is based more than anything on the adequacy of the law which governs MI5's activities, the Security Service Act of 1989. Rather ironically, that is something for which we have Peter Wright to thank. He described in *Spycatcher* what he and his colleagues got up to in London in the 1960s and '70s in the following terms: 'And we did have fun. For five years we bugged and burgled our way across London at the State's behest, while pompous bowler-hatted civil servants in Whitehall pretended to look the other way.' He was describing in dramatic terms what has to be done to carry out eavesdropping and search operations.

To eavesdrop effectively it is obviously important to plant the microphones where they will have the best chance of picking up the targeted conversations and also where they will not be discovered, and that is usually somewhere inside the premises where you expect the conversations to take place. Such operations were carried out long before 1989 and though in those days they were carefully controlled and scrutinised for the appropriateness of the targets and though judgements were made about the balance of risk and reward, and though they were known about and tacitly approved of in Whitehall, the fact remains that those operations had no explicit statutory basis.

When, in 1985, telephone and mail interception had been legislated for under the Interception of Communications Act (IOCA), it had been thought too politically sensitive to legislate for eavesdropping. So although after 1985 the interception of communications on public systems, telephone and the mail, was surrounded by legally based regulatory checks, eavesdropping on private conversations went on as before.

The fact that it had been thought too difficult to legislate for entry into private property did not deter Sir Antony Duff. He took the view that the ambivalent position under which MI5 conducted operations, which were accepted as necessary for the effective protection of the state and were tacitly approved by its political masters, but which were not covered by statute, was totally unsatisfactory. Once the position had been highlighted in Peter Wright's book, he was unwilling to continue to carry out such operations, and those which required entry to property were suspended. The result of that was a sudden loss of intelligence, just at a time when terrorist and other hostile activity was at a peak.

So discussions were set in train in Whitehall which eventually, after Sir Antony had retired, led to the passing through Parliament of the Security Service Act of 1989. Contrary to the way it is sometimes presented, it was MI5 who were very keen to have legislation, so that they could get on with the work they had to do and some members of the government who were very much less keen. Some ministers, including at first Mrs Thatcher, took the view, not altogether surprisingly, that setting out to legislate to allow the secret state to break into people's property for the purpose of planting microphones to overhear their conversations would cause a terrible furore and do the government no good at all. However, they were persuaded that it was necessary to have the power, and if there was to be the power, there must be legislation. Article 8 of the European Convention set out the right of everyone to respect for his private and family life, his home and his correspondence. And it went on to say:

'there shall be no interference by a public authority with the exercise of this right except such as is in accordance with the law and is necessary in a democratic society in the interests of national security, public safety or the economic well being of the country, for the prevention of disorder or crime, for the protection of health or morals, or for the protection of the rights and freedoms of others.'

By the mid-1980s, case law under the European Convention had recognised that a state may set up a security service to provide a covert response to covertly organised threats; but the state must put its security service on a clear legal basis and there must be adequate and effective guarantees against abuse including a means for the citizens to complain and seek redress. Without a law in place to take account of these points, our arrangements in this country appeared to fall foul of the European Convention. So ministers agreed to bite the bullet and legislate, both to put the Security Service on a statutory footing and to provide the power to enter property.

When the idea that we should press ministers for legislation was first proposed, I was very uncertain about it. I was not at all confident that government would be robust enough to legislate to give us the powers we needed and I was afraid that instead, the result of pushing them might be that we would permanently lose a source of vital intelligence. This seemed to me a crucial issue and quite unasked I produced a paper for the first Directors' meeting after the idea had been mooted, setting out the pros and cons and concluding that the arguments came down, just, in favour of the cons.

In those days it was not at all usual to have papers for Directors' meetings. The idea that important policy issues should be debated in an open way was new. Under the old regime, either there were no policy issues, because change was avoided, or those at the top decided everything without discussion. After we had discussed it and I had thought more, I changed my mind and became persuaded that the status quo could not last, and if we did nothing, we would lose the powers anyway. So I then became an enthusiast for the legislation and I sat on a small Working Group, which worked very closely with Home Office civil servants to draft the Bill.

Once it had been decided to legislate, it was clear that the law must do much more than provide the power to eavesdrop. The new law had effectively to replace the old Maxwell Fyfe Directive, under which the Service had worked since 1952, and in doing so it must define the entire task of the Service and at the same time provide the 'adequate and effective guarantees against abuse', which the European Convention required, for all its activities. The draft Bill which we proposed, suitably worked on and smartened up by the parliamentary draughtsmen, was piloted through Parliament by Home Office ministers. The timing of its introduction to the House of Commons was carefully planned. It came in the wake of a revision of the Official Secrets Act, which was focused on by the press and those who took a close interest in civil liberties. So when the Security Service Act came along, many of the natural opponents of such legislation had shot their bolts against the Official Secrets Act, with the result that the Security Service Act had a much smoother ride than might have been expected.

What the Act did not contain, among the various ministerial and judicial oversights it provided, was a parliamentary oversight committee. We thought hard about this and Parliament debated whether it should, but ministers, civil servants and some in the Security Service all felt that would be a step too far at that stage, though it was not ruled out for ever. The opportunity was taken to introduce such a committee in 1994 when MI6 and GCHQ were legislated for in the same way.

Since the passing of the Security Service Act, I have several times been asked by colleagues in other countries to explain to their ministers and oversight committees why it is so important for modern security services to have the power covertly to enter private property. If it was difficult for the UK government to bring in legislation to grant such a power, with the level of the terrorist threat that existed at the time in this country, it was much more difficult for countries where there was apparently very little or no such threat. But terrorists strike against their targets where they perceive the defences are weak. US embassies have been attacked in Africa, British citizens have been kidnapped in India, British diplomats and soldiers have been murdered in mainland Europe. Effective counter-terrorism requires international cooperation, including the provision of adequate powers for security services and police. The important thing is not the provision of powers but that their use should be properly controlled.

That argument cut no ice with the Norwegians, when I made it to their oversight committee in the early 1990s, and as far as I know they still do not have the authority to eavesdrop. In February 1999, I was asked to answer questions from the New Zealand Intelligence Oversight Committee, who were considering legislating to give their security service such powers. The New Zealand security service had, in fact, thought that it had such powers and only when their legislation was challenged in the courts was it discovered that they did not. The hearings in New Zealand were in public, and it was clear what strong emotions are raised by giving to a state body the power to, as it was put 'enter our homes and listen to our conversations'. As someone said in evidence to the Committee, 'While the state imprisons people for breaking and entering, it has the audacity to legislate that it is all right for the secret service to commit such crimes under the pretext of protecting its citizens.' Those strongly held views do not weaken the case for having such powers, but they do serve to emphasise the care which must be taken in using them.

There was considerable relief, not only in MI5 but also in Whitehall when the Act finally got its Royal Assent. Antony Duff had retired by then, and his successor Patrick Walker invited all the ministers who had steered the legislation through Parliament, including the Prime Minister and the Lord Chancellor, to a party in our Gower Street Headquarters, to celebrate.

This was the first time I had had a chance to observe Mrs Thatcher at close quarters. Though I had met her when she visited the Service, as she did from time to time, those occasions had been very stage-managed, and there had not been much opportunity for anything other than formal presentations. Those were the days when the Service was still very careful indeed what it said to ministers and anyone who was to make a presentation at a ministerial visit, let alone a Prime Ministerial visit, had to rehearse it in front of their Director. In fact, Mrs Thatcher's first visit to the Service had gone down in the memories of all those present, not because anyone fluffed their lines or got their facts wrong, but because her whisky was not mixed to the right strength. Apparently she was presented with a glass containing a gold liquid which was very pale indeed. She promptly returned it, demanding something much stronger, much to the embarrassment of those who had spent hours trying to get the occasion perfect but had forgotten to establish the facts of this vital detail.

By the time of the legislation party I was the Director in charge of Counter-terrorism. It was the period when the Provisional IRA was actively trying to kill British servicemen in Germany and my colleagues and I were closely involved in trying to thwart their operations, to identify the terrorists and to get them arrested. Just the night before, there had been an incident at a military base in Germany where the terrorists had been disturbed by a night-watchman while they were setting their bomb, and had fled before detonating it. I was well briefed on what had happened. But before I could open my mouth, the Prime Minister told me all about it at some length and with some intensity, fixing her eyes on a point somewhere over my right shoulder. I recognised points from the briefing note we had sent down to No. 10 earlier that day, but she had got some of the details wrong. For an instant I wondered whether I should correct her story, but it only took me that split second to decide that would not be wise. I am sure that was not the only occasion when cowards like me allowed her to remain misinformed.

Much had happened in the years before the legislation to change the culture of MI5. The recruitment of younger, more open-minded people from varied backgrounds, the increase in the number of women and the gradual abolition of the taboos on what they could do, the crises which had produced a much more open management style – all these influences had begun to lift the veil behind which our predecessors had hidden us and which for years had separated us from the outside world. The legislation had also set in train a course of events with a most profound effect on my own life, in that it led to the formal announcement of my name when three years later I was appointed Director-General. This pushed me into the public eye in a way that I neither expected nor was prepared for.

The first impact of the new law was that for the first time we were required to answer detailed questions from experienced lawyers about why we had reached the conclusions we had and why we had taken this or that action. These were the members of the Tribunal set up under the Act to take complaints from members of the public about anything which they thought MI5 had done to them or their property.

The first few visits of the Tribunal were tense occasions. Each side was sizing the other up. They knew nothing about us or the ethos of MI5 and did not know what unacceptable practices they might find or whether we were going to try to pull the wool over their eyes. We did not know whether they were open-minded, reasonable people or whether they would turn out to have preconceived ideas and axes to grind. Not surprisingly, they took their work very seriously. They asked for, and got, any files relevant to the complaint they were investigating, and spent a considerable time understanding what those unfamiliar papers meant. We, for our part, had to get used to the novel idea that the files, which recorded in detail what had gone on and why, files on which we had written notes and minutes, totally unaware that anyone outside the Service would ever read them, were now being scrutinised by outsiders, albeit within the ring of secrecy.

I welcomed this. We were confident in the integrity of our procedures, we were proud of what we had to show them. After their first visit, which lasted most of the day, we decided that these were indeed reasonable and sensible people and we resolved that the best way to deal with the situation was to embrace the oversight. We would arrange for them to tour the service. They should meet the ladies (and by then men as well), who worked in the Registry; the people who spent hours listening to and transcribing the often extremely crackly and blurred product of the microphones which had been installed under the new law; the desk officers who had to make the judgements about whether this or that person should have a file or be investigated. We would explain everything to them in detail, confident that if they understood the issues, they would, by and large, agree that what we had done had been appropriate. And on the whole they did. I think they were impressed with our willingness to discuss the issues and to open up frankly to their scrutiny. For our part, we had to learn to explain ourselves clearly to people whom we could not assume would necessarily think the same way as we did – and to serve dry sherry before lunch, which, we learned, is the approved drink of the Inns of Court.

In addition to the law, Antony Duff's other great contribution was to secure Prime Ministerial backing for a new building for MI5. During his time as Director-General we occupied nine separate buildings in central London, of which the best known were Curzon Street House and the building at the top of Gower Street, above the Euston Square underground station, both now knocked down. Such a large number of separate buildings was grossly inefficient, to say nothing of the insecurity of regularly moving quantities of highly sensitive files and papers between buildings – this was before the days of computerisation. A fleet of vans drove in a continuous shuttle service from building to building several times a day, but very often when papers were needed urgently they were stuck in a traffic jam somewhere in Mayfair.

The regular shuttle service between Gower Street and Curzon Street did have the great advantage that without too much of a diversion it could pass by Marks & Spencer and staff could hitch a lift to do their shopping. It was seen as a great loss of privilege when, after a prolonged negotiation, Thames House on Millbank was acquired and after the move there was no shuttle service any more.

Tony Duff retired before many of the changes which he instigated had come to fruition, and it was left to his successors to bring them successfully home. He made a massive difference to the culture of the Service, which I was able to build on when I became Director-General and instituted a programme of greater openness. I had reason personally to be thankful to him for having recognised that I was capable of doing the most difficult jobs in the Service. And in particular for having promoted me to what I thought of as the best job in the world, Director of Counter-espionage in the final days of the Cold War.

# 18

By the time I became Director of Counter-espionage, the girls were twelve and sixteen. Even though they did not know in any detail what I did for a living, they knew it was something secret for the government. The arrival of the *New Statesman* reporters at the front door had been only one in a series of strange events they had had to get used to. One evening several years before, the phone rang and I answered it. After I had put the phone down, one of them said: 'What was that?'

'Oh nothing', I said absent-mindedly, 'it was just about someone who thinks he's been stabbed by a poisoned umbrella.'

'Has he?'

'I don't think so.'

'Oh,' she said, and went back to whatever she was doing.

That, of course, was the first notification by the police of the incident when Georgi Markov was poisoned by the Bulgarian Secret Service on Waterloo Bridge. I did not take the reported stabbing seriously at first, though of course it later turned out to be true and a similar case happened in Paris shortly afterwards.

There were innumerable telephone calls at odd times of the day and night, which often resulted in my leaving home unexpectedly. There were occasions when the news reported the expulsion of certain Russian officials for 'unacceptable activities', when I seemed extremely interested and unusually cheerful. And later while the Provisional IRA was bombing London, I seemed always to have an anxious expression and an obsessive interest in the news on the radio, which was often the first notification of an unexpected attack.

Inevitably, the girls got involved to some extent in the life of the Service. They met many of my colleagues, and members of foreign intelligence services too, when I entertained them at home. They and various trusted boyfriends were often roped in as waiters for those occasions, just as in any other household. When I became a Director we used to have the branch planning awaydays at our house in Alwyne Villas. Over the years, the girls got to know my closest colleagues quite well, though they could never remember who was who, and complained that they all seemed to be called Chris or John. Later on, when I became Director-General, they became a lot more involved, as all three of us were swept up in the tide of media interest.

When I started to live on my own I decided that they were becoming too old to be looked after by *au pair* girls. By then, Sophie was only a few years younger than they were, and she resented being told what to do by 'foreigners who can't even speak proper English,' and who could not cook as well as the girls themselves. When one of the German girls, distracted by Harriet and her cousin Beatrice arguing in the back seat over a bottle of orange juice, drove the car spectacularly into a line of parked cars (including a Rolls Royce) outside the gates of Waterlow Park in Highgate, we decided that we would look for some other arrangement. So from then on two local ladies came in, one to clean and one to iron on different days and the girls became latch-key children. We could cope with normal routines, but when something outside the normal occurred, as it very often did, for example if one needed extra maths coaching, or one got into a team and had to be ferried to matches it was particularly difficult. When they were doing the big public exams, they did not get the level of support I would have wanted to give them. Sophie did her A Levels when I had just taken over as Director of Counter-espionage, and Harriet was just starting work for hers when I became Director-General and the press were hounding us.

Like any working mother, I was constantly managing conflicting pressures, trying to be in two different places at once, and apparently succeeding more effectively than even the Scarlet Pimpernel. The result of all this was that the girls learned to look after themselves, to travel around London alone, and to be independent and self-reliant beyond their years.

None of this was made easier because my job as Director of Counter-espionage involved a considerable amount of travelling abroad. Since the beginning of the Cold War, one of the great strengths of the West's counter-espionage effort had been the sharing of intelligence between the closest allies, the UK, the USA and the old Commonwealth. This survived the unfortunate paranoia-feeding between James Angleton and Peter Wright and was the foundation of the 'special intelligence relationship' which exists to this day. So keeping these links as close and friendly as they were was an important task for any Director of Counter-espionage. I paid several visits to the USA, and to Australia, Canada and New Zealand, while my mother came to stay to look after the girls.

Secret services are not usually associated with cooperation and sharing. It sounds like a contradiction. But in a world where the threats get more sophisticated and more global, the intelligence task gets more difficult, and cooperation between intelligence allies is vital and grows ever closer. When MI5 was first set up in 1909 it was expressly forbidden to form any foreign links at all. But even though their task in those days was limited to countering the activities of foreign spies within Great Britain, they soon found that it was very difficult to do this without any support from friendly counterparts overseas. But right up to the Second World War there was only the bare bones of any international security structure and it was not until well on into that war that any really effective security links between allies were put in place, in particular between the UK and the USA. Once those links were set up, however, they considerably increased our combined effectiveness. The exploitation of the 'double cross' spy cases mentioned above, which successfully misled Hitler's Germany and contributed greatly to the success of D-Day, was an early joint effort.

After the end of the Second World War, it was the Cold War that dictated the direction of security and intelligence work and it was clear that any effective defence against the massive and sophisticated intelligence efforts of the Soviet Union and her Warsaw Pact allies could only come about through close collaboration between Western security services. But collaboration against that target was a very sensitive business. There was always the fear that one or other of the Western services might have been penetrated by the Soviet bloc, a fear which of course proved only too well-founded on several occasions. So the links that were established were mostly bilateral, service to service, cautiously and carefully done on a strictly 'need-to-know' basis. The exception to the bilateral rule was the link between the closest Western intelligence allies of the Cold War, the British, the Americans, the Canadians, the Australians and the New Zealanders – the so-called CAZAB link.

When I first joined the counter-espionage branch in the early 1970s, knowledge of this CAZAB link was very closely held. The knowledge of it was imparted to new officers in an 'indoctrination' session, after which their names were inscribed with great formality on a list of those with knowledge. There were a number of such lists of those to whom particularly tightly held information had been revealed and over a career, particularly in counter-espionage during the Cold War, you found yourself on numerous such lists, as you 'needed to know' secret after secret. Each list had its own codeword and unless your name was on the list for any code-worded operation, no-one might speak to you about it and you would not be permitted to see any files. There is nothing new about this, of course. In the Second World War when similar secret operation names proliferated, Winston Churchill cabled home from one of his transatlantic voyages to meet President Roosevelt, that he had been reading *Hornblower* and approved of it. His staff spent days trying to discover which secret plan he was referring to before they realised that Churchill had been reading C.S. Forester's first *Hornblower* book.

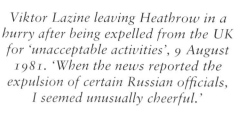

*Viktor Lazine leaving Heathrow in a hurry after being expelled from the UK for 'unacceptable activities', 9 August 1981. 'When the news reported the expulsion of certain Russian officials, I seemed unusually cheerful.'*

*Georgi Markov, later poisoned with an umbrella by the Bulgarian Secret Service, while on Waterloo Bridge. 'I was notified of the incident by the police in a telephone call one evening . . . I did not take the reported stabbing seriously at first, though of course it turned out to be true.'*

*John Major opens the new
MI5 building, 1994.*

Receiving an Honorary Degree
at Exeter University, 1996.

*Celebrating my sixty-fourth
birthday by playing in Tom
Stoppard's* The Fifteen-Minute
Hamlet, *in a barge theatre in
Copenhagen, 1999.*

When you leave, retire or move away to another part of the work, you have to sign off the lists. It feels like a sort of brain washing or mind-hoovering process, but there is sense behind it. It makes it quite clear that after a certain date you have no current information, so if sensitive information gets out, and there is a suspicion that there may be a spy in the organisation, it is easier to narrow down the search. The trouble is that after a time you inevitably forget what list you are on and what particular secret operation each codeword refers to. It was quite a revelation when I retired and someone turned up in my office with innumerable lists for me to sign off which I had totally forgotten about.

The existence of CAZAB and its regular meetings was one of the factually accurate things which Peter Wright chose to reveal in his book *Spycatcher*. Since the end of the Cold War, it no longer exists in that form. The growth of terrorism, and the newer threats like organised crime require cooperation of a totally different type – less discreet, broader, more inclusive and above all more immediate.

In the spring of 1988 I was in Australia for a CAZAB meeting, accompanying Patrick Walker, who was then Director-General, when the Gibraltar operation went down. Also present was the head of MI6, the heads of the CIA and the FBI and the heads of the Australian, New Zealand and Canadian services – the old intelligence allies of the Cold War.

We were a small, élite and oddly assorted bunch, met together to share some of the most sensitive information we had at that time, our assessments of the current counter-espionage threats and the details of current cases. The Americans, both venerable, white-haired judges, political appointees supported by professionals, were the heads of enormous organisations with vast operational and assessment resources to deploy and far more cases to draw on than any of the rest of us. Their then head of counter-espionage was a small, bird-like man of great experience and detailed knowledge, who, unlike his predecessor James Angleton, the alter-ego of Peter Wright, possessed balance and common sense. He had no notes with him but as an aide-memoire would produce a very small shiny black notebook from the top pocket of his casual shirt. I never saw inside it but considering its explosive contents it must have been written in some private code.

The British were the oldest services, next in size to the Americans but much smaller, greatly respected for their professionalism and headed by long-serving intelligence officers. The smallest by far were the New Zealanders, a service of tens rather than tens of thousands, but regarded as well-run and professional and led by an ex-military officer.

We met on an island off the Australian coast, which was inhabited by nothing much except kangaroos and Australian intelligence officers in training. In spite of the relaxed surroundings, the atmosphere was serious. As the only woman present I was mercifully spared the more macho aspects of the occasion, such as ferociously competitive tennis or swimming in icy water off the well-protected beach. Though we were in a remote spot, we were not exactly out of touch. The Americans, as always, had brought their vast teams of communicators and enormous satellite dishes with them. They also had their teams of armed guards who followed the heads of the FBI and the CIA everywhere, clutching their weapons in little handbag-like holders – a level of security that I personally thought was ridiculous, bearing in mind our secure environment.

At the time we had left London, intelligence was just beginning to come in about a team of Provisional IRA terrorists in Spain. Patrick had been keeping in touch as far as he could with what was going on as the action moved to Gibraltar. But the news that the Active Service Unit, as they called themselves, had been killed came as a great surprise and a shock.

That operation provides a classic example of the difficulty of counter-terrorism work. MI5's contribution to such operations lies in acquiring intelligence from a variety of sources and assessing it in order to try, by a combination of knowledge, experience and common sense, to work out what is really going on. The objective in a counter-terrorist operation is to be there first, so that the terrorists can be thwarted and the bomb does not go off. By the nature of things, intelligence will nearly always be partial, so it is rarely clear exactly what is planned. When a crisis develops, when the partial information indicates that a terrorist operation is imminent, it frequently comes down to assessing the risk of doing nothing against that of doing something and possibly getting it wrong.

In the case of the Gibraltar incident, a lot was known about the Provisional IRA's then current strategy, which was to murder British military personnel outside Northern Ireland and Great Britain, because, it was thought, they would be less well defended and the security forces less focused. Much was also known about their chosen methods of attack, amongst which were shooting and car bombings. So when intelligence indicated that a group of known Provisional IRA terrorists was in Spain, it was not difficult to work out that their target might be the British military presence in Gibraltar, and so it turned out to be. Analysis and observation correctly pinned down the precise target and when the terrorists parked their car in the square in Gibraltar where the military band parades took place, it seemed likely, though there was no certainty, that they were intending to explode a car bomb.

In such circumstances difficult judgements have to be made. The risk of making arrests before there is enough evidence to hold or prosecute the terrorists, then having to let them go free to return on another occasion when there might be no intelligence of their intentions, has to be weighed against the obvious risk of letting them proceed with their operation and intervening only at the last minute when their intentions can be proved. These are difficult and stressful decisions, some-times involving risk to members of the public and usually taken without precise information and often under acute pressure of time. They are the day-to-day currency of counter-terrorist operations.

In the case of Gibraltar, as everyone knows, the operation

ended with the shooting and death of the terrorists. This was followed by the discovery that the car that was parked in the square was not the bomb itself, but a car parked to block a space for the bomb which was to be made up in another car from explosives already stored in Spain to be brought in on a later day. That operation was followed by a series of thorough examinations of the actions of all concerned, first at an inquest and then by the European Commission of Human Rights and finally by the European Court of Human Rights, seeking to determine whether the killing of the three terrorists was lawful and whether or not it constituted a use of force more than was absolutely necessary given all the circumstances.

That the inquest decided that the killing was lawful and the European Commission decided that it could be regarded as absolutely necessary for defending others from violence, whereas the European Court by a majority of ten to nine, judged that the killing of the terrorists was not a justifiable use of force in all the circumstances, serves to point up the intense difficulties which attend the conduct of this type of counter-terrorist operation. My complaint against programmes such as *Death on the Rock* is that in their enthusiasm to prove that the state is at fault, they appear to make no attempt to give honest consideration to the difficulties of balancing the risks in operational situations. They look only at what happened and not at what might easily have happened.

A few days later, Patrick and I were cycling gently round the island in a break in the meetings, when he asked me if I would take on the post of Director of Counter-terrorism. He wanted to send the then Director to Northern Ireland to take charge of the Service's work there. This request came as quite a shock to me, and a fairly unwelcome one at that, knowing as I did the many difficulties of counter-terrorism work, not least those I have just described. I had had no previous experience of working in the terrorist field and felt ill-equipped to go in at Director level. But it was flattering to be asked, as it was far and away the most difficult and exposed post at that level. I decided, without much hesitation, to take the risk and say yes.

By this time, MI5 had been working against terrorism for over twenty years. But after my involvement in 1969, as part of the tiny section formed at the very start of the new phase of the terrorist problem in Northern Ireland, my career had gone in a different direction and I had been largely focused on the Cold War. Over those years, of course, terrorism resulting from the situation in Northern Ireland had grown vastly. The Provisional IRA, well resourced by Colonel Gaddafi with arms, explosives and money, had extended its operations out of Northern Ireland to the European continent and the British mainland, and had been regularly seeking armaments, new technology and funds in North America and elsewhere. Loyalist terrorists too had developed their operations and were constantly looking to increase and upgrade their arms and equipment.

While the Northern Ireland terrorist problem was growing, as early as the late 1960s other forms of terrorism had begun to appear. Firstly in Europe, with small, violent national revolutionary groups, like the Red Brigades in Italy and the Red Army Faction in Germany, which were trying to overthrow capitalism through the use of terror. Then at about the same time, in the first manifestations of what came to be known as 'international terrorism', groups started to attack, apparently at random and particularly in Europe, primarily to get the attention of the world's press focused on their particular issue. This began with Palestinian terrorists, and most people saw it for the first time in 1972 on world-wide TV when a group calling itself 'Black September' attacked the Israeli athletes at the Munich Olympics. A key figure at that time was Carlos the Jackal, now languishing in a French gaol.

Palestinian terrorism on an international scale continued for many years, with hostage takings, aeroplane hi-jackings, car bombings and shootings. Even after Yasser Arafat on behalf of the PLO renounced violence in 1988, other so-called 'rejectionist' Palestinian organisations, such as the Popular Front for the Liberation of Palestine and the Abu Nidal group, continued the terrorist operations.

As the years went by, some threats declined but others, quite unpredictably came to take their place. Extremist Islamic terrorism grew during the '80s and with the declaration of the West and America in particular as the 'Great Satan'. Attacks on Western interests took place everywhere and all sorts of groups began to adopt terrorism as a means of achieving their ends, moving round the world to do their business. As Europe started to dismantle its borders, keeping track of them, knowing who was where, became increasingly difficult.

All this terrorist activity presented a great challenge for governments and their security and law enforcement agencies. It was a puzzle to know how best to deal with it, and in most countries it took a long time for sensible and suitable arrangements to be worked out. Some countries, particularly Israel, used special military groups to assassinate the leaders, on the principle that they were 'at war' with the terrorists. Countries of the Soviet bloc sheltered, armed and encouraged the terrorists as a way of weakening the West. Some countries actively used terrorism as an arm of their foreign policy, particularly at various stages, Libya, Syria, Iran and Iraq.

In Western Europe and the USA, governments in their various ways tried to counter it, firstly politically, by ostracising the governments who supported terrorists and by refusing to bargain with the terrorists themselves. Mrs Thatcher took a particularly firm line, though other Western governments were more equivocal. Secondly, they tried to deal with it legally, by prosecuting and imprisoning those they caught, regarding them as criminals, not political prisoners. Thirdly they stepped up all forms of protective security arrangements, such as airline security, and protection for political figures and those thought to be most at risk. And fourthly they relied on their security and police services to get advance intelligence, so that terrorist operations could be thwarted and the terrorists arrested. In extreme circumstances, it was recognised that military assistance would be needed, and crack anti-terrorist squads such as the FBI's Hostage Rescue Team were trained specifically to deal with hi-jacks and other forms of terrorism.

All this meant that MI5 along with other Western security services had had to develop a new approach. The tried and tested techniques used to catch spies and monitor Soviet intelligence officers, which often involved painstaking, long-term investigations, did not quite fit the bill of dealing with people who were aiming to kill. We still needed these traditional investigations to understand the terrorist groups and their aims and methods, so that we could counter them. But they were difficult to monitor, being often a long way away and usually in countries which were sympathetic to them. So, as well as classic investigations, we also had to develop the ability to take rapid action, to react quickly to events as they unfolded.

To increase the chances of success in this difficult field, a way had to be found to distribute highly sensitive intelligence quickly and securely, across state borders, so as to alert whichever country was being threatened or was in a position to take some action. So a network of international contacts had been developed between security services, extending far beyond the traditional cautious, discreet and careful contacts of the counter-espionage field. It was never questioned that friendly countries would take just as seriously terrorism aimed at each other as they would that aimed at themselves. In MI5 we played a leading role in developing these networks.

One of the underpinnings of this new closer relationship in Europe was the group of Heads of European Security Services, which met twice a year. It started as a small, secretive group, but over the years it has expanded and its existence has become known. In its early years it was best known for the extravagance of the hospitality with which Heads of Service entertained each other but later it came to provide the essential glue for the close collaboration at working level between the European services. Meeting and getting to know the other heads of service was a way of judging their professionalism and the standing in their own country of the service they led. If you are to share the most sensitive intelligence, often obtained from human sources in very dangerous positions, you need to know that the service which is receiving it is competent to deal with it professionally and securely.

But all this collaboration, national and international, was not without its problems and did not settle down quickly or easily. One of the difficulties at the beginning was achieving a shared assessment of the intelligence, what it meant and what should be done about it. This is quite vital because there are obviously likely to be enormous problems if one country, on receipt of some intelligence, alerts the government, mobilises the Special Forces, grounds all aircraft and closes the frontiers, while another discounts the intelligence as a fabrication and ignores it. That sort of thing tended to happen at first, but gradually, as contacts developed, as key people met and grew to know and respect each other and as close international friendships developed, such problems became less frequent.

Because terrorist activities were politically motivated and needed a political as well as a security, intelligence and police response, some countries appointed Ministers for Terrorism. In the UK we did not, I am pleased to say. Politically, terrorism was dealt with by the Home Secretary, the Foreign Secretary or the Northern Ireland Secretary, whoever was most appropriate.

Ministers for Terrorism were, from the point of view of the intelligence professionals, nearly always a disaster. They tended to be quite junior and to see terrorism, or at least a high-profile response to terrorism, as a way to further their own political careers. They loved to tour around Europe, calling not only on ministers, but also on police and security services, accompanied by somewhat embarrassed officials from their own countries. They all had their own theses or ideas for solutions, which very often involved creating new pan-European structures to overarch the national bodies which existed already. These new bodies were rarely necessary and often turned out merely to confuse what existed, to cost money and to waste time.

Terrorism is of course an immensely political business. But

MI5 is primarily a security intelligence organisation, not a policy department. Its job is the acquisition and assessment of intelligence and that is its fundamental skill. To deal with terrorism effectively, new intelligence techniques had to be developed. Terrorism required the accessing of information quickly and the old paper files and the endless brown boxes of index cards in the registry of my early career were far too slow. Files were being computerised and programmes were being developed to access them in different ways. The physical surveillance officers had also to develop new techniques. The KGB were gentlemen compared to the terrorists. They were of course well trained and often excellent at avoiding surveillance. Over the years of the Cold War they had acquired an encyclopaedic knowledge of the side roads and one-way systems of London, of the Underground network and the layout of all the stations. But of one thing you could be sure, if they detected surveillance, they would not turn round and shoot. The terrorists were not so well trained, but in similar circumstances might well shoot. So terrorism brought a different level of risk – physical danger to the staff but also of course, the risk of the death of large numbers of members of the public or massive damage to property if the intelligence were inadequate or the assessment wrong.

The need to tackle terrorism was one of the most significant influences in changing the culture and working practices of MI5. By the time I joined the counter-terrorism branch as Director, a new style of MI5 officer had emerged, quite different from those who had been around when I first entered the Service. The modern version was younger, travelled regularly, spoke foreign languages and was easy with open discussion about strategies and cases. The new breed of MI5 officer was comfortable in Whitehall, sitting on committees and discussing issues with ministers and their advisers. As more and more counter-terrorist operations were successful and ended with the arrest and trial of the suspects, giving evidence in court became much more common. Those who were able to meet these new requirements thrived and advanced, those who couldn't either left or became back room players.

During my first few years working against terrorism the main focus was on the Provisional IRA's efforts to kill British military personnel in Germany. The terrorists, in small secure units, would live under cover in holiday cottages in France, Belgium or the Netherlands, and travel into Germany to reconnoitre and attack their targets. Detecting, monitoring and arresting them was a joint effort between the security forces of all the countries concerned and demonstrated how well European security cooperation had developed by that time. Even when we failed to prevent the killings, we frequently managed to identify the perpetrators and a number were arrested though they were not all successfully prosecuted. In the end, the Provisional IRA decided that the losses they were sustaining made their European operations not worth the cost, and they transferred the focus of their operations to Great Britain, where they knew they would achieve much more publicity and impact.

Though a good deal of our resources were focused on terrorism from the situation in Northern Ireland, both republican and so-called loyalist, much was still going on in the international terrorist field. I had not been Director of Counter-terrorism for more than a few weeks when, one evening just before Christmas in 1988, yet another telephone call home, initially answered by one of the girls, sent me off out to work again. PanAm 103 had been blown out of the sky over Lockerbie.

That particular attack caused enormous consternation and distress, partly because it was so unforeseen, partly because so many people were killed, people who appeared to have been selected for death quite by chance, and partly because it drew everyone's attention once again to the vulnerability of air travel to attack and its consequent attraction for terrorists. As always in these cases there was an instant demand for the answer to the question, 'Who is responsible?' followed almost immediately by the next obvious question, 'Will there be another one?' International counter-terrorist arrangements were tested to the limit as many false leads, so-called 'intelligence' and speculation whizzed around the world and 'analysts' emerged from every corner to give their view and intensify public anxiety and political pressure.

In such a fevered atmosphere it was easy to start jumping to conclusions, and we, like others, found that our early assessments later turned out to be incorrect. As always in such cases, it is from the hard, painstaking, detailed analysis that the soundest conclusions emerge. Creating the space for that work to go on, in a fevered international climate, is the difficulty. A team was detached to work closely with the Dumfries and Galloway police (who were faced with the prime responsibility, as the remains of the plane and its passengers came down in their area) and with forensic experts and colleagues in the USA and in Europe.

The investigation was prolonged and difficult and there were a number of false leads. It involved enquiries in many parts of the world and the detailed tracking of the bomb from its making to its explosion. The result was a brilliant fusion of forensic, intelligence and analytical skills, which ultimately resulted in the arrest, trial and conviction of one of the perpetrators.

The division of counter-terrorist responsibilities in the UK which existed when I became Director was imperfect and complicated. It was supposed to ensure that each agency and department had the opportunity to contribute in its area of expertise, while preserving certain principles, namely that ministers were answerable to Parliament and the public for the security of the state, that law and order on the street were the responsibility of the police, that diplomacy was the preserve of the Foreign Office, and that the armed forces came under the Ministry of Defence. What had resulted, as far as the security and intelligence community went, were 'arrangements', set out by the Joint Intelligence Committee, designed in the hope of avoiding confusion of responsibilities and conflicting interpretations of events. The arrangements made MI5 responsible for the collation, assessment and distribution of all intelligence on international terrorism affecting the UK, on Irish loyalist terrorism outside Northern Ireland and on Irish republican terrorism outside the British Isles. The RUC, with whom of course MI5 worked very closely, had the lead responsibility in Northern Ireland and the Metropolitan Police Special Branch (MPSB) was responsible for intelligence against republican terrorism in the mainland of Great Britain.

All this sounds complicated and it was. But that's not too surprising: everything relating to running the country involves networks of liaison between departments and agencies. The important thing is that they work; that on the day everyone knows precisely what their role is and isn't, because no counter-terrorist operation is ever exactly the same as the one before. By the time I became involved, exercises were held regularly in different parts of the country and abroad so that everyone could rehearse their role. If a terrorist incident, a hi-jacking or a hostage situation takes place anywhere in this country, it is the Chief Constable who is in charge, unless and until control is handed to the military. In such a situation, a confusing number of experts and advisers would descend on his patch to help the unfortunate Chief decide what to do, and if he and his staff had not had a chance to practise, they would find it hard to make sense of it all.

When exercises were being planned, there was much enthusiasm among junior staff to volunteer as 'hostages', especially if the exercise was overseas, in Bermuda for example. But they tended not to volunteer twice, as they often returned from playing that particular role having seen nothing of the country they were in, having had no sleep for forty-eight hours, and covered with bruises from having been hurled out of a 'hi-jacked' aircraft or building by their 'rescuers'.

The exercises could be extremely realistic when you were involved at the sharp end. I was once in a room as a 'hostage' along with some cardboard cut out 'terrorists' who were due to be 'killed' when the military burst in to rescue us. I can still feel the wind in my hair as the bullets whistled past me and slammed into my cardboard captor. At the time I had perfect faith that our rescuers knew what they were doing, but now I do occasionally wonder if perhaps I was standing in not quite the right place and my life was more at risk than I knew.

One part of all these arrangements seemed to me to be out of date and damaging. That was that the Metropolitan Police Special Branch had retained the lead role for intelligence, as well as police work against the Provisional IRA's operations on the mainland of Great Britain. This was a historical anomaly, which had survived the taking on by MI5 of lead responsibility for intelligence gathering, coordination and assessment work against all other forms of terrorism outside Northern Ireland. Through the work we had done against the Provisional IRA's European campaign and with the RUC in Northern Ireland, we had learned a lot about how to counter their operations, and felt we had much to contribute to doing the same thing in Great Britain. Frankly, in my opinion, neither the intelligence-gathering techniques nor the assessment skills of the police were, in those days, up to scratch. But this was an extremely delicate issue to address without causing a furore. The Metropolitan Police, with whom we worked extremely closely and cooperatively in many fields, would inevitably regard any attempt to change the status quo as treachery. Losing their cooperation would not be in anyone's interests. What's more, it seemed likely that all the Chief Constables, through their powerful association ACPO, would line up together in supporting the Metropolitan Police and opposing any change. I had many discussions with colleagues about what to do and concluded that whatever the difficulties we must not let the issue drop. Our attitude was in marked contrast to that of our predecessors. Although I have no direct knowledge of this, it was widely said in MI5 that, at the time the Brighton bomb almost killed Mrs Thatcher's cabinet at the Conservative Party conference in October 1984, there would have been the opportunity for the Service to take on the intelligence role against Provisional IRA activity in Great Britain, but our predecessors had not wanted to take on the responsibility, because they were afraid of criticism if they failed.

Eventually, after many discreet conversations, the Cabinet Office, having gained the support of No. 10 Downing Street and the military, set the ball rolling to bring about a change. The Home Office was charged with looking at the whole issue and, true to form, set up a working group, with representatives of all interested parties arguing for their own interests, which ensured that the process was not only prolonged but bloody. The working group eventually produced an ambivalent recommendation, which no-one understood and everyone interpreted differently. Ultimately, the Prime Minister and his advisers forced through the change and MI5 took on the role. I think it was the IRA mortar bombing of No. 10, which came close to killing John Major's cabinet, which clinched it as far as he was concerned.

Those negotiations were long drawn out and uncomfortable for everyone involved and left relations with parts of the police quite rocky for some time. Many senior police officers chose to see it all as a trial of strength, which ultimately they lost, though others thought the changes were right and were extremely helpful and supportive throughout. The whole episode was made more difficult by hostile leaking to the press as the discussions went on, and I acquired a reputation as a ruthless and wily manipulator of Whitehall, of which I was rather proud, though I don't think it was very accurate.

As the election of 1992 was called, we were still uncertain what would happen. It seemed to everyone very likely that the Labour Party would win, and all the discussions and issues would have to be aired again for new Labour ministers. However, the Conservatives won the election, Kenneth Clarke became Home Secretary and accepted the recommendation when it came onto his desk, and the changes went through.

However, patience was not one of Kenneth Clarke's virtues, and, having agreed to the change, he wanted instantaneous results. In the summer of 1992, just after the decision had been taken, but before it had been implemented and while we were still engaged in difficult and detailed discussions with the police on exactly how we would discharge our new responsibilities, I, by then newly appointed as Director-General, was summoned down to the Home Office. Kenneth Clarke questioned me grumpily on why we had not yet made any noticeable difference to the level of IRA activity. I had to tell him that such things took time. We would make a difference in due course. He just had to wait and give us support and encouragement.

I don't think he found the advice very palatable. For Home Secretaries life is full of the nightmare of unpredictable disaster, so it is not surprising if they are rather jumpy. On another occasion, when I went to explain to Kenneth Clarke that we wanted to use a building in a residential part of London as a garage for cars, involving much increased traffic movement, he painted for me a nightmare picture of the large-scale protests on the street that would result, from mothers with placards pushing babies in buggies, fearful that their children would be run over. As it turned out there were no protests and everything went ahead as planned.

But of course, having taken on a responsibility, we had to work hard to deliver. Making sure we could, and that we had and retained ministerial support, occupied the first part of my time as Director-General.

## 19

I left Counter-terrorism at the end of 1990 on promotion to one of the two Deputy Director-General posts which existed at the time. I was appointed on the retirement of David Ranson, a long-time Security Service officer who had made his reputation in the counter-subversion branch at the time of the 1974 miners' strike and had been very involved in the early days of the Service's work in fighting international terrorism. His retirement turned out to be sadly short, as he died only a couple of years later.

My promotion to Deputy Director-General was the first time I seriously wondered if in fact I might end up as Director-General. It still seemed to me that the other deputy, Julian Faux, was much more likely to be given the job than I. He was responsible for the operational and investigative work, had served in Moscow and had run the surveillance section. More recently he had directed the surveillance operation against Michael Bettaney which led to his arrest in 1984. Julian kept a velvet glove pinned to his office wall to remind him that in earlier days he had been accused of being rude to senior officers. My job, in charge of the support side – finances, personnel and recruiting, accommodation and all the general underpinning – was dull in comparison. It is tempting to think that it was because I was female that I was given the 'soft' subjects but I don't believe that was the reason. The fact that I was a female had almost ceased to be relevant to the progress of my career by this time. As far as colleagues in the Service or in Whitehall went, I did not think it was an issue. Some of the police still found it difficult to treat a senior woman like a normal human being, and felt the need to treat all engagements with me and senior female colleagues as trials of strength they had to win, though by that time there were a considerable number of more up-to-date senior police officers who did not have that problem. Abroad, attitudes differed. Mediterranean colleagues, who were often generals or admirals, tended to be charmingly gallant. In Northern Europe, being female was not an important factor and even the French had by then ceased to hide pregnant women behind screens. The Danish intelligence service had been headed up by a woman for a few years by the time I became Deputy Director-General. I had yet to find out about the attitudes of our Cold War opponents.

By the time I left Counter-terrorism, I was exhausted. The level of terrorist activity in both Irish and international arenas had increased to the point where, when I left, we decided to split the branch in half and two Directors were appointed to do the job I had been doing.

I felt that what I needed more than anything else was a break before I took up my next post. I asked for and was given a short sabbatical to go off and polish up my French; I had been taking conversation lessons already for some time. So just after Christmas 1991, I set off to France in my ancient Beetle Cabriolet car to take a course of lessons at the Chamber of Commerce school in the Market Square in Lille. The French loved the Beetle, and whenever I stopped someone would come up and offer to buy it. In those days I had no commercial instinct and I never pursued their offers.

Setting off to France, I felt more carefree than for very many years. I left the girls and MI5 behind with no qualms at all. Sophie was by then at university and Harriet went off to stay with a cousin. It was a wonderful feeling to have no responsibility for anything or anyone except myself. I stayed with a young family in a small house in the outskirts of Lille and had their young son's bedroom. He had piled up all his stuff in the corner when he vacated his room for me, and somewhere among it all was some sort of electronic gadget which played a tune at 3.30 every morning. I never found where or what it was, so I never managed to turn it off. But this did not matter because although it usually woke me up, I had no difficulty in my responsibility-free state of mind in going back to sleep again. Even Desert Storm, the invasion of Kuwait, which I watched on the TV news, seemed remote from me, though I knew that my colleagues would be very much on the alert for any terrorist strikes by Saddam Hussein or his friends on his enemies in the West.

In some countries, even those with a far less serious terrorist threat than we had, it would be remarkable that the deputy head of the internal security service could go off totally alone and unprotected on such an 'ordinary' sabbatical abroad. It was thanks to the anonymity which had been until then a feature of a career in MI5 that I was able to do so. My hosts and the teachers at the school had no idea what I did for a living, though, as ever, my job made ordinary human relations rather difficult. The teachers were anxious to help me with particular vocabulary that would be useful in my profession, but I did not think it would be appropriate to ask them for the vocabulary for surveillance and running agents and tapping telephones. So I represented myself as some kind of an expert in physical security, and engaged the Manager of the Chamber of Commerce in earnest conversation about locks and security systems, which I did not know a great deal about in English let alone in French. When, only a year later, there was much publicity about my appointment as the Director-General of MI5, they were surprised to discover whom they had been harbouring.

I pottered about Northern France in my little car on those dark, freezing-cold January days, and watched Lille readying itself for the arrival of the cross-channel trains. And on the way home, I stopped in Bruges and re-visited the museums which I had known well when we lived in Brussels, and watched the ducks sliding on the frozen canals. But all too soon it was time to go back to work, and I returned to the gloomy Gower Street offices, where I had last worked as Director of Counter-espionage, feeling little enthusiasm for my new job.

Resource management was not something that appealed to me at all. The Treasury was beginning to take a close interest in the resourcing of the intelligence agencies, thinking, rightly, that over the years we had got away with less rigorous scrutiny than other departments, because we had been able successfully to hide behind our veil of secrecy. So the late 1980s and early 1990s marked the introduction of a whole new system of resource and priority scrutinies, which would have made our predecessors pale. Their objective had been to keep such things away from Whitehall, particularly the Treasury, on the grounds, which they successfully held for a remarkably long time, that it was all too secret for anyone except the most closely involved to know anything about.

In the 1970s, when Michael Hanley was Director-General, we heard tales of the DG becoming apoplectic at the insensate demands of Whitehall for information to substantiate and justify resource requirements. To do them justice, he and his successors were not seeking to cover extravagance, or anything worse, it was just that they had no faith in Whitehall as it then was to understand what the task of the intelligence agencies was, and to resource it properly. It was another manifestation of the distance and suspicion which existed in those days. Nor did that lack of openness lead to profligacy; I believe it was quite the opposite. In their desire not to raise their heads above the parapet, our predecessors may well have failed to introduce changes which might have cost money, when perhaps they should have done. The housing of the Service in so many, rather unsuitable buildings was an example.

But in the late '80s, as Mrs Thatcher got to grips with public expenditure, the veils of secrecy were gradually being torn away. Each year, a new system was tried for scrutinising the expenditure of the intelligence agencies. In fact the administrative time, thought and energy which went in to tackling the subject was in our case totally out of proportion to the sums involved. But it had by then become a sort of challenge and, as far as we were concerned, the torture of the public expenditure round got more and more refined as the years went on.

Within the Service we started to make huge changes in our management processes, not only financial management but also the way we managed our staff. We greatly improved our assessment of staff performance, we introduced performance-related pay, we made our separate businesses cost centres with their own budgets and performance targets. In doing that we took advice from a wide range of senior managers in different fields, not only in the public service. Because our business was regarded as mysterious, such people were interested to come and meet us and give us advice. So as time went on, we felt we had a good story to tell to the Whitehall scrutineers. But that did not make the process any less agonising.

The system that had been put in place meant that the staff of the Intelligence Co-ordinator in the Cabinet Office were responsible for the first scrutiny of our plans. Then the Treasury moved in, and questioned everything in that suspicious, combative manner which was the professional style of Treasury officials in those days. They cultivated an incredulous tone of voice, designed to make one feel an idiot and I had to force myself not to get cross, which was exactly what they wanted. The whole process culminated in the heads of the intelligence agencies having to appear before a committee of the ministers of those departments which were the 'customers' for their product, the Home Office, the Foreign Office, the Ministry of Defence, the Northern Ireland Office etc, with of course the Treasury in attendance. It was a sort of refined 'Star Chamber', where the ministers had all been provided by their officials with the most awkward questions they could think up. To the unfortunate scrutinee, it seemed like a sort of competition of beastliness. You knew that whatever you were proposing, you would be given less, and drawing attention to the comparative cost to the country of a successful IRA bomb in the City of London and a few more thousands of pounds spent on counter-terrorism never seemed to work. I came away wondering ruefully why I had put so much effort into stopping them all getting blown up.

Even the most normally pleasant and friendly people

seemed to change when public expenditure was involved. When John Major was briefly Chancellor of the Exchequer he visited us for a briefing with his Treasury officials. All was going well until I, knowing it was my turn to speak next and unsure of a figure I thought he might question me about, wrote a note to my colleague sitting next to me, who I thought would know the answer. John Major noticed, stopped the person who was speaking, and accused me fiercely of 'cross-briefing', whatever that meant. I felt like a schoolgirl who had been caught cheating in an exam. My later encounters with John Major when he was Prime Minister were much more friendly.

By the time I retired, the scrutiny process had been refined further. The 'Star Chamber' grilling had been written out of the script, and things had become much less aggressive. The version in operation at that time culminated in the three agency heads and the Cabinet Secretary and his staff meeting the Chief Secretary to the Treasury and his staff in his office in the Treasury. It was never a pleasant occasion, but when William Waldegrave was Chief Secretary, at least he managed to make it more humane by offering us sandwiches and a glass of wine. Previously we had not even been offered a cup of coffee. Although the questions were no less searching, he smiled and was polite and friendly, which was a much more effective way of getting at the facts than the rather bullying style that had been in vogue previously. But he took a real interest, and was well informed, and comfortable with the subjects we were discussing.

A main responsibility for me in the year I was one of the Deputy Director-Generals, was to conclude successfully the work on Thames House, the building which Tony Duff had acquired to house the whole Service, and get us moved in on time. Thames House had had many occupants since it was built speculatively in the 1930s, including the Department of Energy during the 1984 miners' strike. To make it suitable for MI5, with its special needs, there was major work to be done. It effectively had to be rebuilt internally, two buildings had to be joined together and a road permanently closed. Some elegant panelled rooms and art deco staircases covered with original 1930s linoleum had to be preserved and in some cases removed and replaced. It fell to me, first as Deputy Director-General and then as Director-General to preside over the refurbishment and the move into the new building, though the hard work was done by others.

At first the government had hoped that both MI5 and MI6 would fit into Thames House, but when that proved clearly impossible, a new building was acquired for MI6 too, so they could move out of their squalid 1960s block in Lambeth, Century House, which was falling to bits. The exotic Terry Farrell building on the Thames, now well known because of its appearance in a James Bond film, was identified as their future home.

Like all huge building projects, particularly in the public sector, the Thames House refurbishment had been fraught with difficulties throughout. Initially, there had been a great deal of discussion in Whitehall before it was finally decided that the building should be acquired to re-house MI5. That meant that when the building was ultimately purchased, the purchase cost was higher than it might have been if decisions had been made earlier. Initial estimates of the cost of converting the building, which were done by the Property Services Agency, had taken no account of the special requirements of the Service, nor of the fact that the building contained, as well as a number of listed features, a considerable amount of asbestos. Inevitably, when it was finally decided that we were to be the occupants, the conversion costs were greater than had been originally envisaged. Mrs Thatcher became alarmed at the rising costs and, concerned that we might be ordering gold-plated taps for the toilets, persuaded Stuart Lipton of Stanhope Properties to cast his eye over the project. There were no gold-plated taps, but with his expert knowledge and experience, he was instantly able to achieve large cost savings and he remained as our adviser until the project was completed. With his help, when a final budget was set, we succeeded in completing the project on time and within budget, but only at the cost of detaching some of our best intelligence officers to work in the project team, rather than against our intelligence targets. All their brains, determination and covert skills were needed to bring the project safely home and towards the end it was clear that dealing with the building industry was just as tricky as dealing with the KGB. It struck me then and it strikes me now that the public sector does its building projects in a curiously inefficient way.

There was one thing I had to do as Deputy Director-General which I could not possibly have foreseen, which compensated me for all the above and turned out to be the most fascinating of all the things I did in my time in MI5. During 1989, with startling speed, the communist governments of the former allies of the Soviet Union in what was then called Eastern Europe began to unravel, and the Cold War, which had dominated the work of MI5 for the whole of my working life, came to an end. The suddenness with which it all happened had not been foreseen by the intelligence services of the USA or Europe or of the Soviet Union itself. But when it happened, it had a dramatic effect on all intelligence professionals in both East and West.

For our part, we saw both threats and opportunities in the new circumstances. In spite of the increasing amount of work we had been doing against terrorism in recent years, many people still associated MI5 with the Cold War, and began to assert loudly that there was no longer any need for it and it should be disbanded. We felt a need to explain ourselves and to justify our existence in a way that we had never felt before. But we also saw huge opportunities in the situation, and we sat down with colleagues in MI6 to consider how to turn it to our advantage.

In particular, we saw an opportunity to offer help to our former enemies in the intelligence and security services of the former Soviet bloc countries, to adapt themselves to working in democracies. They were going to need to convince the citizens of their newly democratic countries that they had changed, and that instead of working against the people to keep totalitarian governments in power, as they had under communism, they were now working for the citizens, to protect democracy. If security services were to exist in these countries and were to be effective, and it was important for the preservation of the new world order that there should be security systems in place, they would have to learn rapidly how to work within a system of laws and controls. The new governments needed help too in putting together appropriate systems of laws and oversights to control those services. We in this country had quite recent experience of setting up systems which were working well. We had up-to-date advice to offer.

They would also need advice on recruiting and training new people to staff their services. Many of the Cold War veterans were either not suited to working under a democracy or were fatally tainted by their activities under communism. The important advantages to be gained seemed to all of us to make it worthwhile putting resources into this work. By making allies of these people we could help the diplomatic initiatives that were then under way to develop friendly relations with the new democracies. In our own professional field, we hoped that we could convince the new intelligence services that by allying themselves with us, they would no longer feel it necessary to spy on this country, which would save us resources for more important things, while also enabling us to clear up some of the old cases of the past and assure ourselves that no harm was still being done. But also, very importantly, because their former communist governments had often helped and harboured terrorists as a way of damaging the West, they had information which would be invaluable in countering terrorism. So, with the encouragement of the Foreign Office and working closely with colleagues in MI6, we moved swiftly to contact our former enemies and to offer friendship and assistance. After a time, we found ourselves in an *Alice Through the Looking Glass* situation, training and advising Bulgarians, Hungarians, Poles; the representatives of services who had been our enemies all my working life.

I was responsible for our own in-service training, so I was frequently called upon to preside over the end-of-course dinners for our new allies. They must have regarded us and particularly me, a female, as something from another planet, our style and ethos was so different from theirs. I remember making a light-hearted speech at one dinner, telling some Bulgarians, I think it was, that one of the great advantages they now had in this post-Cold War era was that they would soon have a female at the top of their service. They gazed at me in stony silence and did not at all see the joke. But the speeches of thanks which our guests made were both emotional and touching. They had very recently been through the most earth-shattering experiences. Their world had been turned upside down, and if we found it all astonishing, for them it was many times more so. I was presented with an eclectic collection of cap badges and other insignia and objects engraved with friendly messages from organisations with which I had never expected to have anything but the most hostile relations. It was a very exciting and quite bizarre period.

This was particularly true when I found myself in the headquarters of the intelligence service who would have imprisoned and possibly killed the volunteer who had been my very first agent case ten years earlier, had they found out what he was doing. Much vodka and whisky was drunk far into the night as we swapped stories about the sorts of things, though not the details of cases, we had been trying to do to each other during the Cold War. But I also found it deeply satisfying to see these former totalitarian states, who had oppressed their citizens for so long, coming to terms with democracy. On one occasion I attended a dinner at the British Embassy in Budapest to which the Ambassador had invited the Hungarian intelligence oversight committee, set up under their new legislation. It had only just been created and comprised people from both wings of Hungarian political life, which meant that on that committee were old communists and former samizdat writers who had been political enemies for years, all cautiously eyeing each other up but sincerely trying to work together in that most sensitive area of political life, national security.

That was unexpected enough. But far and away the strangest experience of my working life was a visit I paid in December 1991 to Moscow to make our first friendly contact with the KGB. Some months before, Douglas Hurd, who was Foreign Secretary at the time, had met the man whom Gorbachev had put in charge of the KGB following the failed coup against him, Vadim V. Bakatin. Douglas Hurd had recognised that Bakatin was a true democrat who was sincerely interested in reforming that organisation. He asked him, in the spirit of the times, if he would like some people from the British Security Service to go over and talk to the KGB about working in a democracy. He said he would. I was delighted to be asked to lead the team. We were three, myself, a colleague from MI5, a man who had spent much of his Security Service career in counter-espionage work against the Soviet intelligence services and whose hatred of communism was matched only by his love of Russia and its language, and an official from the Home Office. Together we set off on what was for all of us a unique experience.

It is difficult to describe the excitement and incredulity that we felt at the events that were taking place in Russia in those last days of 1991. Suddenly everything was turned on its head, nothing seemed fixed and nothing was impossible. It was breathtaking for me, after more than twenty years spent combating the activities of Soviet intelligence, to be setting off to Moscow to meet them for what we hoped would be friendly talks. It was obviously equally amazing for the other side, though I think they looked at events rather more cynically than at that time we did. We were met at Sheremetyevo airport by a KGB team led by a man whom, I found out later when I got back home again, I had already come across once before. He had been a member of the KGB office in New Delhi in the 1960s when I was a locally engaged clerk-typist working in the MI5 office there and, as one was required to do, I had written a note which was faithfully stored on a file in the registry, reporting that I had encountered him. I am not sure he knew that we had met before as he did not refer to it. There he was clutching a small bunch of red roses, a traditional gesture of greeting – I gathered later that they had agonised over whether as a senior professional woman I would be insulted or flattered to be offered flowers. While we waited in the VIP lounge for our luggage to appear, we made stilted conversation, none of us quite sure what tone to adopt for this remarkable occasion.

We stayed with the British Ambassador, Rodric Braithwaite, in the embassy just across the river from the Kremlin. We arrived just as winter gripped Moscow, and from my bedroom window I watched as over the few days we were there the river turned first to ice and then to a snow field.

There was a sense of complete unreality in the embassy, a reflection of what was going on in the street outside. Everything was changing incredibly fast and no one knew what would happen next. The USSR was in its terminal stages (by the end of December it had ceased to exist) and the leaders of the Soviet Republics had agreed to form the Commonwealth of Independent States, but what that would mean in practice was not clear at all. Out on the street, there was every sign of economic breakdown. Little old ladies were selling a single tin of soup or a pair of worn shoes. In the Gum department store practically all the shelves were empty; there was hardly anything at all to buy. No-one knew what the rouble was worth, and prices at the tourist stalls in the Arbat where we bought the then current version of the Russian doll – a big Yeltsin, containing Gorbachev, Khrushchev, Stalin and a tiny Lenin in the middle – varied minute by minute.

Inside the British embassy the old Cold War feel of being in a hostile environment was still much in evidence. All the security rules were still in force, but attitudes were already changing and a new self-confident approach to security was taking over. It was as though the old enemy was beginning to lose its teeth. So though we went into the safe room to discuss with the embassy staff the strategy for our meetings, and though everyone was still conscious that there were microphones everywhere and that all the Russian staff were working for the KGB, there was far less concern about what they overheard than there had been. In fact, we all took rather a delight in speaking freely. The rules of the game had completely changed. At dinner in the embassy dining room on our first night there, conscious that we were being overheard, we spoke quite openly about the KGB and how we judged they were reacting to the new situation. I caught one of the women who were serving our dinner looking at a colleague and raising her eyes to the heavens at our conversation – or was it to the large crystal chandelier which hung over the table and was no doubt picking up everything we said?

Our meetings with the KGB were held in their headquarters in Dzerzhinsky Square, a complex of large, forbidding buildings which also includes what had been the Lubyanka prison, over the years a place of torture and death. The statue of Felix Dzerzhinsky, founder of the Cheka, the predecessor organisation of the KGB, had not long before been dragged off its plinth by the mob and carted off to rust in a park somewhere. My colleague, who has a well developed imagination, muttered, 'Can't you sense the blood in every stone?' as we went through the door. We were shown to a meeting room, where Mr Bakatin welcomed us at the door. At a long conference table, what seemed like an immense line of KGB officers, all male of course, was drawn up on one side. We assumed they were a mixture of the First Chief Directorate, the foreign intelligence service, the counterparts of MI6, and the Second Chief Directorate, the domestic security service, our own counterparts. Four rather isolated chairs had been placed on our side, for the three of us and our interpreter. It was an eerie atmosphere as we sized each other up, and there was much smiling and handshaking and remarks about historic moments. But in fact, on both sides, we were rather like wild animals suddenly being presented with their prey in circumstances where they couldn't eat it. We had been watching each other for years, competing and trying to catch each other out. But for those few days we were all friends, though the friendly feelings did not run very deep in some of those present.

We had come with prepared scripts about the need for laws and oversight in democracies, the ostensible reason for our visit, and with some requests. Mr Bakatin invited us to give our presentations and make our requests, then he would leave and let us, the 'professionals', talk to each other. We went through our description of the laws and regulations which controlled the activities of the intelligence agencies in the UK. These were met with polite incredulity by our KGB interlocutors. I then made my requests.

Over the years, members of the staff of the British embassy in Moscow and their families, who for the most part lived in blocks of flats reserved for the staff of foreign embassies, had been subject to harassment of various descriptions. It was clearly done either by or with the tacit support of the KGB. Flats had been entered when their occupants were out and obvious signs of someone's presence had been left around. Freezers had been turned off, and small things broken. Possessions had been removed and returned on another occasion – a favourite trick was to take away one shoe of a pair and then bring it back a few weeks later. Quite frequently, the tyres of diplomatic cars parked outside flats were punctured or other damage was done. The idea presumably was to frighten and unsettle the people concerned. Sometimes the harassment was more threatening. When diplomats or their wives were driving in and around Moscow, they were very frequently followed by surveillance cars, that was expected, but sometimes those cars drove dangerously and threateningly close or even, apparently on purpose, hit the car they were following. My request was that if, in this post-Cold War era, we were to get closer and cooperate, that sort of behaviour should stop.

Mr Bakatin's response to my opening remarks was friendly and welcoming. As for my request, he said that he would do what he could to look into the harassment, but in a surprisingly frank admission of his position, he added that he doubted whether he would be able to do anything about it. Turning to the man who had been in charge of the welcoming party at the airport, my one-time acquaintance from Delhi, he said that he knew that when enquiries were made, he would be told that it did not happen. That turned out to be true. Before we left, we were told that if such things occurred, it was not the KGB which was responsible. For a time after our visit such incidents became much rarer. I believe that later on they started again.

Mr Bakatin lasted only about six months in that post, and by January 1992 his imminent departure was announced. Others tried to push ahead with his reforming policies but eventually after a couple of years things began to go slowly into reverse and the successor organisations to the KGB took on many of its characteristics. Bakatin has since written a book about his time in charge, *Izbavleniye ot KGB* (*Getting Rid of the KGB*). But when my own appointment as Director-General of MI5 was made public, shortly after our visit to Moscow, he was still in post. Amongst all the congratulations I received, the letter from him, still head of the KGB, was the one I most enjoyed. It seemed the crowning unexpectedness of that whole unexpected period.

I recently had a rather extraordinary sidelight on that episode. In the autumn of 1999, I visited Kazakhstan with a delegation from BG plc, on whose Board I sit as a Non-Executive Director. We had gone there to look at the work the company and its partners are doing on the oil and gas fields in the north of the country. The very competent security men who were looking after us, who were employed by Group 4, were all ex-KGB men. They knew exactly who I was and we developed a very friendly rapport on the basis of our past employment. I told them I had been to Moscow to visit their headquarters in 1991 when Bakatin was the Chairman. 'Ah yes,' they said. 'That was a very low period for the KGB. We thought all our influence was being taken away.'

The KGB in Moscow were not at all interested in our presentations about laws and oversight arrangements. They could not wait for Mr Bakatin to leave so we could get down to discussing the protocol they wanted me to sign, which would set out the terms of our future collaboration. I got the very obvious impression that if I had signed such a document, as a few Western services did, it would have been used as part of a public relations campaign the KGB were engaged in to prove their democratic credentials to their own citizens. It was obvious from all the meetings we had that at that stage, not surprisingly, they had little idea where they or their country were going.

On the second day we had meetings in another building within the Lubyanka with what we took to be the intelligence services of the group of independent states which was just being formed. There was no clear explanation given at any stage of who anyone was or what they represented. When we asked how they intended to organise themselves and operate now the USSR was being abolished, they just did not know.

In the gaps between our meetings, we sightsaw in temperatures colder than I had experienced. We filed past Lenin, still lying in state in his mausoleum, paid our 'respects' at Stalin's memorial and went inside the marvellous cathedrals in the Kremlin, where religious services were again being held. While we did so, we were followed around closely by some part of the KGB, clearly not the A Team, as they were fairly conspicuous. 'Perhaps,' we thought, 'they are making sure no harm comes to us,' but I think it more likely that in that massive bureaucracy, people were merely doing what they always did.

One afternoon we drove out to Chekhov's house outside Moscow. It was clear that we had got there before the local surveillance officers expected us. When we arrived we were the only group present, but a few minutes after we had gone into the house, there was a sound of running feet and suddenly a panting lady joined us, trying, without much success, to appear like an interested tourist looking round the house. In the evening we attended the Bolshoi ballet, sitting in the front row of the stalls in gilt armchairs, reserved for guests of the KGB.

As well as the request for an end to harassment, I wanted to establish what scope there was for a reduction in the espionage attack by the KGB on this country. It seemed to me not unreasonable to expect that if the Cold War was over, there should be less aggressive spying. This was a matter for the First Chief Directorate, the foreign intelligence arm of the KGB, so on the second evening of our stay, the head of the First Chief Directorate, Mr Primakov, later Russia's Foreign Minister and briefly Prime Minister, invited me to a meeting to discuss that topic. My small party and I drove in the Ambassador's Rolls Royce to what seemed in the dark to be a rather leafy suburb, to what I took to be a KGB safe house.

It was difficult to avoid the feeling that we had somehow slipped into a James Bond film and that reality had become confused with fiction. It was a dark, cold and snowy night. As I was taking off my snow boots in the hall, Mr Primakov materialised on the stairs to welcome us. We went upstairs to a lamplit sitting room, furnished with heavy curtains and drapery behind which anything could have been lurking. We had a brief, rather cool discussion. I asserted that in the new post-Cold-War conditions, there was much scope for co-operation on security matters, like terrorism and serious organised crime. However, if there was to be true co-operation, the level of KGB espionage on the UK should be reduced. Mr Primakov made it very clear that in his view that was a ridiculous idea. I was barking up completely the wrong tree. Espionage would continue to be necessary, for the defence of Russia, and they would continue to engage in it at whatever level they chose.

It was clear that the conversation was not likely to be very fruitful, so we called it a day before too long and he disappeared behind the draperies. When I regaled the Ambassador later with my account of this meeting over dinner, another frisson passed through the waitresses.

We went once more to that house the next evening for a farewell dinner with our new KGB 'friends' and the Ambassador. Mr Primakov did not reappear, but a fair cross-section of the others we had met did. I sat next to the man who was heading the KGB's PR department, who advised me most sincerely, but surely with his tongue firmly in his cheek, of the need for intelligence services to be more frank and open. A couple of years later, one of his successors in that post was reported to have said, 'There are friendly states, but no friendly intelligence services,' a sentiment which characterised the nature of our 'cooperation' with the Russians for years to come.

Much champagne was drunk on that occasion and innumerable toasts, with many references to the number of women in top positions in the UK, along the lines of 'Your Queen is a lady, your Prime Minister is a lady and now in MI5, dear Mrs Rimington, we have a lady.' I made a speech in English, my colleague and the Ambassador made speeches in Russian. Everyone on the KGB side made a speech in one or the other language. The wheel had come full circle from the cocktail party in the Russian embassy in New Delhi in 1968.

If the level of later cooperation had matched the level of bonhomie that night, we would between us have cracked the problems of terrorism and organised crime for all time. Unfortunately it did not and it took several years for any real collaborative work to be done with the KGB's successor organisations, the SVR and FSB, and when I left MI5 in 1996, cooperation had still not reached any significant level. In the new democratic Russia many of its former officers have joined new élites of various kinds and are making reputations and fortunes for themselves.

That will surely always remain the most extraordinary period of my life. Up to that point, it was inconceivable that I would ever visit the former Soviet Union or the countries of Eastern Europe, let alone that I would meet our opposite numbers there. For someone in my position, travel there, even on holiday, was prohibited until the early 1990s. The nearest I had got was looking over the wall into East Berlin in the early 1980s, seeing the desperately run down blocks of flats on the other side, the spikes and dogs in no-man's land and the guards in the watch towers, and thinking how awful it was. Yet ten years later I met my German colleagues in East Germany at the hotel in Potsdam where Churchill, Truman and Stalin met in 1945 to organise the occupation of Germany.

I still find it hard to get used to being able to travel freely behind the former Iron Curtain. My feelings persisted into the summer of 1999 when I spent a holiday in Poland and found myself being punted on a raft down the river which forms the boundary between Poland and Slovakia. It was unimaginable, when I first worked in MI5 that that could ever happen, unless I had been under cover on some operation.

# 20

When I got back from Moscow in the middle of December 1991, there was still no news about who was to succeed as Director-General. Speculation was growing, as everyone knew that the then Director-General's sixtieth birthday was in February and that was when he would retire. But one day, shortly before Christmas, after a meeting, I was asked to stay behind and he said, 'Congratulations. You are to be the next Director-General.' By then, it did not come as a great surprise to me, but thinking about it now, it is, to say the least, rather strange that no-one had thought to ask me if I wanted the job. Whatever process had brought us to the point of my being told that I'd got it, this certainly was not open competition. No applications had been asked for and I had neither applied nor been interviewed, or not knowingly at any rate. What would have happened if at that late stage I had said I did not want it, I don't know. But I did not say that, though it soon became clear that what I was being offered was something of a poisoned chalice.

At the same time as I was told that I had got the job, I was also told, almost by the way, that the appointment and my name were to be publicly announced, and the announcement would be in the next few days. It did not take me a moment's thought to realise that there was likely to be a sensation. It was the first time the appointment of a Director-General of MI5 had ever been formally announced. What's more, I was a woman and the first woman to hold the post, and that alone was bound to cause a stir. When I had recovered from the shock, I said, 'I'm not sure this is a very good idea.' I rang up the Permanent Secretary at the Home Office, Clive Whitmore, to tell him so. But he seemed to think I was making a lot of fuss about nothing and anyway, 'The Prime Minister has agreed,' he said. It was clear that the powers-that-be in Whitehall had taken all the decisions and had signed up the ministers and trying to unscramble anything at that stage would not be a good way to start my period in office.

Unfortunately for me, they had been so focused on taking the decision that they seemed to have given no thought to the impact it would have, or how the inevitable furore should be handled. I asked what arrangements had been made to brief the press. Apart from the announcement, which was not to be accompanied by a photograph, for security reasons – the Provisional IRA were active in Great Britain at the time – nothing was laid on. It was not envisaged that I would give interviews and comment from me was to be restricted to a two-line statement of pleasure as part of the press statement.

Even I, inexperienced in the ways of the media as I was in those days, thought that was rather asking for trouble. The principle behind making the announcement was one I approved of. It was the logical outcome of the Act of Parliament which had been passed in 1989 to put the work of MI5 on a fully legal basis. The post of Director-General had thus become a statutory one and so, the thinking went, the public had a right to know who was holding the appointment. Truth to tell, there was also a good 'equality' angle to the story, which the government's advisers had not missed. But the way the announcement was handled was a disaster, though as it turned out not a PR disaster, but a personal disaster for the girls and for me. Though I think we managed to turn it later to an advantage for MI5, its effect on our personal lives was permanent.

I decided that Harriet and I would go away from home the day of the announcement and stay away for a couple of days to let the furore die down, as I rather naïvely thought. Sophie was away at university. So we parked the dog with the security staff at the office and went to stay in a hotel in Half Moon Street, just round the corner from our Curzon Street office. We watched the TV news that evening, as they tried with difficulty to cope with the government's announcement. They had no photograph, nobody knew anything about me and they didn't know who to ask for a comment. In the end John, who as Director-General of the Health and Safety Executive occasionally appeared on TV when there was a disaster of some kind, agreed to comment. He told an astonished nation that they were lucky to have someone like me to look after them.

It was an extraordinary experience. Having spent all my career being anonymous and trying to keep in the shadows, saying as little as possible about myself or my work, I suddenly saw myself plastered all over the TV and the newspapers. The appointment became an international story and our contacts all over the world were sending us articles from newspapers from Hong Kong to Buenos Aires.

Unfortunately, I had not managed to contact Sophie to tell her what was going to happen, and she later told me that she was sitting in her digs that evening with the TV on in the corner of the room when she suddenly realised that they were talking about her mother. She said, 'I thought you must have done something wrong, because I knew you were not supposed to talk about your work.'

After a couple of days, during which the story continued to run, Harriet and I got fed up with cowering in a hotel. It was too uncomfortable and we were worried about the dog, so we packed up, collected him from the office and went home.

The trouble was that Ian Fleming and John le Carré, depending on your taste in reading, had done their jobs too well. They had convinced us all that the world of intelligence was full of intrigue and excitement involving men like Alec Guinness or Sean Connery. When a middle-aged woman popped up as the only representative they had ever been told about, looking as someone said to me 'as if you could have been a teacher', no-one knew how to react. Their readers thought MI5 was just like the spy stories; that it had not changed since the days of Vernon Kell before the First World War. Not surprisingly, they did not know things had moved on. By saying nothing at all about ourselves and what we did, we had allowed the myths to continue. The semi-covert handling of the announcement of my appointment had merely made things worse.

But there's no doubt at all that most of the excitement was caused because I was a woman, not at all what the spy story writers had told them the head of MI5 was like. The press was all over the place on this angle. At first, the headline writers tried to get me back where women belonged, in front of the kitchen sink. 'Housewife Superspy', said one. 'Mother of Two Gets Tough with Terrorists' and 'Queen of All Our Secrets' were some other efforts. Then we had the love interest. 'MI5 Wife in Secret Love Split', proclaimed the *Sun*. When the girls heard this on the *Today Programme*, they rushed out to buy the *Sun*, behaving just as the headline writers intended, thinking they were about to learn something amazing and scandalous about my private life. How disappointed they were when they found that all it said was that John and I were living separately.

Then I became 'Woman of Mystery', and people were invited to phone in if they knew anything about me. Later on I became a hard-eyed manipulator of Whitehall. Even later still, I was repackaged as 'M', Ian Fleming's Head of MI6, and played by Judi Dench in several James Bond films. The Oxford Union asked whether Judi Dench and I would appear together to address them, I can't remember on what subject, but, as ever, the substance would have mattered less than the appearance.

That was the beginning of one of the most uncomfortable periods of my life. The press inevitably found out very quickly where we lived. Lots of people in Islington knew us. The children had lived there most of their lives and had many friends and we had lived in the same street for nearly ten years by then though the neighbours had no idea what I did for a living. They were very surprised indeed to find that the quiet lady who lived in the house up the road had turned out to be someone famous.

Photographers camped outside the house, determined to be the first to get a photograph. In the absence of anything better, the *New Statesman*'s blurry picture of me walking up the street in the black-and-white coat got lots of outings. The coat itself had long ago gone to a jumble sale but at that point it could probably have been sold for a large sum, the hype was so great. Before long the photographers succeeded, as inevitably they would, and several desperately unflattering pictures appeared of me unloading my shopping from the boot of the car on a Saturday morning, wearing tatty old jeans and a Barbour and looking as dishevelled as most people do in those circumstances. Some of the newspapers, entering into the spirit of things, printed their snatched photographs with a black band across my eyes, which made me look a lot worse. One of those pictures appeared in one newspaper to illustrate an article about British women in public life, asking why they always looked so much worse than the French. The French were represented by a photograph of Elizabeth Gigou, then the French Minister for Europe, leaning nonchalantly on her office desk, beautifully coiffured and wearing Dior, Yves St Laurent or something similar. That taught me what all women in public life have to learn fast, that you'd better look as good as you can, whatever you are doing, in case there is a telephoto lens about. Otherwise you risk looking ridiculous, and whatever institution or organisation you represent looking ridiculous with you. When I see Cherie Blair, slimmed down by remorseless exercise, stoically wearing her designer clothes on holiday, I know how she's feeling.

After that, it was open house for the press and in due course the *Sunday Times*, fresh from its triumphs over the revelations about the marriage of Prince Charles and Princess Diana, chose to do an in-depth enquiry into my private life. Using a private investigator, they obtained details of my bank account – they even put some small sum of money into it under a spoof Russian name which they claimed was that of the head of the KGB – a list of the numbers which had been called from my home phone, which branch of Marks & Spencer I bought my Saturday shopping from, and various other things. I was rung up on a Saturday morning by a *Sunday Times* reporter, who told me proudly that they had obtained the information by covertly following me around and that they were going to publish it, on the grounds that it was in the public interest to know how vulnerable I was to terrorists. He added that if they wanted to they could get details of my medical records too. I was not sure what the public interest angle in that would have been but at the time it did not seem worth complaining, though I did later make a complaint to the Data Protection Commissioner, without any noticeable result.

The situation became even more heated when a small conference centre at the top of our street took a booking for a conference with a security theme. It had nothing to do with us or with any part of government, but the Islington police judged that security protection was needed, and closed the road with barriers and police cars. Not surprisingly, the neighbours and the local paper, the *Islington Gazette*, connected this with my presence in the road, and everyone began to regard me as a thoroughly undesirable neighbour. People with whom I had been on nodding terms for several years, suddenly started to say things like: 'I wish you wouldn't go to work just as I'm taking my daughter to school,' with the clear implication that if someone tried to shoot me and missed, they might hit them. Another neighbour wrote to the *Islington Gazette* to complain that my helicopters, ceaselessly circling overhead were keeping his family awake. The helicopters were part of the policing of the Arsenal football matches and had nothing at all to do with me. I went to a meeting of the neighbours, to try to calm all this down, but I did not have much success, in fact I think I made matters worse. When one of the neighbours on the other side of the road let in a press photographer and a large picture of our house appeared prominently in the *Independent*, there seemed no option but to pack up and go. With the level of Provisional IRA activity at the time, it was clearly not safe for us to stay.

Having decided we had to move, the question became where

to? Though it had long been the custom for certain ministers and military Chiefs of Staff to have secure accommodation provided for them, no such arrangement had previously been necessary for the heads of the intelligence agencies, who had until then been protected by anonymity and lived the life of ordinary private citizens. This was a new situation, and it took many discussions in Whitehall and some time to sort out. But though it was uncomfortable for us, it was a bit of a joke for others that the Director-General was wandering around the town, living out of a suitcase, with nowhere to lay her head. In an article in the *Spectator* about my brush with the *Sunday Times*, Auberon Waugh told the probably apocryphal story of Roger Hollis, the Director-General under Macmillan, who lived in an unguarded house in Campden Hill Square in West London. At one point, according to Waugh, the Prime Minister's private secretary took to telephoning him at home and saying, 'Aha, villain! I know your secret,' then hanging up. The calls were eventually traced to the Prime Minister's office and there was a great stink.

After the *Independent* photograph, my security advisers wanted me to go quickly while they assessed the situation, so we – Harriet, dog and I – moved into a flat at the top of some offices we had in those days in Grosvenor Street. It was the most uncomfortable and unsuitable place to be for any length of time. To take the dog for a walk, you had to descend several floors in a lift and walk through miles of corridors, past the guards to the street. It was practically impossible for Harriet to invite her friends in to see her. We felt as though we were in prison. In the daytime, the dog had to come into my office, where the security guards looked after him. After a bit they made him an honorary member of their team, as Alpha 7, with a pass on his collar showing a photograph of a dog, which they had cut out from a magazine. He went on the regular security patrols with them and was rather proud of his new status, but he was the only member of the family who was enjoying himself.

As part of the process, we went to look at a Whitehall

building, where some of the ministers who need particular
security protection live. There was one vacant flat, which it
was thought for a time we might have. But when Harriet saw
that cavernous place, with its immense, high rooms filled with
the most decrepit, albeit antique, furniture, and realised that
all her friends would have to pass the scrutiny of armed
policemen to visit her, she burst into tears and said that
whatever happened she was not going to live there. Even
though I pointed out what a splendid view we would have of
the Trooping of the Colour, she was not to be persuaded. For
her it had all become just too much. I began to worry that if
this went on much longer, I was going to lose all my family.
That was a sacrifice I was not prepared to make, for my career
or the country. So we went back home to consider what to do
next.

It was tough for the girls. Harriet was just starting work for
her A Levels. She was often alone in the evenings during that
period when I was working late or away and she was scared
stiff. She told me later that she did not know what she was
more afraid of, the press at the front door or creakings on the
stairs in the evenings, which might be the IRA creeping in at
the back. It was not Harriet the journalists were after, so
though she had to run the gauntlet of the photographers, she
could go in and out of the front door with impunity. But while
we were sticking to the 'no photograph' policy, I had to slink
out through the gate at the back, into someone else's garden,
and reappear out of the side door of a house in the next street.
It was all very disruptive to my daily schedule.

Sophie had a rough time too, even though she was away. A
flat in north London where she sometimes stayed with friends
was raided by the anti-terrorist squad who were looking for a
group of IRA suspects in connection with the bomb at
Harrods. She was not there when the police broke in, but her
friends were spread-eagled on the floor and taken in for
questioning. Not surprisingly, they all thought she was to
blame and no-one believed the truth which was that the police
had raided the wrong address. That story, which featured

under prominent headlines in most newspapers (typically in the *Daily Star* as 'Spy Chief Girl in IRA Cop Gaffe') convinced some journalists that there was no smoke without fire and that if she was not a terrorist she must belong to an extreme left wing student group. They demanded interviews on the grounds that it was in the public interest. Some turned up unannounced at the door of a remote cottage where she was living at the time, when she was there alone, and without saying who they were, thrust cameras and a microphone into her face, confusing and terrifying her.

The advice continued to be that we should move, and that advice became more urgent when some men who were arrested in connection with one of the bombing raids in London proved to have a newspaper cutting which made it clear where we lived. So we put the house on the market. Clearly we were never going to be able to live there again. We went underground, an ironic outcome of greater openness. Our new covert life was not easy, particularly for the girls. It is difficult to lead a normal young life if you have to be careful all the time whom you invite to the house, and give your telephone number to. Their particular worry centred on their car. It was registered and insured in another name, and they were always worried in case they were stopped by the police or had an accident. They used to say before they went out, 'Now just tell me again, Mum, who am I?'

The whole of my time as Director-General was dogged by our unsettled living arrangements, because even when it was agreed where we should live, it was a place that needed a lot of work to make it habitable. Harriet and I camped there surrounded by builders for more than a year. Our first Christmas dinner there, nearly two years after I took up the job, was held in a room furnished with garden chairs and lit only by candles in bottles.

I bought another house for my retirement, but unfortunately I was just beginning to move myself in, during the winter before I retired, when something froze in the roof over a long weekend when I was away, and the next thing I knew was that all the ceilings had collapsed and the place was a total wreck. The massive damage was only discovered when a neighbour rang the estate agent who had sold me the property, and through a circuitous route the news came into my office that water could be heard running in my house. I was in a meeting with the Prime Minister at the time, introducing my successor, so a colleague went to investigate. When he opened the door, water was pouring down the stairs and out of every door frame and light fitting, there was about a foot of water in the basement and all the carpets were squelching. They hardly dared tell me what had happened, and I was forbidden to go and look, until pumping and debris-clearing operations had finished. All that took more than a year to sort out. So my last few months as Director-General, just like my first years, were overshadowed by living problems.

The initial excitement of the announcement of my appointment took a long time to die down. More than a year after I was appointed things were still quite hysterical. I was invited to one of HM The Queen's regular lunches for people in public life. There were a number of famous people there, including the then manager of the England football team, Graham Taylor, and Linford Christie. However, the press got wind that I was there, and assembled at the gates of Buckingham Palace to take my photograph as I left. At the time, on the advice of my security advisers, we were still pursuing the 'no photograph' policy, so with the connivance of the Royal Household, I slunk out ignominiously through the Royal Mews after lunch was over. But that did not put the reporters off, and we had, 'Oh to be a Fly with the Spy at the Palace', covering an article about what I might have said to my fellow guests.

For the first few years I was bombarded with requests to make public appearances of various kinds, all of which were most unsuitable for a public servant and a successor of Vernon Kell. By every post came invitations – would I appear on *Wogan* or the *Clive Anderson Show* or *Have I Got News for You?* Would I be interviewed by *Vogue*, or be a guest on

*Masterchef* or sit on the sofa with Richard and Judy? I had no illusions that most of it was because I was a woman, and the press still liked to play to what it perceived as the sexism of its readers. None of the male Permanent Secretaries in Whitehall was asked to do any of it and nor did I take up the invitations.

There is no doubt that our first steps into openness could easily have been better handled. But there's also no doubt that there would have been far less fuss had I been a man. When later on the names of the heads of the other two intelligence agencies, MI6 and GCHQ, were publicly announced, there was hardly a ripple, though by then some of the lessons of handling such announcements had been learned. When I retired and my successor was named, we had become much more adept at these things and as he was a man and the announcement was expected, thankfully he had none of the same furore to put up with.

In spite of the media reaction, to my colleagues and the intelligence community, in this country and abroad, my appointment came as no particular surprise. Nearly half the staff of MI5 was female by that time and although many of them still worked as clerks and secretaries, there was also a fair percentage of women in the intelligence officer and other professional grades, though they were not as well represented at the top as they will be in the near future. I have made fun of some of my male colleagues of the '70s, describing them as old-fashioned and traditional in their attitudes, but whatever criticisms can be laid at the door of some of them, I had been allowed to progress up the hierarchy without ever feeling that to get on I had to pretend to be or to think exactly like them. Whatever popular fiction would have us believe, there is no typical MI5 officer, no overpowering 'house style', to which everyone is required to conform. On the contrary, diversity, individuality and even eccentricity have always been tolerated, provided that there was a clear willingness to work within the operational and legal rules.

By the time I became Director-General, MI5 had been through a series of huge institutional shocks, bringing about big changes in its culture, the type of people it employed and the way it managed its resources, both human and financial. Even our task was changing. As we moved away from the priorities of the Cold War and with legislation and oversight, we began to emerge uneasily from behind the veil of secrecy which had hidden us for most of my working life. We had coped with all this change with what I think in retrospect was quite surprising sang-froid, calmly getting on with the task in hand. But there was a strong sense that though we had moved on a long way, we had not yet arrived anywhere. As Director-General I had been turned into a public figure; we were about to move to a new high-profile building and to take on, quite publicly, major new terrorism responsibilities. In marketing jargon, where should we position ourselves in this new world order? Who were we now? My role would be to find an answer to that question. The chaotic start to my period as Director-General made this urgent both professionally and privately.

As Director-General my approach was collegiate, a style which I found worked well, although, as I have learned in the last few years, it is scorned by many of our business leaders. It is a style which comes more naturally to women, who tend on the whole to feel more able than many successful men to look for and create consensus, and more inclined to ask for and listen to advice. The Board of Directors became a group of equals where our strategies and policies were discussed, a far cry from the Directors' meetings I had attended some years before. I encouraged my Directors to behave corporately and not as barons each representing their own fiefdoms, though they needed little encouragement on this as they all had views on the issues and were anxious to air them. We also listened to the advice and experience of people from various walks of life outside the public service; I was determined not to fall into the mistake of earlier days in allowing ourselves to be cut off from the outside world.

We went off to the country for the first ever Board 'Awayday', and over a weekend we did our SWOT analysis (Strengths, Weaknesses, Opportunities and Threats) and sang songs round the piano in the evenings. The management gurus would have been proud of us. Many things emerged from that occasion and its successors, which produced a strategic agenda. But the one thing that emerged most clearly, not least as a result of the intense interest of the press in my appointment and the nonsense that many of them wrote, was the huge gap between the perception of MI5 and the reality.

As long as I could remember, we had suffered from ill-informed and often hostile comments on our affairs. It was in large part our own fault because we had never commented and never sought to put the record straight, though some of us had long thought that we should, and there's no doubt that silence had harmed our reputation and with it, to some extent, our effectiveness. External perceptions mattered more than they had in the days of the Cold War. Then secrecy was more important than public understanding. Now the balance had changed. As MI5 moved more and more into work against terrorism, it was inevitable that more of its activities and investigations would come to public attention, whether we liked it or not, if only through trials in the courts. It was important that juries and judges believed the evidence our officers would give. If their entire knowledge of MI5 was based on James Bond films or John le Carré novels, or even on the sort of reporting which was at that time common in the press, they might think not a word we said could be trusted.

In any case it was undermining for the morale of the staff, who were being called on to work hard in sometimes dangerous circumstances, to see misleading and silly stories about what they were supposedly doing continually appearing in the newspapers. I had got fed up with the 'MI5 Blunders' headline, which seemed to be permanently made up and ready for use above any story in which the intelligence services figured. So the task was to get rid of that headline once and for all and to raise the level of debate about security matters. It was a mission to inform, using my high public profile as a way of doing it.

Clearly, an effective intelligence service cannot be entirely open about itself. Details of specific operations, techniques, the names of agents must always remain secret. But there is much that can and should be aired about the need for secret organisations in a democracy and how they should be controlled. There were risks, and many people ready to warn of them, not least some members of the Service who feared that greater openness would raise the profile and therefore the risks of terrorist attack. And they had a valid point. It was a question of balancing the risks and the rewards. 'It will be a slippery slope,' they said. 'You may think you can set boundaries on what you will say, but the press will push remorselessly and you'll find yourselves saying more and more.' 'A wise virgin keeps her veils,' Simon Jenkins warned us in *The Times*.

I felt entirely confident about the story we had to tell and reasonably confident that we could stick to the boundaries we had set ourselves. We were an effective, well run, legally based and overseen organisation, of which the country could and should be proud. Like any organisation, we would not always get everything right, but when we did not, we were prepared to explain ourselves. We listened to the warnings, but decided that an even wiser virgin knows exactly how many veils she can cast off while remaining safe.

So an openness programme was drawn up in the hope of getting us off the back foot and into the lead. We did not take advice from PR consultants, but worked it out for ourselves. The various steps were obvious, though they were not achieved without a considerable amount of angst elsewhere in the system. A first step was to publish a booklet about MI5, putting some facts into the public domain for the first time. It is now in its third edition. The process of getting the first edition off the stocks would have made a good episode of *Yes Minister*. After much debate about the principle and the content – every word of the draft text was scrutinised in case it said something that somebody might regret at some time in the future – Whitehall reluctantly acquiesced and the Home Office even agreed that when it was published, I should present it to the media at a launch conference at the Home Office.

The project had been kept a close secret. The journalists were summoned to the Home Office for an undisclosed announcement. When they found out, they seemed both amazed at what was happening and bemused by it. Though the launch looked like a press conference, and I answered all the questions, the assembled journalists were told by the Home Office that they must not say in their newspapers who had briefed them. The journalists all knew who I was and telling them that they could not say so introduced an unnecessarily farcical element into the proceedings. It was not a very auspicious beginning to our openness programme, though the booklet was well received.

That extraordinary ruling resulted from the nightmare in Whitehall at the time that if they did not keep a very close rein on me, I would end up answering questions about security policy and usurping the Home Secretary's role. Despite the anxiety about any public appearances I made, I was perfectly clear where my role ended and the Home Secretary's began. If any proposal for a public appearance was put to the Home Office for clearance, a major lecture for example, the answer would come back, usually after much correspondence had been exchanged and weeks had gone by, 'The Home Secretary agrees, provided that you don't answer questions.' What terrible faux pas they expected me to commit in the course of answering questions I never discovered, and of course I gave many talks on less formal occasions, which were not cleared, when I always answered questions. It was illogical and a pity because it gave the impression that I was only prepared to talk to a prepared text.

The afternoon of the booklet launch I took a photocall at the Home Office with Michael Howard, then Home Secretary, and for the first time authorised pictures appeared in the newspapers. The photographs were accompanied by much comment about my personal appearance and what I was wearing, but the comment I enjoyed most was a letter in the

*Spectator* from someone who wrote to say that as a result of disclosures made in the name of 'openness', he found himself fancying the head of MI5.

From then on my life became an open secret. Though for security we still lived under cover and I used a false name in many everyday situations, I began to be recognised in the street and, like many women in public life, I also acquired my quota of telephone and letter stalkers, some of whom are still with me. Casual social contact and even transactions in shops required a snap decision about whether I should give my real name or an alias. If one or other of the girls was with me that decision obviously covered them too, something they found uncomfortable and annoying. They hated the level of intrusion of work into our private lives, caused by the security requirement.

After the booklet launch, I began to accept invitations to lunch with the media, and I realised that often on those occasions the hosts were just as apprehensive as I was. An early occasion was at ITN and prominent among the guests was Jon Snow. He proceeded to interview me over the lunch table as if I had been on *Channel 4 News*; he seemed amazed that I was a normal person and even said that he had expected me to be more like Rosa Kleb, the KGB officer in *From Russia With Love* who attacks James Bond with the knives in her boots. I went again to ITN later to do an off-the-record question and answer session over lunch and when I finally retired, they presented me with a game they had created, based on Monopoly, which was called 'MI7 – The Game for MI5 Chiefs'. The Angel Islington, Mayfair and the other properties around the board had been replaced with 'Bugging Kit', 'False Passport', 'Spy Satellite' and other tools of the trade. You lost £40 if you left your unlocked briefcase on ITN's newsdesk, though you won £100 when *Channel 4 News* alleged that a certain MP was a KGB agent. I played 'MI7' with some colleagues just before I retired and we imagined the headlines, 'MI5 Board of Directors Plays ITN's Game'.

When at the end of 1993 I was asked to do the next

Dimbleby Lecture on BBC TV, it seemed to fit perfectly into the strategy we had adopted. It would be a high-profile, dignified opportunity to put some basic facts on the record and to raise some issues which might generate a decent debate, for example how security services should be controlled in a democracy and how far it is appropriate for the state to intrude on the privacy of the few to protect the safety of the many. These were issues about which many people had opinions, but so far because of our own secrecy the debate had not been well informed. The title 'Security and Democracy. Is there a conflict?' seemed appropriate. People would be able to see me, hear me speak and they could form their own judgement of what I said. What's more, I would not be offending against the Home Office restriction on my answering questions.

But when I asked for agreement to do the lecture, all the same anxieties that had surrounded the booklet were raised again. After a prolonged period of gestation and much consultation, the answer came from Whitehall that ministers had agreed. But when we had drafted the text, everyone with any angle on anything I wanted to say had to be consulted and every word was picked over and brooded on. At one stage I feared that I would end up by merely opening and shutting my mouth and saying nothing at all. I had a meeting with the then head of the Foreign Office, David Gillmore, who appeared to have been briefed by his officials to object to practically everything about any foreign country, presumably in case someone should be upset. In the end, Robin Butler, the Cabinet Secretary, managed to ensure that I could say everything I wanted to say.

Appearing on TV to talk about MI5 was quite a dramatic thing to do, and I was extremely nervous. But I felt that it was a seminal occasion in terms of our relationship with the British public. On the whole I was pleased with the reaction. It was not all favourable of course, but some of it, at least, was serious. *The Times* published the text of the lecture in full and other papers and magazines printed articles discussing the issues. However, inevitably, one or two journalists wrote about my clothes and one wrote that I had very big ears, and that these must be useful for covert communications.

Our greater openness with the press and the public eventually attracted the attention of Parliament. Under the 1989 Security Service Act, which provided legal oversight of the Service's work, no provision had been made for any form of direct parliamentary scrutiny. It was the Home Secretary who answered to Parliament for our activities. This was always seen as likely to change in time, but ministers of the day were not enthusiasts for a parliamentary committee, which would inevitably require their attendance as well as ours to answer questions. However, certain members of the Home Affairs Select Committee were eager to add the Security Service to the scope of their scrutiny. Barbara Roche, at the time a member at the Home Affairs Select Committee, hearing that I had been to lunch with various newspapers, invited me to have lunch with her at the House of Commons. This invitation somehow got into the public domain, and had I accepted, which I was rather keen to do, the occasion would have risked becoming a political statement about parliamentary oversight. Instead, it was decided that the Home Affairs Select Committee could come to our office in Gower Street for a briefing and lunch. However, it was made clear that this did not imply an acceptance on the part of the government of any jurisdiction by the Committee over the Service.

Members of the Committee accepted the invitation in that spirit, and agreed among themselves that they would keep the details of the briefing confidential. However, the press soon got wind that they were coming, and a Keystone Cops situation developed, as the cars we had sent to the House of Commons to bring the Committee to our offices in Gower Street were pursued by photographers and reporters on motor bikes. Apparently, we had not told the Committee members where they were going, not through any wish to keep it a secret, but merely because it had not occurred to us as they were being driven there, which made it seem all the more mysterious.

Meanwhile, in the calm of my office I knew nothing of the excitement down at the House of Commons, until a rather breathless and shaken Committee arrived. Entering into the spirit of the occasion, our dining-room cook had put 'Reform cutlets' on the menu. The menu card was purloined by one of our guests, Chris Mullin I think, and in the absence of hard information about the content of the meeting, the menu became news and was reported in various newspapers and a satirical version of it later appeared in *Private Eye*. Kenneth Clarke complained to me later that Reform cutlets were very old-fashioned – the joke had apparently passed him by.

At the time, I had on the wall of my office a framed quotation from Edmund Burke, which I had inherited from one of my predecessors. It read: 'Those who would carry on great public schemes must be proof against the most fatiguing delays, the most mortifying disappointments, the most shocking insults and worst of all the presumptuous judgement of the ignorant upon their designs.' I was rather embarrassed about this and hoped no one would notice it, but as luck would have it, Chris Mullin did, and later sent a message asking for the wording. I did not give it to him, as I suspected it would only turn up later in some sardonic article. Instead, I removed it.

Though in many ways that was a bizarre occasion, it was also a historic one, in that it marked the first formal direct contact MI5 had with Parliament, other than with ministers or shadow ministers. The Home Affairs Select Committee did not in the end acquire oversight responsibility for MI5. In 1994, the Intelligence Services Act, which provided a legal status for our two sister services, SIS and GCHQ, brought in a new parliamentary oversight committee, the Intelligence and Security Committee, to take on the parliamentary oversight function for all three services.

I became Director-General in February 1992. On 9 April the general election was called. In the period before a general election, the heads of departments customarily offer a briefing to shadow ministers. The odds were on Labour winning the 1992 election and it seemed likely that Roy Hattersley would become Home Secretary and my boss, so I invited him to visit us. I prepared carefully for his visit, conscious that it was he who had said of us in parliament during the debate on the 1989 Security Service Bill, that we were the worst security service in the world. I was determined that we should present the friendly, open and relaxed face, which was actually us and not appear defensive in the face of his criticism. I had the office specially polished up and acquired some potted plants to make it look, I hoped, warm and welcoming. I even removed a sword which had been presented to my predecessor by one of the East European security services at the end of the Cold War, because I thought it looked too militaristic. After all the trouble I took to create the right impression, I was mortified to hear him talking about the occasion in a quiz show on the BBC recently; the best he could do was to describe my office as gloomy. But that relationship was not to be. Labour did not win the election and Kenneth Clarke became Home Secretary.

Dealing with the politics at home and relationships abroad took a good deal of my time. I have mentioned the group of European Heads of Service but there was another group to which we belonged which met much less frequently but was altogether more exotic. That was the Heads of Commonwealth Security Services. The year in which I became Director-General it met in Kampala. The Ugandans looked after us superbly, but a detectable tremor went through the assembled company on the first night when at the welcoming cocktail party in the hotel grounds, we were told that the pleasant grassy hollow where we were taking our drinks was the former killing field where Idi Amin's men had slaughtered their opponents before throwing them into the river. The long-legged Maribou Storks, which perched precariously on all the trees around, watching us in a menacing way, had apparently first arrived in the centre of town in those days, attracted by the rotting corpses. The delegates were housed in two separate hotels and I was pleased to be told that it was the other one, not the one I was staying in, that was Idi Amin's HQ. However, one of our fellow delegates was effectively deprived of a sound night's sleep for the duration of the conference, when he realised that the room we were being told of, where opponents of the regime had been tortured before being killed, was the very same room he had been allocated.

The Commonwealth Security Conferences – I attended two during my time as Director-General – were characterised by the very different security concerns of the delegates. At that first one, there was earnest discussion of a topic close to the hearts of some of our African colleagues, how to convince governments that there should be continuity of the security service when the government changed – in other words how to prevent the service becoming the tool of the party in power – an issue which mercifully I had never had to contend with. At the second such conference I attended, the gap was even wider. When each country was asked to say what was their top priority security concern, I said, 'Terrorism', and the Namibian delegate said, 'Cattle rustling'.

Alongside all the political activity and foreign liaison, we had to get on with what we were there to do – the security intelligence work. The major task during my first year as Director-General was to implement the decision that had by then been taken that we should take over lead responsibility for intelligence work against Irish republican terrorism on the mainland of Great Britain from the Metropolitan Police Special Branch. As soon as we had finalised the details with the Metropolitan Police, which took some time, we needed to move quickly and start to try to make a difference to the level of intelligence available, so that any terrorist attacks might be thwarted. Thanks to the Treasury's attentions, and our own analysis over the preceding few years, we had a very good idea of where our resources and costs lay, which was a great help when almost overnight we had to redirect about 25% of our effort away from the targets of the Cold War and into supplementing our existing counter-terrorist effort. Making such a change is not as radical as it may sound. The fundamentals of intelligence work are the same whether you are working against terrorists or spies. The intelligence tools are the same, the assessment skills are the same, but clearly, there is much to be learned about any new intelligence target, although we already had considerable experience working against this one in both Northern Ireland and continental Europe.

Working extremely closely with the Metropolitan Police Special Branch, in circumstances where not all of them were pleased with the change of responsibilities, was not always easy. At the beginning, we sent some of our staff down to Scotland Yard to sit in with some police teams. They were mostly female, not because of any desire to make a sexist point, but because they were the people who had been doing similar work in the Service and had the best background to make a good contribution. They got some first-hand experience of how women were treated in the police. There were small harassments of various kinds and one report came back that one of our officers found a pile of dirty washing on her desk one day, with the instruction that she was to wash it. I heard that she threw it out of the window, and was not harassed again.

The middle of a bombing campaign in Great Britain was not the best time to take on this new work and inevitably it put us in a very high-profile position. By its nature, intelligence, especially on such a well-trained, well-equipped and secure organisation as the Provisional IRA is hard to come by. In his *Autobiography* John Major has set out in detail the complex policy he was pursuing during these years to try to bring peace to Northern Ireland. Our job, with our other intelligence and police colleagues, was to try to ensure that he and his advisers had the best possible supply of intelligence to help them weave their way through the complexities. This meant that from time to time I brought him very unwelcome news about operations being planned or imminent, which sometimes we did not have enough intelligence to be sure of preventing. On such occasions he would look grave and say, 'I'm relying on you,

Stella,' and I would go back to my colleagues and say, 'The Prime Minister is relying on us,' to which they would reply, 'Gosh, thanks,' as they went off to do their job.

During all that period I never felt that the political agenda in any way affected what I could or could not report. No-one ever tried to put any pressure on me to report only what they wanted to hear, or to slant intelligence briefings to fit the political agenda. In fact the only time in my whole career when I ever felt that sort of pressure was in my dealings with the Americans over Northern Ireland, though the FBI were always immensely cooperative and helpful, and responded magnificently to our many requests for operational assistance. But just before I retired, I was given a very hostile grilling in Washington by the then President's national security team, who clearly had their own view of the rights and wrongs of the situation in the island of Ireland, their own sources of information, and their own political agenda. They did not wish to hear anything from me which did not fit with it and I had no confidence in what they would do with anything I told them. It was a novel, unwelcome and scary experience for me.

In all my dealings with John Major I never felt that there was any chance that he would blame us if we were unable to prevent a terrorist attack. He understood that there is no such thing as 100% intelligence or security and provided we showed professionalism, the right skills, the right strategies, and had not made some stupid mistake, he would back us up. This support was very important. When intelligence operations are successful and prevent a terrorist incident, no-one knows anything about it. It is very rare in those circumstances for anything to be said in public. The priority is to preserve the sources of intelligence. However, when intelligence fails to prevent an incident and a bomb does go off, there is a very high-profile disaster for all to see. That will inevitably happen from time to time and during those first few years we failed to prevent an attack on the City of London, the bombing in Docklands with which the Provisional IRA signalled the end of its ceasefire in 1996, and the bombing of the centre of

Manchester later in that year. I was in New Zealand, attending a conference, when the Provisional IRA detonated its Docklands bomb. I was at Auckland airport in February 1996, just setting off for a weekend break in the Bay of Islands to which I was greatly looking forward, when news of the Docklands bomb and the IRA's announcement that its cease-fire was over, came over the mobile phone. I went straight from Auckland airport to the local office of the New Zealand Security Service and sat there with my New Zealand colleagues in a state of shock watching the destruction and chaos in London on CNN, waiting to hear when I could catch a plane back to London. I set off home that evening, on one of the gloomiest journeys of my life, a journey that seemed to go on for ever. I went straight to a meeting in Michael Howard's office to review the situation, not that there was much for us to say at that point.

Staff morale can be quite fragile in circumstances where there can be no public praise for success, when a planned terrorist incident does not take place, but failure is there for all to see, in glass-covered streets and ruined buildings, and sometimes also maimed and dead people. We took it hard when we failed, even though we did not expect always to succeed. But the readiness of the Prime Minister to come and thank the staff when they had some success known only to a very few was very reinforcing.

When I first went to call on John Major to be introduced by my predecessor, he saw us in a sitting room, which at the time he used as a small meeting room, but he seemed un-comfortable there and complained rather grumpily that it smelled. Whatever was causing the smell was apparently incurable, as after that when I went to call on him he was always in the Cabinet Room, sitting at the long table and looking rather lonely. Not surprisingly, he often seemed rather gloomy, and I rarely brought him good news. But he used to enjoy pulling my leg, which he succeeded in doing quite well when I was new. He once asked me with great solemnity how many telephone interceptions we were doing without a warrant. I was rocked back at the idea that the Prime Minister should for a moment think that his Security Service was intercepting telephones without a warrant. Or, on the other hand, that if I were the sort of person who would lead an organisation that broke the law, I would calmly tell him about it when he asked. But when I got to know him better, I realised that he liked to ask this sort of question just to see how I would react. In similar vein, he once asked me solemnly which Members of Parliament we were investigating. By then I knew him better and I knew what he was up to. He knew perfectly well that if I had ever thought that there was a need to investigate any, he would have been the first to know about it.

Much later, as things began to get very difficult with his Europhobe MPs, he used to ask wistfully whether I had any techniques for dealing with dissidents that I could pass on. By then I felt quite sorry for him and I would come back thankful that I was leading a team of colleagues who were supportive, who broadly thought the same way about the issues we were dealing with and were united about the way to go about tackling them. He on the other hand seemed isolated, surrounded by people who were looking primarily to their own self interest, and who even if they were broadly supporters could not be relied on not to undermine him behind his back. I was profoundly thankful that I was not in politics. But in spite of it all he still kept his sense of humour and just before I left he got me to join in playing a joke on Marmaduke Hussey, then Chairman of the BBC. I was at No. 10 for one of our regular briefing meetings; the Prime Minister's next appointment was with Duke Hussey. A few days earlier the BBC had broadcast a leaked document, which the government regarded as damaging and they were rather put out. The Chairman had been called in to account for the BBC's actions. 'Let's give him a shock,' said the Prime Minister. 'You stay on and be in the room when he comes in. Then he'll think he's really in trouble.' So, when we came to the end of our meeting, Alex Allen, John Major's Private Secretary at the time, showed in Duke Hussey.

On seeing me, perfectly on cue, Duke said, 'My God, it's not that bad is it?' The Prime Minister roared with laughter and I left them to it.

However, my observation of government ministers was that they were chronically exhausted. This showed more and more as the parliamentary term wore on. I don't think I am any more boring than other people, so perhaps it was because many of my meetings with ministers were to brief them, rather than to ask them to take decisions, that I frequently found myself talking to a zombie-like figure, slumped in his chair, with drooping eyelids and a whey-coloured face. Michael Howard's way of dealing with his lack of sleep was to rock and lurch in his chair, which was slightly disconcerting until you realised what he was doing. John Major once admitted during a briefing meeting that he just could not keep awake and I left. Douglas Hurd used to sink far down into his chair and hood his eyes so you could not tell whether he was awake or asleep.

The middle of my time as Director-General was over-shadowed by a great tragedy for the whole intelligence community. On 2 June 1994 I had just got home from work at about 7 p.m. and was thinking about telephoning my brother to wish him a happy birthday when the phone in the kitchen rang. It was the Duty Officer. He said, 'There's some bad news.' That is a phrase I hate. All sorts of possibilities went through my head. Had one of the girls had an accident? Had a mortar bomb blown up Whitehall again?

It was bad. A helicopter was missing on its way from Northern Ireland to Scotland. It seemed likely, said the Duty Officer, that it was the Chinook carrying colleagues who were working in Northern Ireland, with RUC and Army personnel, on their way to their annual conference. Efforts were being made to find out whether it was indeed that helicopter and if so, precisely who was on board, but things looked grim. Meanwhile the television was carrying the story and the wives and families of those who might be involved were ringing up desperately for news.

A dreadful evening began. It took some hours to confirm that it was the Chinook and that everyone on board was dead. The helicopter had come down on a remote headland on the Mull of Kintyre, near the lighthouse, but miles from anywhere else. It was a dark, misty night and pouring with rain. I spoke on the telephone to the wives of some of those who had been lost, but what comfort could I give? A couple of days later I went over to Northern Ireland to call on the bereaved. It was a terrible time. The families were heartbroken and the colleagues of those who had died were stunned with grief. We could do no more than sit silently with each other. I felt both grief and responsibility, as the leader of the organisation which had unwittingly sent them to their death.

Then began a dreadful period of weeks of funerals. I will never forget the funeral of the Head of Special Branch of the RUC, a great colleague of my Service and a dedicated police officer. It took place in Newtownards, on a dark, rainy Northern Ireland day. After the service the mourners lined up behind the coffin to walk to the graveyard, as is the custom in Northern Ireland. The uniformed officers of the RUC and the military walked first in the cortège, behind the coffin, and then came the civilians. I walked behind an RUC officer and I watched the rain pour off his cap and down the back of his uniform jacket in big drops. What a terrible day.

Then there were the funerals of our own staff, some of them men with a lifetime of public service behind them, others young men with promising futures and young wives and families. Their families had not known exactly what their husbands, fathers, sons or brothers did but they had trusted us to look after them. And we had not done so. It was a very bad feeling, which I will never truly get over.

I retired from MI5 in April 1996 after twenty-seven years as a member and just over four years as Director-General. I left a very different organisation from the one I joined as a Junior Assistant Officer in 1969. I started out in a fairly lighthearted spirit, enjoying what I saw as the eccentricity of it all and thinking it might be fun. Before long, it became much more serious and I grew to be convinced of the fundamental importance of the job we were trying to do and involved intellectually in tackling some of the difficult issues that the doing of it raised in a democracy. I lived through some big institutional shocks and helped to manage the consequent changes; the four years I was Director-General saw as much change as any previous period. By the time I left in 1996, I was confident that anyone joining would feel that they had become part of a modern, accountable and respected organisation, clear about its role and responsibilities and professionally competent to carry them out with probity, imagination and drive. I felt proud of the contribution I had made to achieving that.

# POSTSCRIPT

Sixty is the magic age for retirement in the public service, but as I had been given a four-year appointment as Director-General, I was nearly sixty-one when I left MI5. I have met many people whose retirement is all planned out well in advance – they have their house, their garden, their building project or their DIY tasks all lined up and their dream cruise ready booked. My retirement did not begin well. When I came home on my final day, with a box full of junk from my office and a bunch of flowers from my colleagues, I was taken aback when Harriet said, 'Well is that it then?' and burst into tears. I was surprised she was so upset, but it was because her whole life for many years had been so affected by my job – where and how we lived, her relationships with her friends, her own sense of danger and insecurity – that she could not believe that it could all end in what seemed to her such an anticlimax. If anyone deserved a medal from a grateful State, she did.

But of course it hadn't ended. Because my flooded house was still in ruins and my successor needed to move into the official premises, Harriet, the dog and I moved into a sort of holding bay, a small flat beneath one of the Service's operational properties. There we lived for nearly a year, surrounded by most of our possessions in large cardboard boxes and tea chests. Unfortunately for me, the operational task they were performing in the upstairs flat was being done twenty-four hours a day, directly above my bedroom, and it seemed to involve constant walking about on very creaky floors. What's more, they changed shifts at 6 a.m. I learned something I had not until then appreciated, that MI5 officers are particularly cheerful in the early morning. The shift changes were accompanied by loud greetings and the sound of the kettle being put on. The dog, who had never learned great discretion, in spite of his time as an assistant to the security officers, used to bark very loudly to accompany the shift change, so my early months of retirement were not nearly so restful as I had hoped.

As my retirement date had drawn near, I had begun to wonder how I was going to keep myself amused. I did not see myself being comfortable sitting knitting in a rocking chair after all I had seen and done. My first idea was that I might take a leaf out of the book of the Foreign Office who seemed particularly good at getting their ex-Ambassadors berths as Masters of Oxford and Cambridge colleges and try for such a post. While I was thinking about it, a small advertisement appeared in a Sunday newspaper, seeking applications for the Mastership of Emmanuel College, Cambridge, to succeed Lord St John of Fawsley. I put in an application though I am sure now that the advertisement was not expected to produce serious applicants. Indeed, the selection process had hardly begun before it became clear that a majority of the Fellows had already decided to elect one of their own number. They wanted a counterbalance to what they saw as the flamboyant style of Lord St John's Mastership, which, as they described it to me, had been characterised by Royal visits and a building and restoration programme of Renaissance proportions, though accompanied, as they admitted, by formidable fund-raising.

Nonetheless, I decided, partly for interest's sake, to go through the selection process. The whole procedure had a rather mediaeval touch, consisting as it did of a series of 'trials'. First there was trial by dinner. After dinner at High Table, one was required to converse in the Common Room with Fellows, moving from group to group so they could sum you up. It was quite a bizarre occasion. The Fellows, a few in suits or sports jackets but most in something very much scruffier – jeans and pullovers or similar – all covered by the ritual black gown, looked out of place and uneasy as they sat with their port in an 18th-century panelled room, which had been painted in bright, flat designer colours chosen by the outgoing Master. He had had most of the public rooms of the College and the Master's Lodge decorated in the same style. Indeed, the Master's Lodge had had the unusual honour for a college building of being featured in *Homes and Gardens*.

'Do you like it?' I asked innocently looking round the room. 'No,' they said firmly, and went on to complain that they had been unable to do anything in the face of Lord St John's determination to smarten them up. It was a complaint which sat oddly with what I had been told of the governance structure of the College, namely that no decisions at all could be taken except by agreement of all the seventy or so Fellows. Lord St John had clearly found ways of getting round that.

Then there was trial by presentation. The idea of this was that candidates, having met the Fellows at dinner and having been indoctrinated into the financial accounts, would make a speech to the assembled company, setting out what they would do if they became Master. Although, as I now know, this sort of event is normal in the selection process for the Heads of Colleges, it seemed very odd to me to be required to present one's plans before one had even arrived. True to form, I told them I thought they were old-fashioned and needed a bit of modern management, which was clearly not what they wanted to hear. The internal candidate was duly elected, as had, of course, always been intended.

The whole process was interspersed, in the case of my candidacy, by leaks to the press about my progress through the trials, and comments, made no doubt by supporters of other candidates, about the immense levels of security it was assumed my presence would require. Security, it was said, would be of so intrusive a nature that academic life would become impossible. When, at an advanced stage of the selection process, the Provisional IRA let off a huge lorry bomb in Docklands, marking the end of the particular cease-fire they were engaged on at the time, those against my candidacy claimed justification. Not for the first time the

Provisionals had intervened in my affairs and I was never to find out what made the academic world tick.

Having failed in that enterprise, I began to receive enquiries about joining the Boards of some companies as a Non-Executive Director, as well as many enquiries from charitable organisations. I eventually took up some of these and thus began my third career, as a portfolio person.

In many ways this was to be the most surprising part of my life. Having spent the last few years of my career in the Security Service pursuing an 'openness programme', attempting to explain who we were and what we did, and above all what we did not do, I was surprised at how few of those people I now encountered had absorbed any of the messages I thought we had been giving out loud and clear. Most were confused about the difference between MI5 and MI6, which I suppose was not all that surprising. But I was amazed by how many regarded me with caution and concern on the assumption that I must know everything about everybody's private life.

This attitude was typified for me by an episode which occurred just after I retired, and which I mentioned in an article I wrote shortly afterwards in *The Times*. I went to a dinner given by the De La Rue Company for the London diplomatic corps. Much of the business community was there. I was at the same table as the Ambassador of a country formerly part of the Soviet bloc. He had been observing me with some interest during the first course, and just as the main course arrived, he suddenly announced to the table at large, 'She knows the names of all my mistresses.' A frisson went round the table and I could see all my fellow guests thinking to themselves, 'Perhaps she knows the names of all my mistresses too. And what else does she know?'

Many people I now met assumed that my main contribution to the corporate world would be in providing information about security risks and how to manage them. It did not seem to occur to them that having managed a major programme of change in one of the most secret parts of the state, I might have some skills that would be relevant to managing companies. Though I found that surprising at first, I think now, three or four years on, that I understand better why this was. It is just one example of the profoundly imperfect relationship and the lack of understanding which exists between the corporate world and the public service.

In my last few years in the public service we were continually being told that compared with business we were inefficient, slow, risk-averse, wasteful and a number of other uncomplimentary things. Successive Prime Ministers have brought in senior business figures in an almost tutorial role, to demonstrate and explain to the public service how to improve the way it does things – how to manage itself and its business better. Many of these relationships have eventually ended in disillusion or misunderstanding. Various ideas have been adopted, some suitable, some not. Where they have not been suitable, it has often been because businessmen and consultants quickly become baffled, and sometimes irritated, by the sheer complexity of public issues and by the requirements of accountability, which are key to the way the public service conducts itself. Public administration is not free to move, as may seem at first sight best, to solve single issues. The single issues have always to be seen as parts of other bigger issues. And the public service cannot be casual or slaphappy about establishing precedents – you are dealing with people's rights and people's expectations.

In MI5, being somewhat to the side of the mainstream, we were freer to pick and choose from the management models which we observed succeeding or failing in other areas. Though many outside commentators had views on precisely how we should be made accountable, for the most part businessmen were less eager to enter our business to tell us how to conduct it than they were in other parts of the public service. With us they knew they didn't know what it was all about, with other areas they thought they did.

But, after having been told so firmly and for so long that the corporate world was the model we should all be adopting, I was both surprised and sometimes disappointed by what I found when I joined it and met a cross section of people at the top of British business.

My observations relate to no one company in particular nor to every company I have come across. I don't think I was particularly surprised to find that levels of personal ability and skill are still no higher even in the best companies than they are at equivalent levels in the public service. But how long can that last, given the huge and increasing difference in remuneration levels between the two sectors? Clearly companies must offer levels of reward which will attract and retain people capable of running them, and that means rewards on an international scale. I have no problem with that, provided that the rewards are related to performance. But, given the extent to which, in business, it is remuneration which is the prime motivator, and the prime way of establishing a person's status, it does seem to me very unhealthy that such a huge difference exists between the public and private sector. How can company bosses take seriously, for example, Permanent Secretaries who are content to work for remuneration similar to that received by comparatively low level staff in their companies? The truth is that in many cases they don't. One Chairman of a company said to me, 'We don't want an ex-Permanent Secretary on our Board. After all, all they do is what they are told' – a breathtakingly inaccurate version of the job of the head of a government department. Nor do many senior people in business understand the motivation of those whose satisfaction comes, as it still overwhelmingly does in the public service, from a sense of personal achievement or of service to the public. I am sure many cynics will sneer at that characterisation of the senior civil service, but it is still largely true.

I was surprised to find a very inadequate understanding in business of the value which is available, free, from the government machine. I am not talking only about the deep understanding which exists in the Foreign Office about foreign governments, about key personalities and the issues which are likely to affect events in different parts of the world. There is also the information and assessments of the Home Office and the police, to say nothing of the Security Service about domestic issues, tensions, and pressures, all of which are very relevant to long term business planning and can be accessed. But there are other things too. Various parts of the public service know a great deal about balancing complex pressures, managing risks, assessing information and how an organisation can know what it knows by the effective storage and accessing of information. All these skills are vital to businesses, some of which, in my observation, are not particularly good at them. But, as far as I have seen, many business leaders have little understanding of what is available, or any real understanding about how to access it. If any attempt is made to do so, it is either delegated to a fairly low level in the company or done at second hand, through consultants. As a result, it is not used to the best advantage in the formulation of business strategies, to the disadvantage of UK plc.

Of course, I was not surprised by the dominance of men in British boardrooms. It is a well-known fact and it is changing; though it is changing very slowly. But, given the journey through life I had already made, I *was* surprised by the extent to which in 1996, there was still an *issue* about women on Boards. It was quite a few years since I had been aware of being regarded as an oddity, as a female in the public service. Even my European colleagues, the Heads of the European Security Services, had come to accept me as one of them. And although there were not large numbers of women at the top of the civil service, those that were there were certainly not there for politically correct reasons. They were neither patronised nor discriminated against, but treated just like the men. So I was frankly amazed to be told by the Chairmen of several companies, 'We need a woman on the Board.' It was clear that those Chairmen did not much care what woman, nor did they perceive that 'a woman' might have just as much to contribute as 'a man', and that she would certainly be just as different from another woman as two men would be from each other. And I was astounded when the Chairman of one British plc said to me, 'I think we need a woman on the Board, but I am afraid I would not be able to persuade my fellow Directors of that.' It was an unexpected, and unwelcome flashback to find myself addressed as 'dear' by the distinguished Chairman of another. Needless to say those were not companies I wished to have anything to do with.

I was also very surprised, perhaps I shouldn't have been, by the style of some of the men who run British business today. In the early part of the century great businesses were built by giants of men. Such men had imagination, drive and conviction and could inspire the thousands who worked for them, all of whom knew exactly who was the boss and would follow him. Their style was autocratic, and based on a conviction of their own rightness. And those who *were* right built very successful businesses indeed. But that style will no longer cut the mustard in the much more complicated and fast-moving circumstances of the new century. Yet a significant part of the British corporate world seems to me still to be hankering after such men. A new model has not yet emerged. So there are still too many around who appear to believe that in order to lead, it is necessary to know the answers to all questions immediately; that listening is a sign of weakness. Such people have little idea how to lead by delegation, how to place power and responsibility at the appropriate level or how to use the skills of the frequently very talented and enthusiastic teams they have assembled around them. As a result, those talented people, if they stay, gradually lose their ability to take decisions appropriate to their level of pay and responsibility, and look upwards instead for someone to tell them what to do. I was struck too by the focus on day-to-day management of crises, the absence of long-term strategic planning or the ability to recognise or manage complex issues in some of the companies I came across.

This probably struck me all the more forcibly because it is quite a different pattern from what I had been used to. The public service has not bred 'great men' in the same mould. Instead it has organised itself to try to make the best use of all its talents and to manage complicated public business through distributed power centres. The potential weakness of that system is delay, turf battles, passing the buck. One of its strengths is the ability intelligently to apply the corporate memory to new situations. Of course, business and the public service have quite different jobs to do and it will be a disaster if either slavishly apes the other. But it is a big mistake to think that business has a monopoly of wisdom.

And what of the role, which I currently play, Non-Executive Director? It's a role about which there is almost as much confusion as there is about my former career. There have been Non-Executive or independent Directors on the Boards of companies for years but it was only with the Report of the Cadbury Committee in 1992, following some spectacular corporate failures and frauds in the late 1980s, that their role became clearly associated with ensuring proper control of the way companies are run, 'corporate governance' to use the jargon.

Since then, other Committees have sat and made other recommendations about the running of companies, many of which have given further specific responsibilities to the Non-Executive Directors – for setting appropriate remuneration for the executive Directors, for monitoring the audit arrangements of the company and for making recommendations on appointments to the Board, to say nothing of monitoring the strategic direction of the company, ensuring there are effective policies in place and that resources are properly allocated. All this to be done in a volatile and uncertain environment where change is continuous and in an increasingly transparent environment, where the names of Non-Executive Directors appear regularly in the newspapers, accompanied by accusations of incompetence, fat-cattery and of acting as though their position carries only benefits and not responsibilities, particularly when anything seems to be going wrong in a company.

Non-Executive Directors, the informed outsiders, have become the linchpins of the system as the private sector moves from the days of the great autocrats, when it was run without any effective accountability, and tries to develop some appropriate system of oversight. Indeed, so much responsibility has now been piled on Non-Executive Directors that not surprisingly, there seems to be little agreement about anything to do with them. Armies of consultants hold innumerable conferences, breakfasts, dinners, to discuss the role of the Non-Executive Director, the qualifications and skills required, where they should be found, how they should be appointed, how much they should be paid. It is a burgeoning industry.

The job has certainly moved on a lot from the early days of Non-Executive Directors, when anecdotal information relates that they were appointed by the Chairman largely as people he could rely on to support him. I suspect that in those days the job in many companies consisted largely of glancing through a few papers, going to a meeting, saying 'Jolly good show, Chairman,' and going off for a good lunch. But it has now swung so far the other way that it is beginning to look unrealistic to place all those different responsibilities on a small group of people, particularly as many of them sit on or chair the Boards of three, four or as many as eight different companies. It may just be possible to do that when everything is going well, but when things get complicated it clearly is not. But it is not easy to find people with the necessary skills who will take on these roles as the responsibilities increase.

So is it possible to be an effective Non-Executive Director or are you just there to blame when things go wrong? Not so much fat cat as fall guy. I learned a lot from observing how the eminent judges who were the first outside scrutineers of MI5 went about it. They arrived knowing nothing about the intelligence world or the people who worked in it, with the responsibility of investigating complaints. They started by asking for all the files relevant to every complaint they had to investigate. And all the files were given to them. In some cases that might mean thirty volumes stuffed with papers. It was clearly impossible, in the time they had available, to read everything in the thirty volumes, so eventually they settled for summaries of information. In other cases there might be no papers at all to see, if, as happened not infrequently, the complaint was from somebody who had never been investigated and was not known to the Service.

How were they to know if the summary was accurate, or, if no papers were produced, that there genuinely were none? Knowing they could not know everything, they had to work out some way of judging whether what they were being told was likely to be true. They did that by going round meeting people at all levels in the organisation on all sorts of occasions both formal and informal. They questioned and listened far more than they talked. They looked at the processes and the way things were done. They used their judgement and experience to weigh up what they heard, not only what was said, but also who was saying it and what that revealed about the ethos and state of the organisation. They managed with no difficulty to do that without in any sense compromising their independence of judgement. And that is what I have tried to do as a Non-Executive Director.

So I have attended recruitment days, talked to focus groups on this and that, flown to oil and gas platforms and visited many different parts of the companies I am now working with, and the companies who work with us. And, to my great surprise, I spent my sixty-fourth birthday abseiling off a ski lift in Norway, on a Change Management Course, and later in the same week playing Claudius in a production of Tom Stoppard's *Fifteen-Minute Hamlet* in a barge theatre in Copenhagen. Many more traditional Non-Executive Directors would be surprised and shocked at that level of involvement, and it is far more than was envisaged when the system was first introduced but I don't know how the job as it now is could be done effectively without it.

I spent many years working in an organisation which when I joined it had hardly any external regulation at all, except for Home Secretaries who, in those days, seem rarely if ever to have sought to find out what was happening. By the time I left, it was, in common with other parts of the public service, highly regulated, with a complex pattern of accountabilities and oversights – ministerial, judicial, administrative and parliamentary – as well as that of the media, with its long ears and very long purse. I contributed to the development of that regulation and worked under the system which resulted. I believe it was effective, though no system of regulation is perfect and like all healthy systems it will develop and change as time goes on. It is arguable, though it will never be a popular line of argument, that the public service as a whole is now over-accountable. It does seem to me to be a characteristic of contemporary thinking that when something goes wrong, rather than addressing ourselves to the reason for failure, we instinctively rush to add another layer of regulation and oversight. Over-regulation can be the enemy of imagination and inspiration. And perhaps even worse, by enforcing conformity to more and more rules, we give the impression that no more is required, and thus risk ultimately eroding honesty.

# EPILOGUE

Since I was turned into a public figure by the government in 1991, I have had to balance secrecy and openness in my public and private life in a way that has been difficult to get right and often uncomfortable both for me and my family. Much has been written since then about me and the job I did, frequently by people who have never met me, but until now I have said little publicly about myself and written less. This book is me in a way that most of the rest has not been. I am not and never was 'Housewife Superspy', but a 20th-century woman who by chance found herself at the centre of some great national events and some big social changes. My story illustrates, in a sometimes extreme form, the balancing act that many modern women have to perform between the requirements of home, career and family. Most women don't resolve the conflict to their own satisfaction and neither have I.

In telling my story, I also hoped to cast some light on a part of what is called the 'secret state' from a different, more down-to-earth angle than the usual breathless, conspiratorial one. I wanted to show what it was really like to work in one of these much fictionalised organisations through a period of great change and modernisation. For me, it has made for an active life, in some ways a stressful life, but a life full of interest and I have never been bored. I hope that alongside the serious issues, some of the fun of it all comes out in this book.

I shall be very sorry indeed if my publishing my auto-biography has permanently damaged my relationship with the Service I worked in for twenty-seven years and for which I have a very high regard. Some of those who are working for it now are my former colleagues. Many others will know little or nothing about me or the period I have described, when much of what they now take for granted was being developed. If they are, as I expect they are, the same sort of balanced, sane and sensible people I spoke of at the beginning, with a well-developed sense of humour and a down-to-earth approach to difficult issues, they will be getting on with the job they have to do, and not spending much time worrying about this book. That is certainly how I would want it to be.

# INDEX